SIGHT UNSEEN™

robert tinnell   bo hampton

AG
SIG

SIGHT
UNSEEN

Created by   Robert Tinnell and Bo Hampton
Story by   Robert Tinnell
Art by   Bo Hampton
Lettering by   Jack Armstrong
Design by   Michael Anderson

ACKNOWLEDGEMENTS
Jim Bissett, Jim Demonakos, JonKaras/Infinity Management International,
Joe Keatinge, Todd Livingston, Mark Miller, Ron Peppentenzza,
Eric Stephenson, Shannon Tinnell, Neil Vokes, Mark Wheatley
- R.T.

Donna and Herb Barnes, for their unflagging support for the project—Teresa
Hampton for being the one I love and Josef Komenda at Lulu.
- B.H.

Image Comics, Inc.

Publisher   Erik Larsen
President   Todd McFarlane
CEO   Marc Silvestri
Vice-President   Jim Valentino

Executive Director   Eric Stephenson
PR & Marketing Coordinator   Jim Demonakos
Accounts Manager   Mia MacHatton
Art Director   Laurenn McCubbin
Production Artist   Allen Hui
Traffic Manager   Joe Keatinge
Production Assistant   Jonathan Chan
Production Assistant   Drew Gill
Administrative Assistant   Traci Hui

www.imagecomics.com

"To Messers. Straub, King, and McCammon for leading
the way with their words...and maestros Bava, Fisher, and
Romero for doing the same with their pictures... you were my
teachers all. I humbly submit this work in gratitude... "

- RT

" For Joseph Snider, a constant friend..."

-B.H.

"The concept behind the glasses is a working hypothesis for developing glassware based on the natural abilities of canines to see and hear into that portion of the electromagnetic spectrum, where ghosts exist within. We have verified that ghost voices can be heard in the ultrasonic frequency range. We have proven that when ghosts are present, the EMF fields will increase three to five hundred percent over the ambient intensity levels. An implant that increases our sensitivity to a higher frequency range is not science fiction, but is currently being prototyped by scientists. Glasses to see the dead are just a step away from the reality of today."

Dr. Dave Oester, Ph.D.
International Ghost Hunters Society/Author,
America's Haunting Book Series

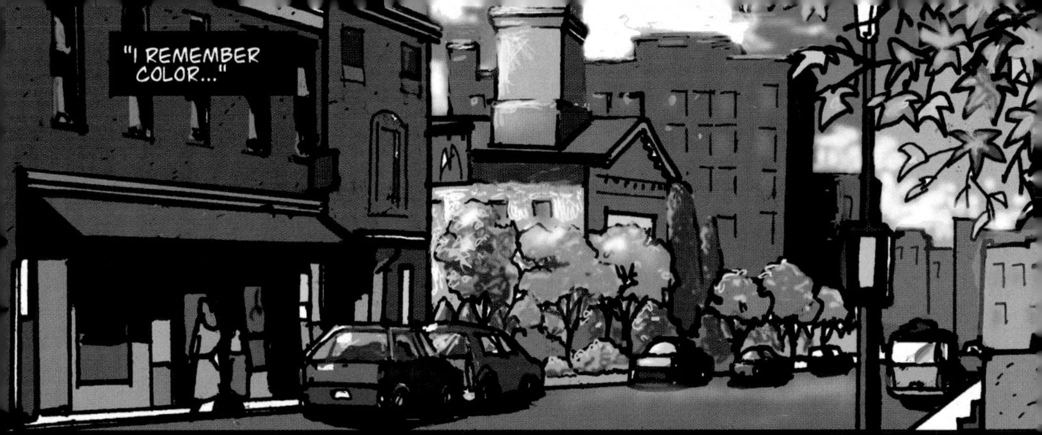
"I REMEMBER COLOR..."

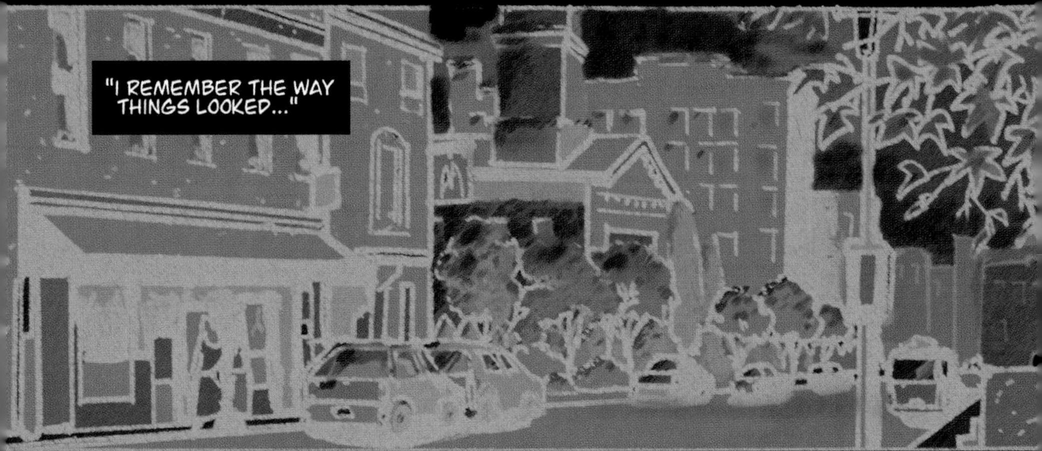
"I REMEMBER THE WAY THINGS LOOKED..."

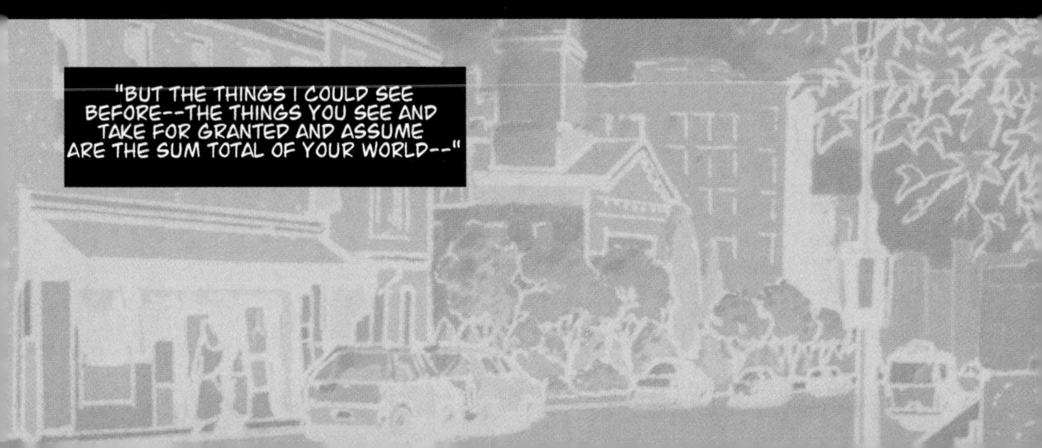
"BUT THE THINGS I COULD SEE BEFORE--THE THINGS YOU SEE AND TAKE FOR GRANTED AND ASSUME ARE THE SUM TOTAL OF YOUR WORLD--"

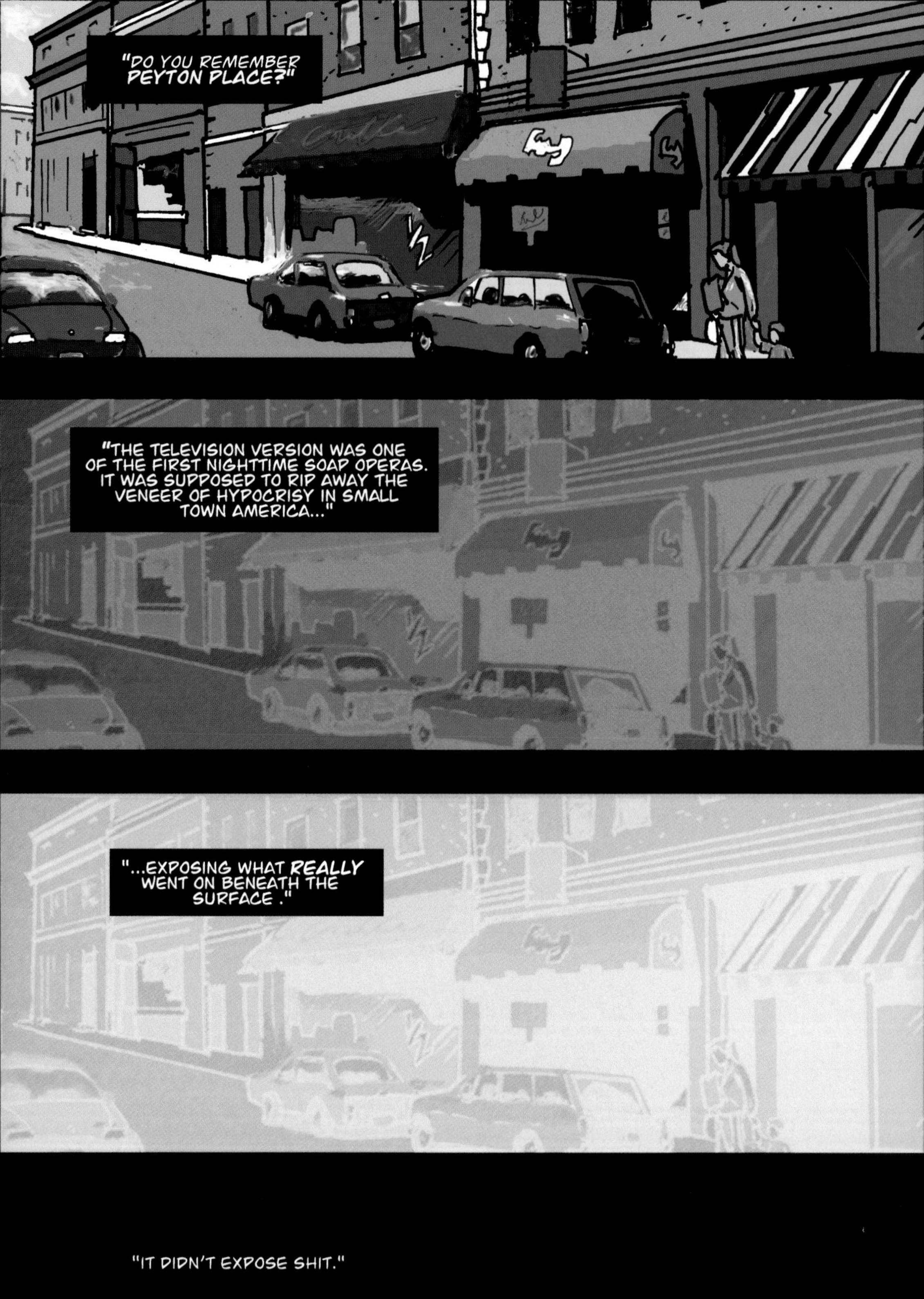
"DO YOU REMEMBER PEYTON PLACE?"
"THE TELEVISION VERSION WAS ONE OF THE FIRST NIGHTTIME SOAP OPERAS. IT WAS SUPPOSED TO RIP AWAY THE VENEER OF HYPOCRISY IN SMALL TOWN AMERICA..."
"...EXPOSING WHAT REALLY WENT ON BENEATH THE SURFACE."
"IT DIDN'T EXPOSE SHIT."

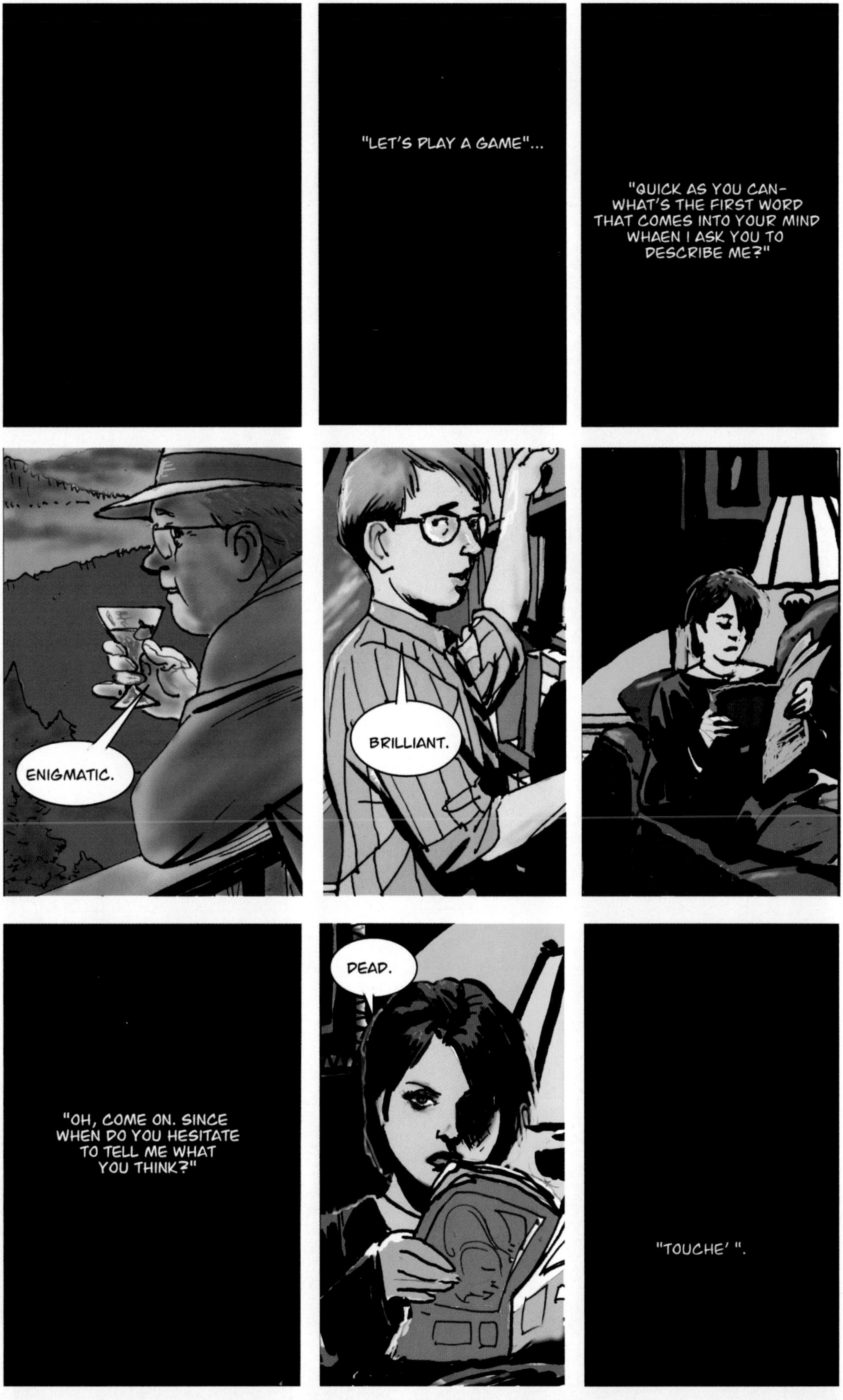
"LET'S PLAY A GAME"...
"QUICK AS YOU CAN- WHAT'S THE FIRST WORD THAT COMES INTO YOUR MIND WHAEN I ASK YOU TO DESCRIBE ME?"
ENIGMATIC.
BRILLIANT.
"OH, COME ON. SINCE WHEN DO YOU HESITATE TO TELL ME WHAT YOU THINK?"
DEAD.
"TOUCHE' ".

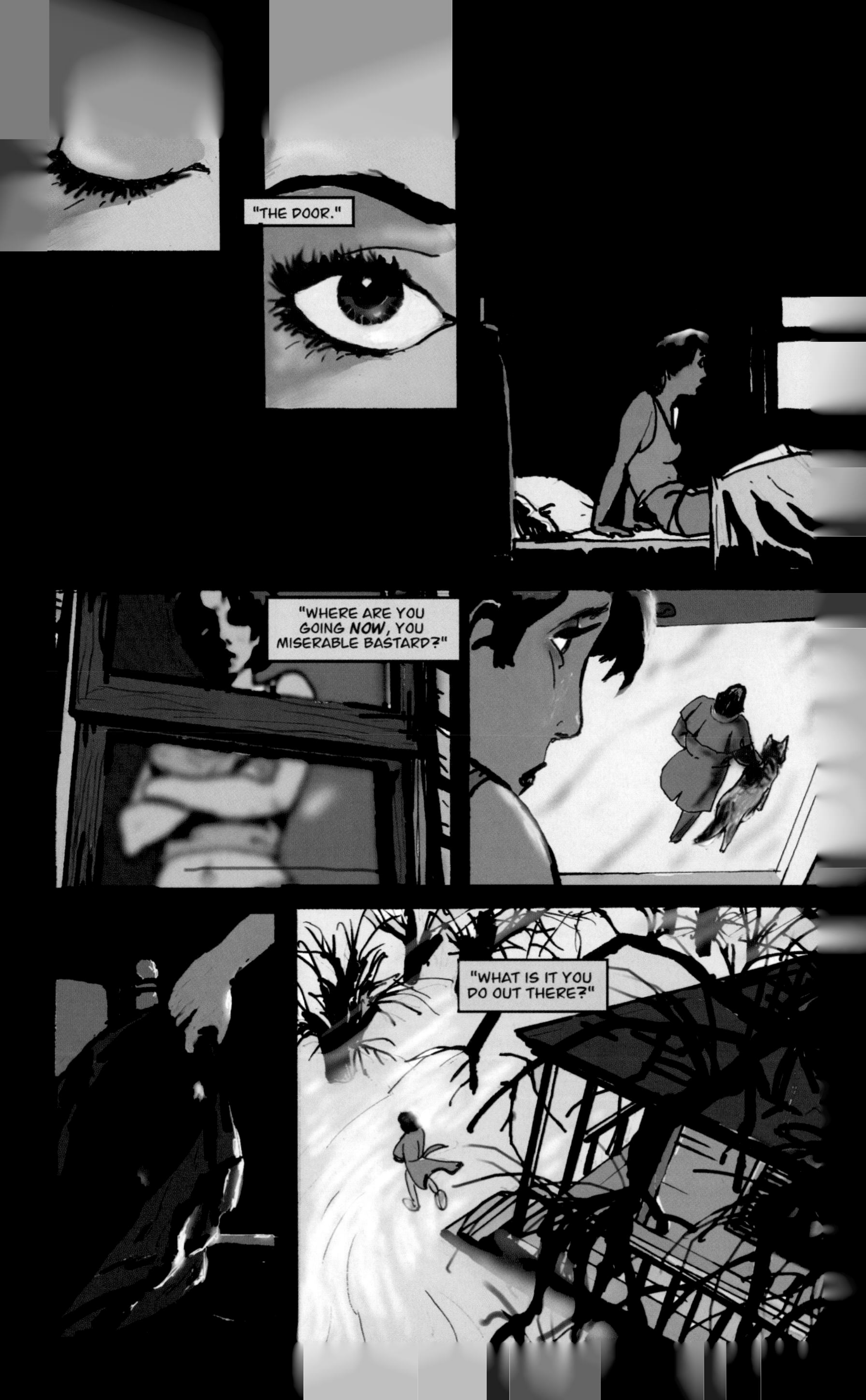
"THE DOOR."
"WHERE ARE YOU GOING NOW, YOU MISERABLE BASTARD?"
"WHAT IS IT YOU DO OUT THERE?"

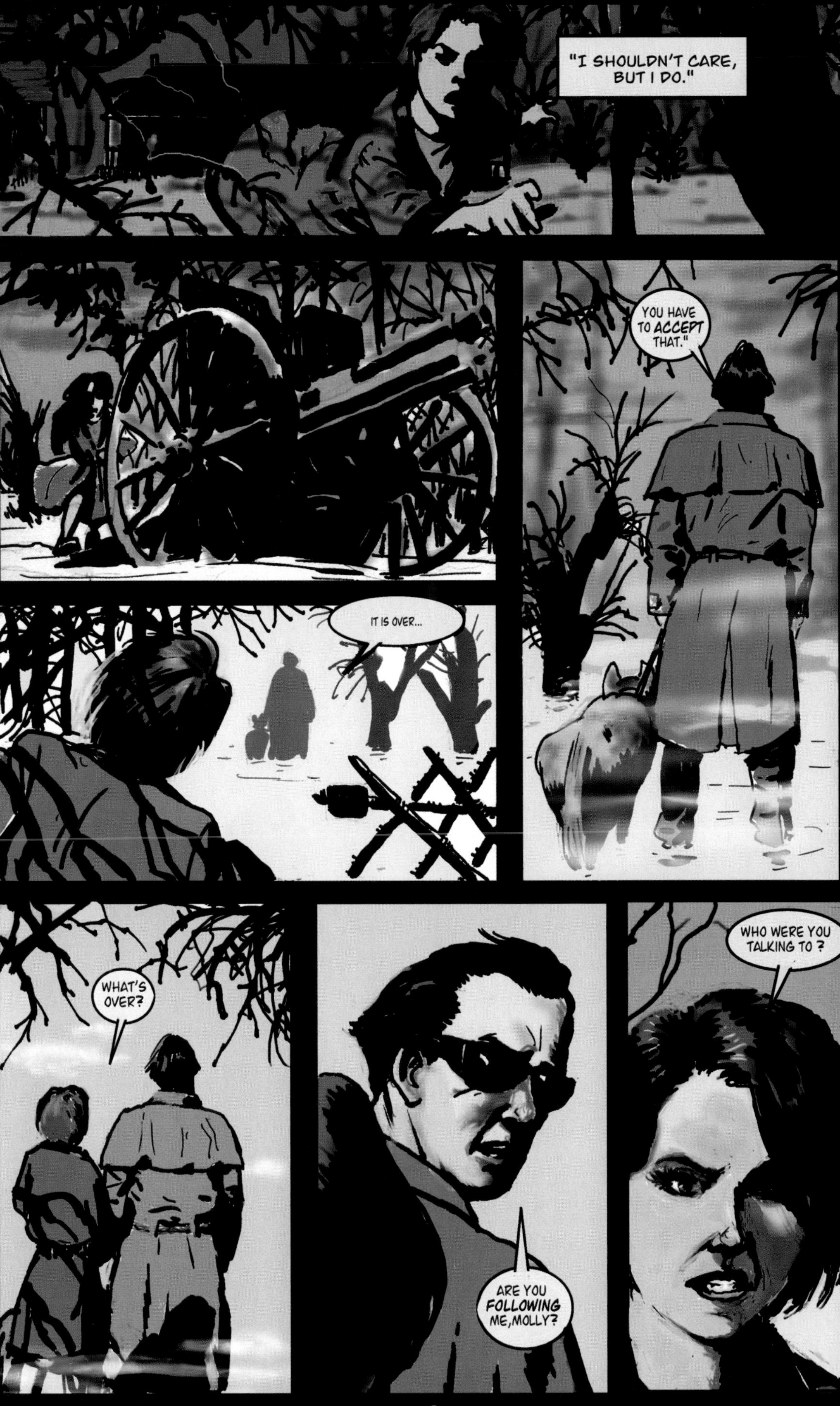
"I SHOULDN'T CARE, BUT I DO."
YOU HAVE TO ACCEPT THAT."
IT IS OVER...
WHAT'S OVER?
ARE YOU FOLLOWING ME, MOLLY?
WHO WERE YOU TALKING TO ?

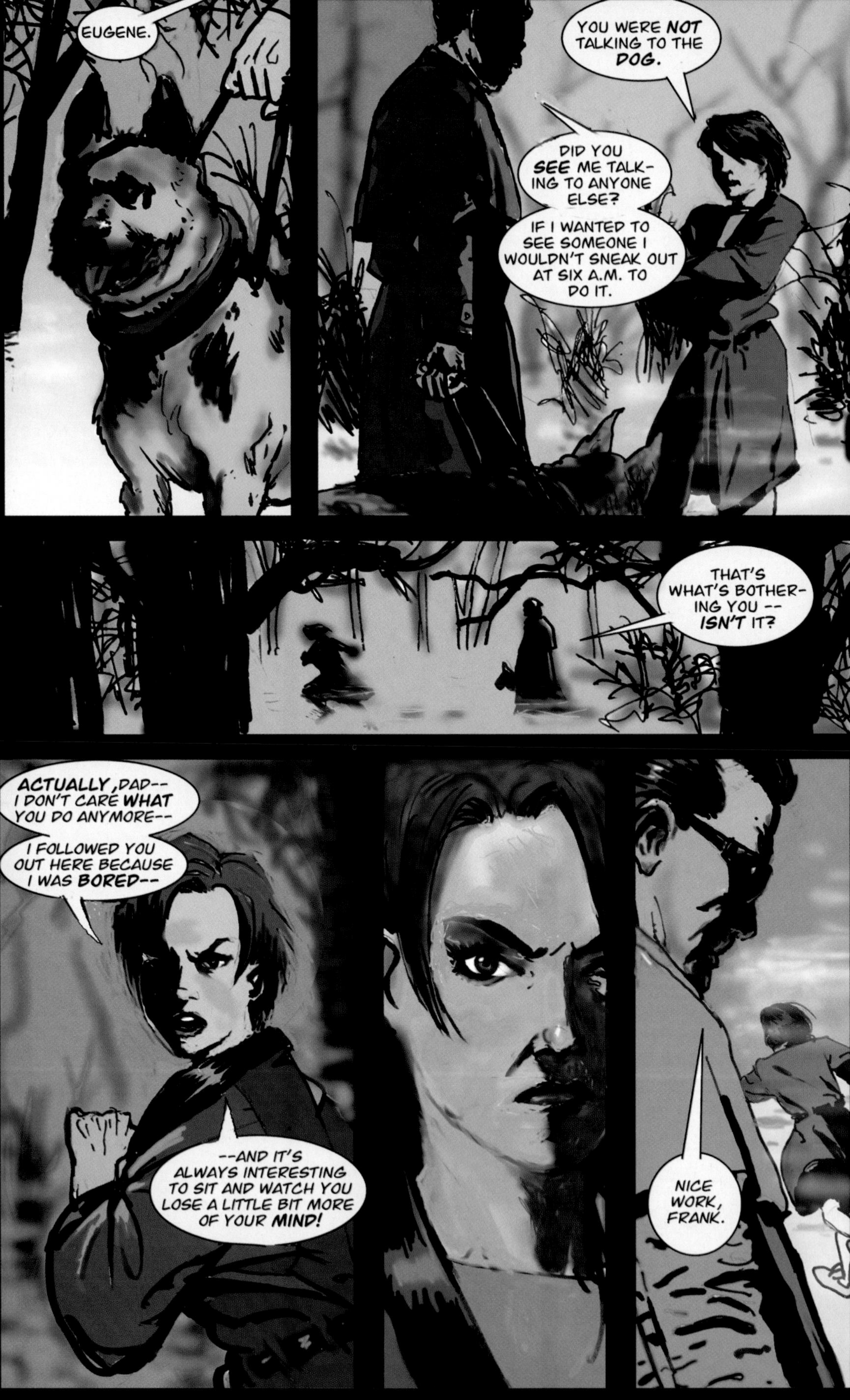
EUGENE.
YOU WERE NOT TALKING TO THE DOG.
DID YOU SEE ME TALKING TO ANYONE ELSE?
IF I WANTED TO SEE SOMEONE I WOULDN'T SNEAK OUT AT SIX A.M. TO DO IT.
THAT'S WHAT'S BOTHERING YOU -- ISN'T IT?
ACTUALLY, DAD-- I DON'T CARE WHAT YOU DO ANYMORE--
I FOLLOWED YOU OUT HERE BECAUSE I WAS BORED--
--AND IT'S ALWAYS INTERESTING TO SIT AND WATCH YOU LOSE A LITTLE BIT MORE OF YOUR MIND!
NICE WORK, FRANK.

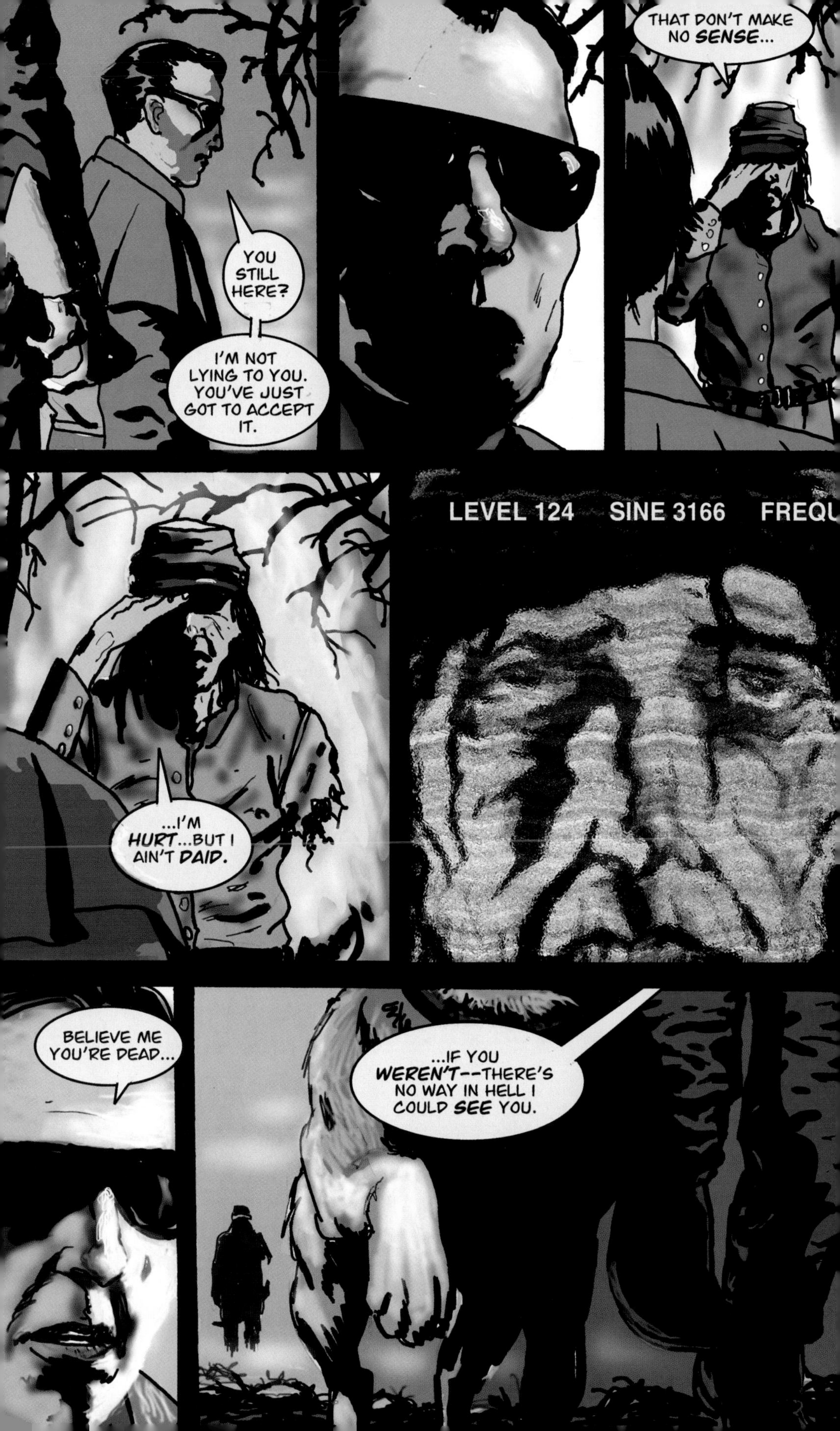
YOU STILL HERE?
I'M NOT LYING TO YOU. YOU'VE JUST GOT TO ACCEPT IT.
THAT DON'T MAKE NO SENSE...
...I'M HURT...BUT I AIN'T DAID.
LEVEL 124 SINE 3166 FREQU
BELIEVE ME YOU'RE DEAD...
...IF YOU WEREN'T--THERE'S NO WAY IN HELL I COULD SEE YOU.

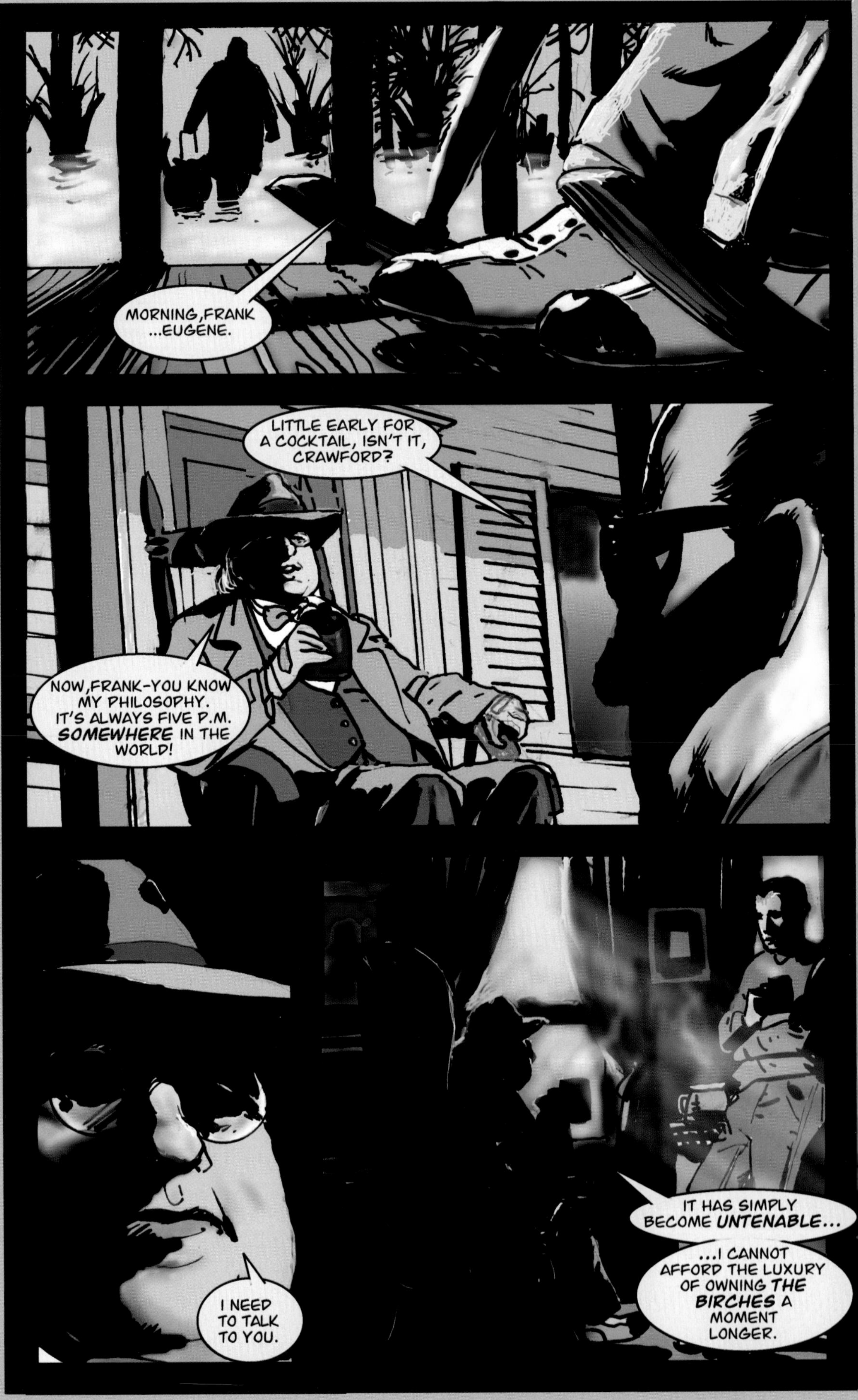
MORNING, FRANK ...EUGENE.
LITTLE EARLY FOR A COCKTAIL, ISN'T IT, CRAWFORD?
NOW, FRANK-YOU KNOW MY PHILOSOPHY. IT'S ALWAYS FIVE P.M. SOMEWHERE IN THE WORLD!
I NEED TO TALK TO YOU.
IT HAS SIMPLY BECOME UNTENABLE...
...I CANNOT AFFORD THE LUXURY OF OWNING THE BIRCHES A MOMENT LONGER.

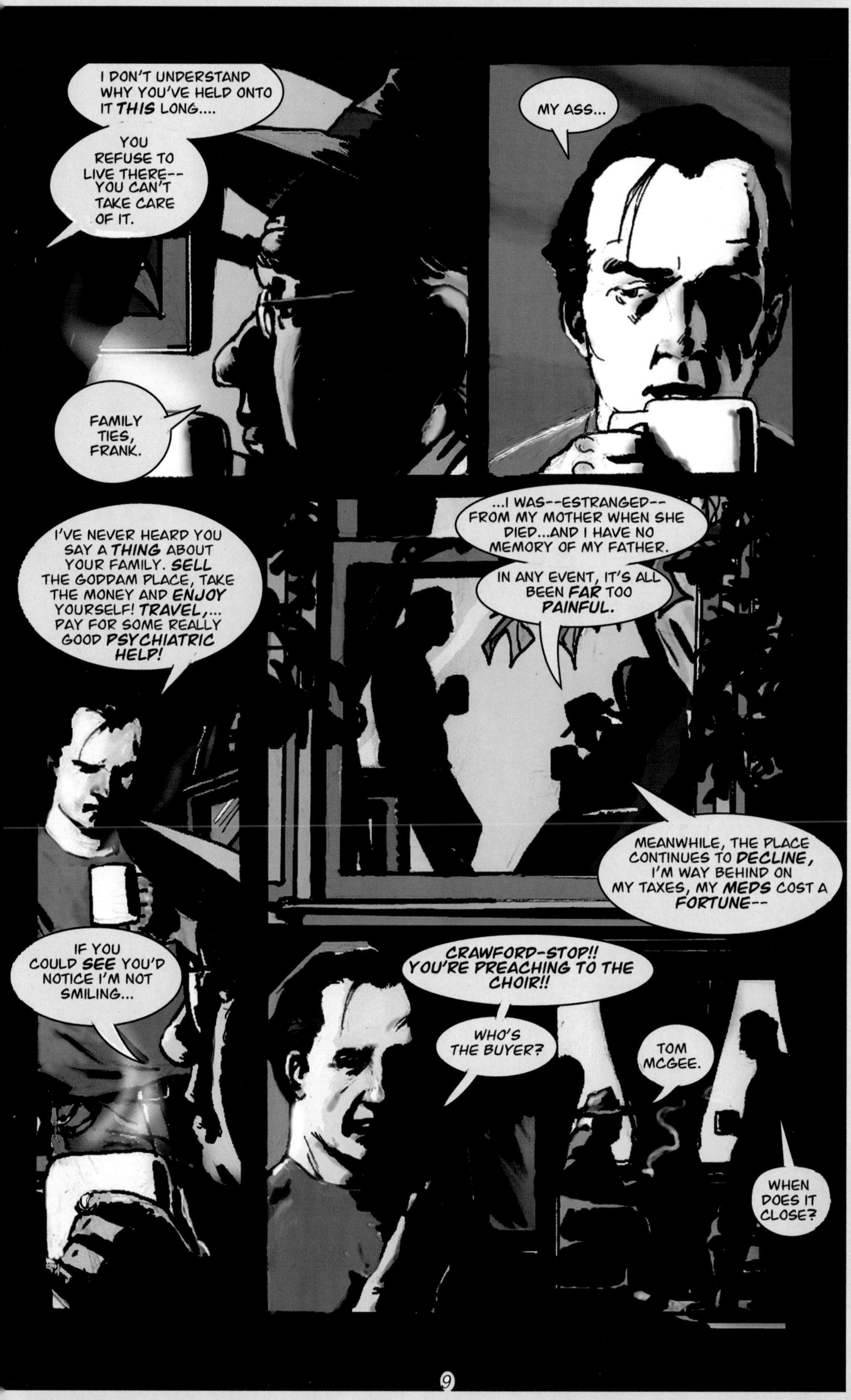
I DON'T UNDERSTAND WHY YOU'VE HELD ONTO IT THIS LONG....
YOU REFUSE TO LIVE THERE-- YOU CAN'T TAKE CARE OF IT.
FAMILY TIES, FRANK.
MY ASS...
I'VE NEVER HEARD YOU SAY A THING ABOUT YOUR FAMILY. SELL THE GODDAM PLACE, TAKE THE MONEY AND ENJOY YOURSELF! TRAVEL,... PAY FOR SOME REALLY GOOD PSYCHIATRIC HELP!
...I WAS--ESTRANGED-- FROM MY MOTHER WHEN SHE DIED...AND I HAVE NO MEMORY OF MY FATHER.
IN ANY EVENT, IT'S ALL BEEN FAR TOO PAINFUL.
MEANWHILE, THE PLACE CONTINUES TO DECLINE, I'M WAY BEHIND ON MY TAXES, MY MEDS COST A FORTUNE--
IF YOU COULD SEE YOU'D NOTICE I'M NOT SMILING...
CRAWFORD-STOP!! YOU'RE PREACHING TO THE CHOIR!!
WHO'S THE BUYER?
TOM MCGEE.
WHEN DOES IT CLOSE?

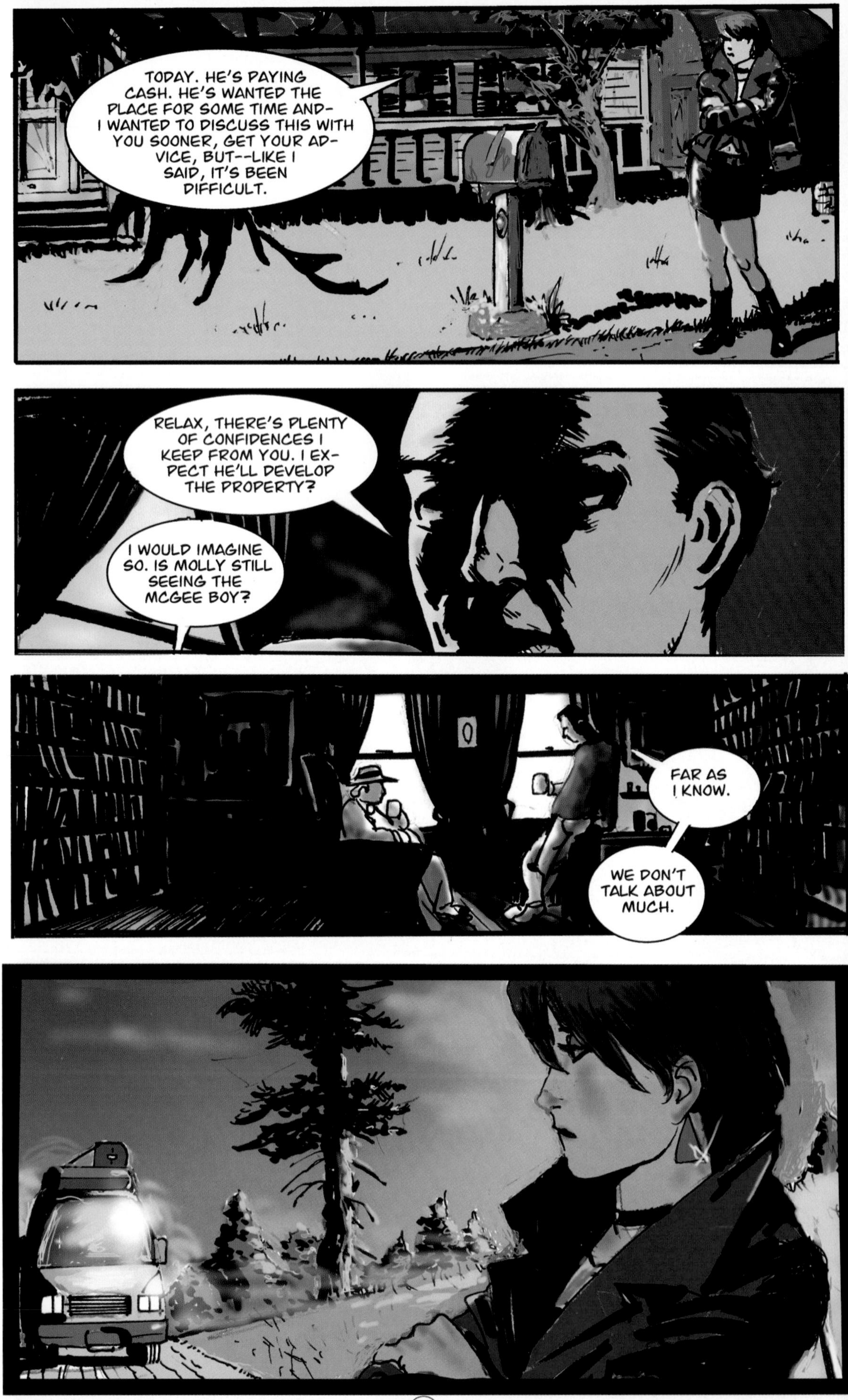
TODAY. HE'S PAYING CASH. HE'S WANTED THE PLACE FOR SOME TIME AND-- I WANTED TO DISCUSS THIS WITH YOU SOONER, GET YOUR AD-VICE, BUT--LIKE I SAID, IT'S BEEN DIFFICULT.
RELAX, THERE'S PLENTY OF CONFIDENCES I KEEP FROM YOU. I EX-PECT HE'LL DEVELOP THE PROPERTY?
I WOULD IMAGINE SO. IS MOLLY STILL SEEING THE MCGEE BOY?
FAR AS I KNOW.
WE DON'T TALK ABOUT MUCH.

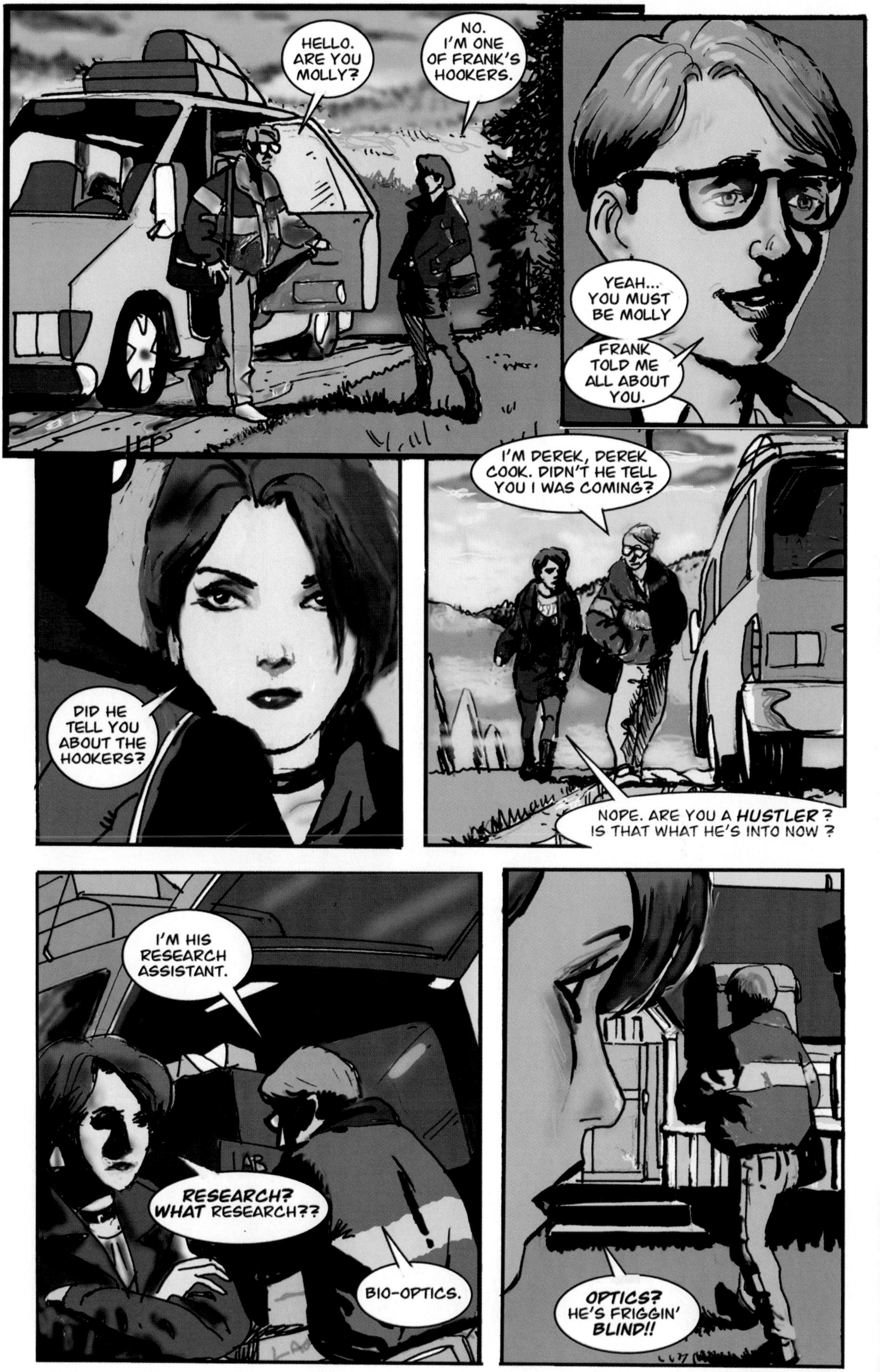
HELLO. ARE YOU MOLLY?
NO. I'M ONE OF FRANK'S HOOKERS.
YEAH... YOU MUST BE MOLLY
FRANK TOLD ME ALL ABOUT YOU.
DID HE TELL YOU ABOUT THE HOOKERS?
I'M DEREK, DEREK COOK. DIDN'T HE TELL YOU I WAS COMING?
NOPE. ARE YOU A HUSTLER? IS THAT WHAT HE'S INTO NOW?
I'M HIS RESEARCH ASSISTANT.
RESEARCH? WHAT RESEARCH??
BIO-OPTICS.
OPTICS? HE'S FRIGGIN' BLIND!!

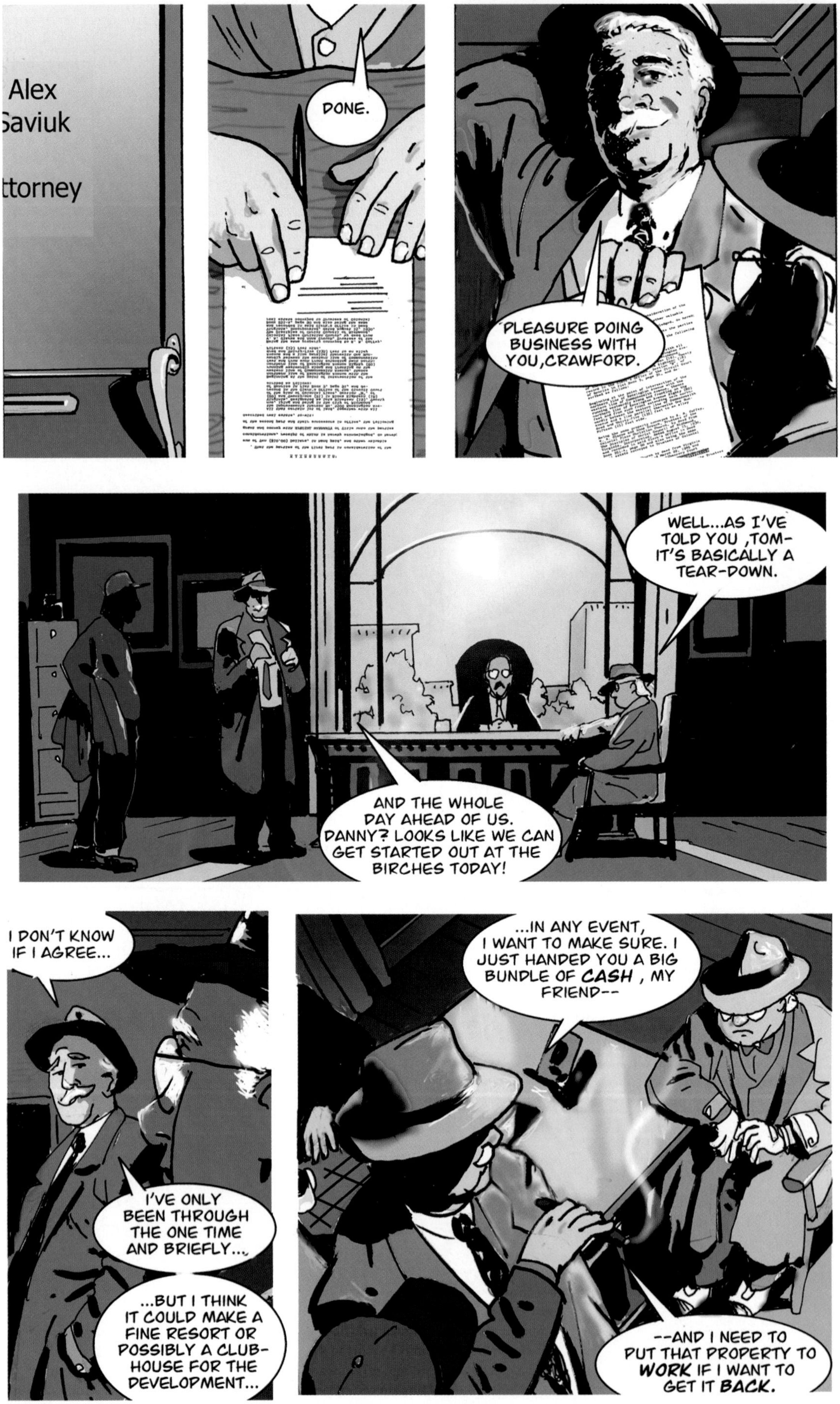
Alex
Saviuk
ttorney
DONE.
PLEASURE DOING BUSINESS WITH YOU, CRAWFORD.
WELL...AS I'VE TOLD YOU ,TOM-IT'S BASICALLY A TEAR-DOWN.
AND THE WHOLE DAY AHEAD OF US. DANNY? LOOKS LIKE WE CAN GET STARTED OUT AT THE BIRCHES TODAY!
I DON'T KNOW IF I AGREE...
I'VE ONLY BEEN THROUGH THE ONE TIME AND BRIEFLY...
...BUT I THINK IT COULD MAKE A FINE RESORT OR POSSIBLY A CLUB-HOUSE FOR THE DEVELOPMENT...
...IN ANY EVENT, I WANT TO MAKE SURE. I JUST HANDED YOU A BIG BUNDLE OF CASH , MY FRIEND--
--AND I NEED TO PUT THAT PROPERTY TO WORK IF I WANT TO GET IT BACK.

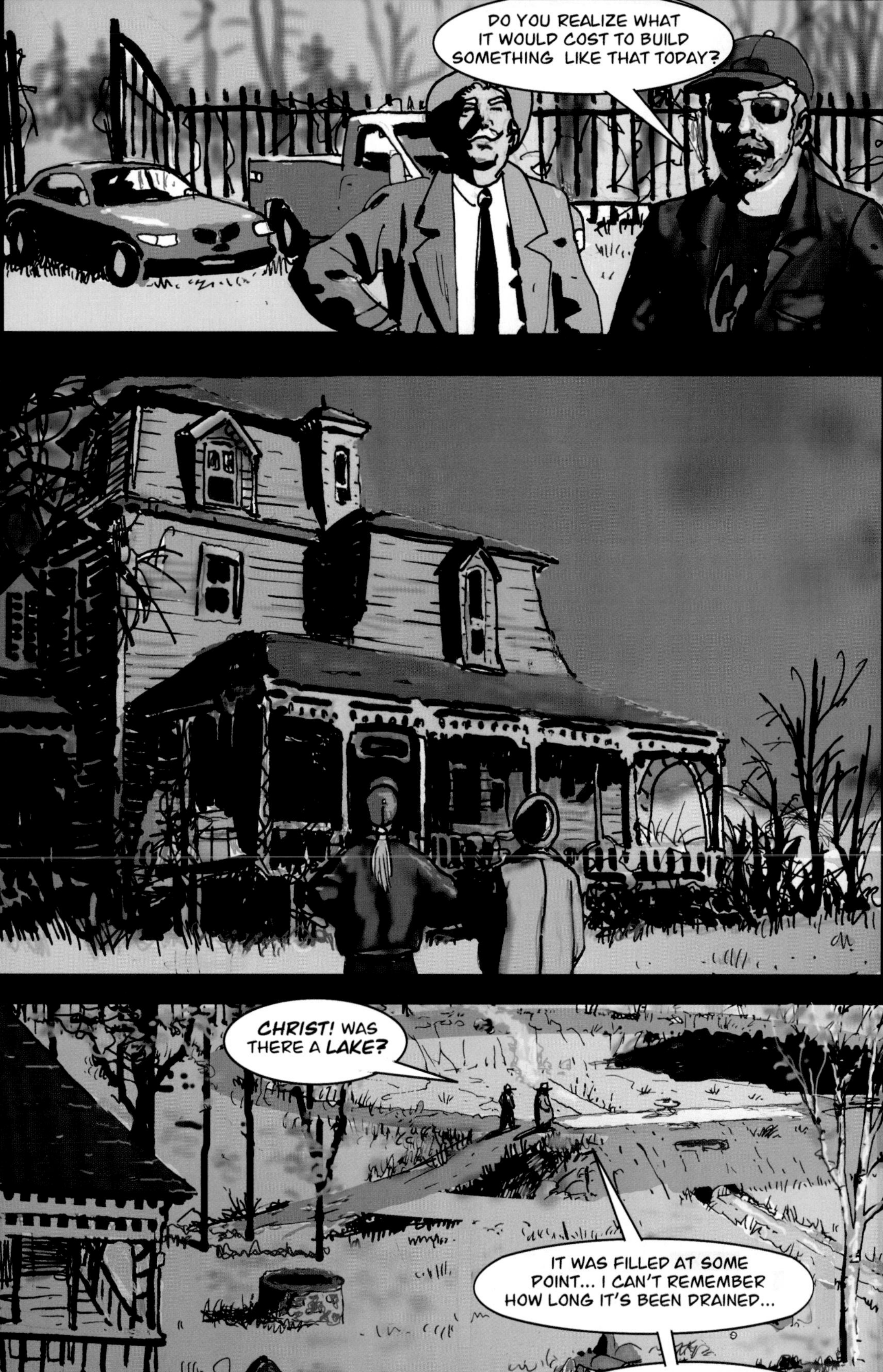

DO YOU REALIZE WHAT IT WOULD COST TO BUILD SOMETHING LIKE THAT TODAY?
CHRIST! WAS THERE A LAKE?
IT WAS FILLED AT SOME POINT... I CAN'T REMEMBER HOW LONG IT'S BEEN DRAINED...
I'M THINKING IF WE FILL IT--SMALL AS IT IS--WE COULD MARKET LOTS AS WATERFRONT!

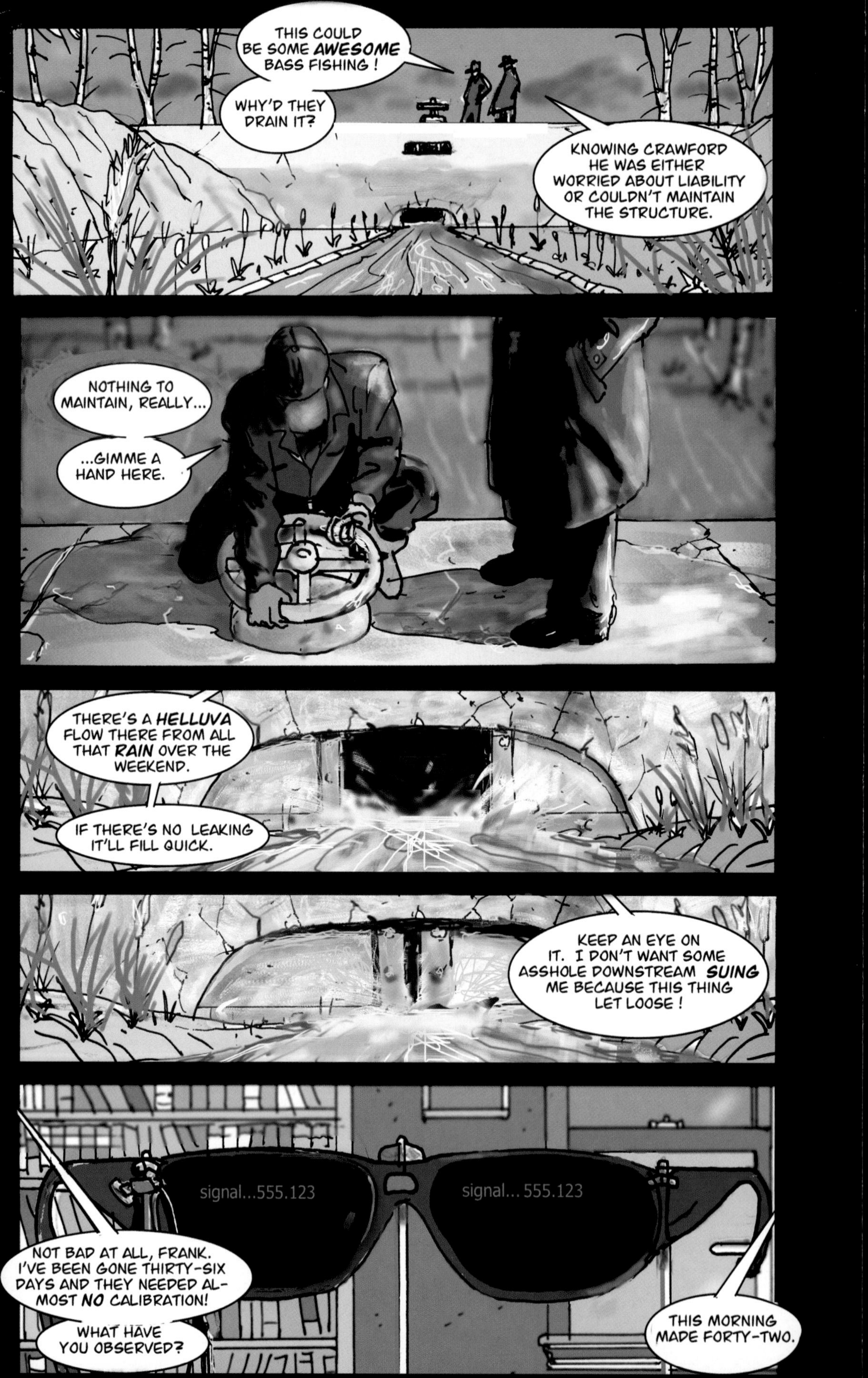
THIS COULD BE SOME AWESOME BASS FISHING !
WHY'D THEY DRAIN IT?
KNOWING CRAWFORD HE WAS EITHER WORRIED ABOUT LIABILITY OR COULDN'T MAINTAIN THE STRUCTURE.
NOTHING TO MAINTAIN, REALLY...
...GIMME A HAND HERE.
THERE'S A HELLUVA FLOW THERE FROM ALL THAT RAIN OVER THE WEEKEND.
IF THERE'S NO LEAKING IT'LL FILL QUICK.
KEEP AN EYE ON IT. I DON'T WANT SOME ASSHOLE DOWNSTREAM SUING ME BECAUSE THIS THING LET LOOSE !
signal...555.123
signal... 555.123
NOT BAD AT ALL, FRANK. I'VE BEEN GONE THIRTY-SIX DAYS AND THEY NEEDED AL-MOST NO CALIBRATION!
WHAT HAVE YOU OBSERVED?
THIS MORNING MADE FORTY-TWO.

JESUS! I CAN'T WAIT TO SEE THE *EMF* READINGS!

I FORGOT IT A FEW TIMES.

JUST TELL ME YOU HAD IT OUT THERE AT LEAST *TEN*--WE NEED SOME NUMBERS!

WHERE'S THE *METER?*

I HOPE THIS THING REGISTERED ACCURATELY.

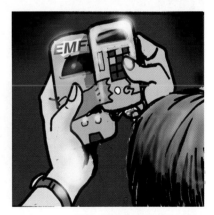

...WOW

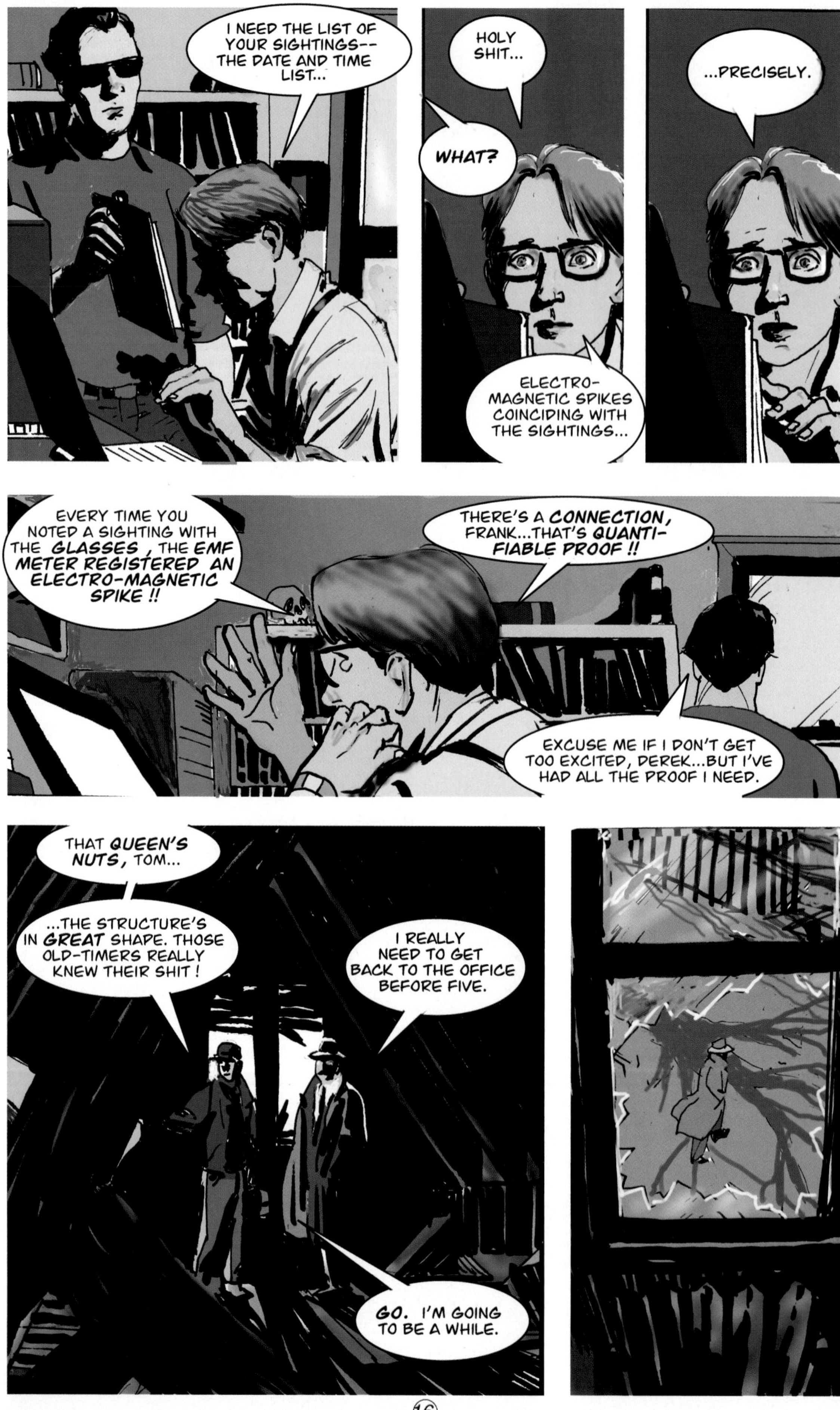
I NEED THE LIST OF YOUR SIGHTINGS-- THE DATE AND TIME LIST...
HOLY SHIT...
WHAT?
ELECTRO-MAGNETIC SPIKES COINCIDING WITH THE SIGHTINGS...
...PRECISELY.
EVERY TIME YOU NOTED A SIGHTING WITH THE GLASSES, THE EMF METER REGISTERED AN ELECTRO-MAGNETIC SPIKE !!
THERE'S A CONNECTION, FRANK...THAT'S QUANTI-FIABLE PROOF !!
EXCUSE ME IF I DON'T GET TOO EXCITED, DEREK...BUT I'VE HAD ALL THE PROOF I NEED.
THAT QUEEN'S NUTS, TOM...
...THE STRUCTURE'S IN GREAT SHAPE. THOSE OLD-TIMERS REALLY KNEW THEIR SHIT !
I REALLY NEED TO GET BACK TO THE OFFICE BEFORE FIVE.
GO. I'M GOING TO BE A WHILE.

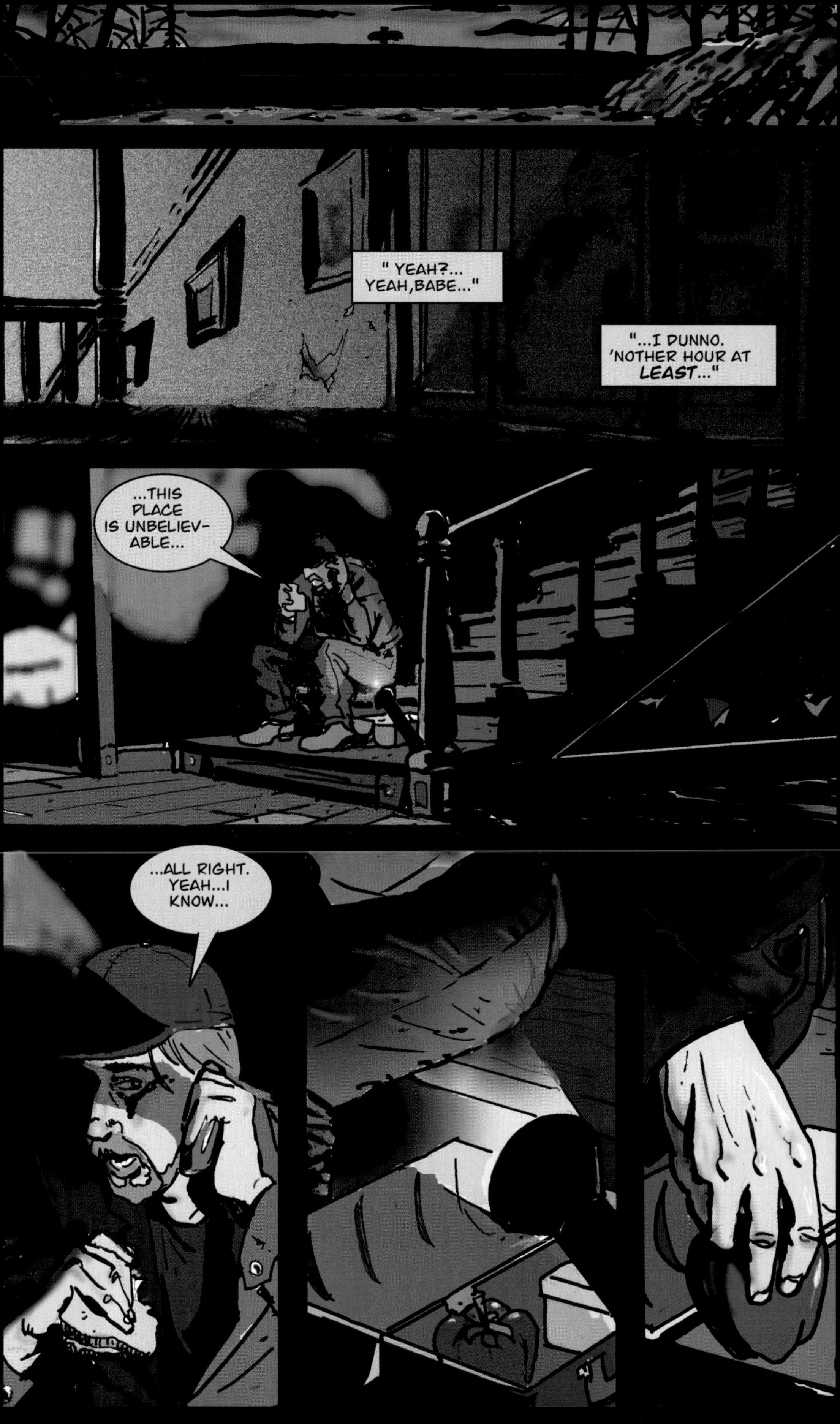
" YEAH?...
YEAH,BABE..."
"...I DUNNO.
'NOTHER HOUR AT
LEAST..."
...THIS
PLACE
IS UNBELIEV-
ABLE...
...ALL RIGHT.
YEAH...I
KNOW...

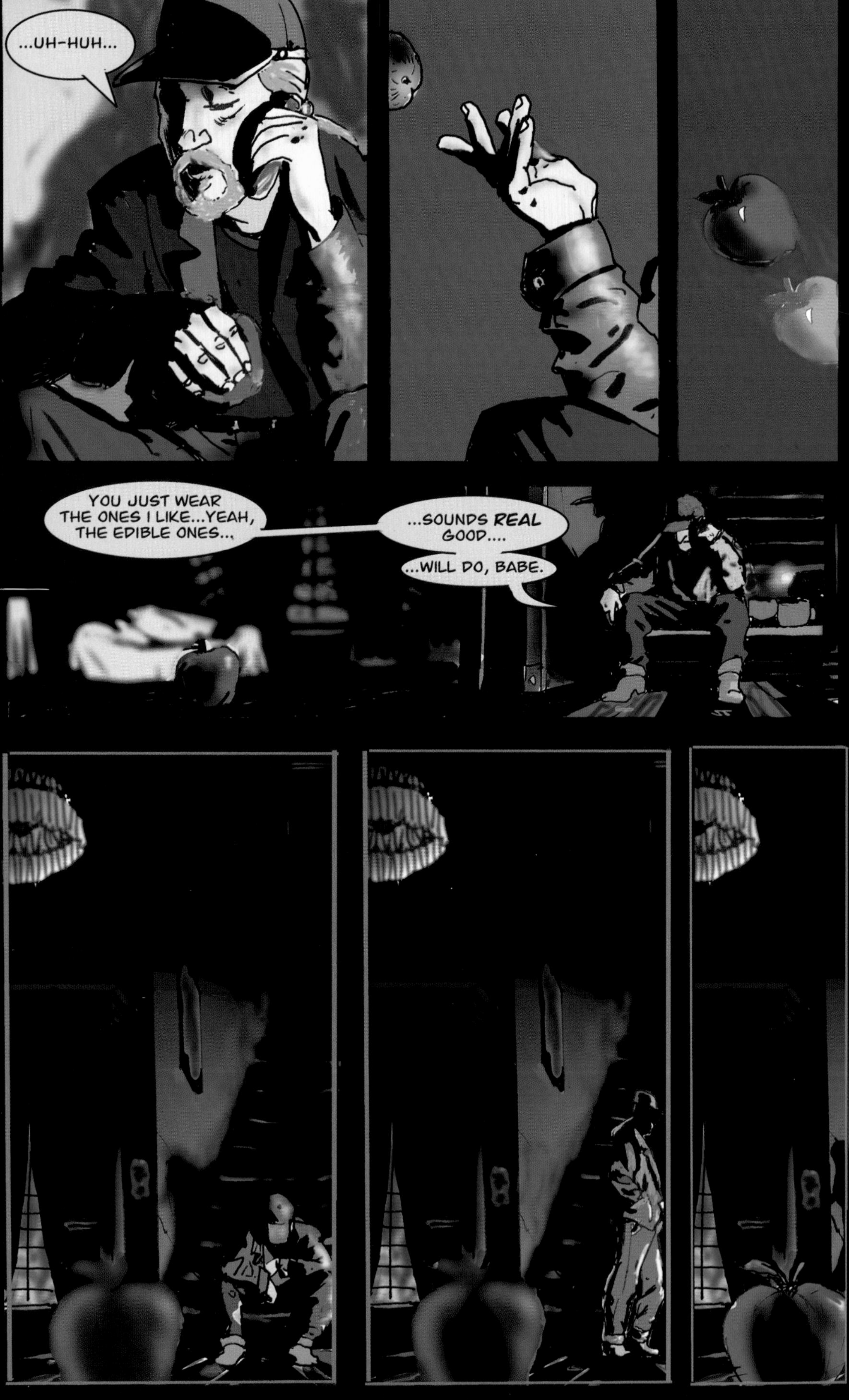
...UH-HUH...
YOU JUST WEAR THE ONES I LIKE...YEAH, THE EDIBLE ONES...
...SOUNDS REAL GOOD....
...WILL DO, BABE.

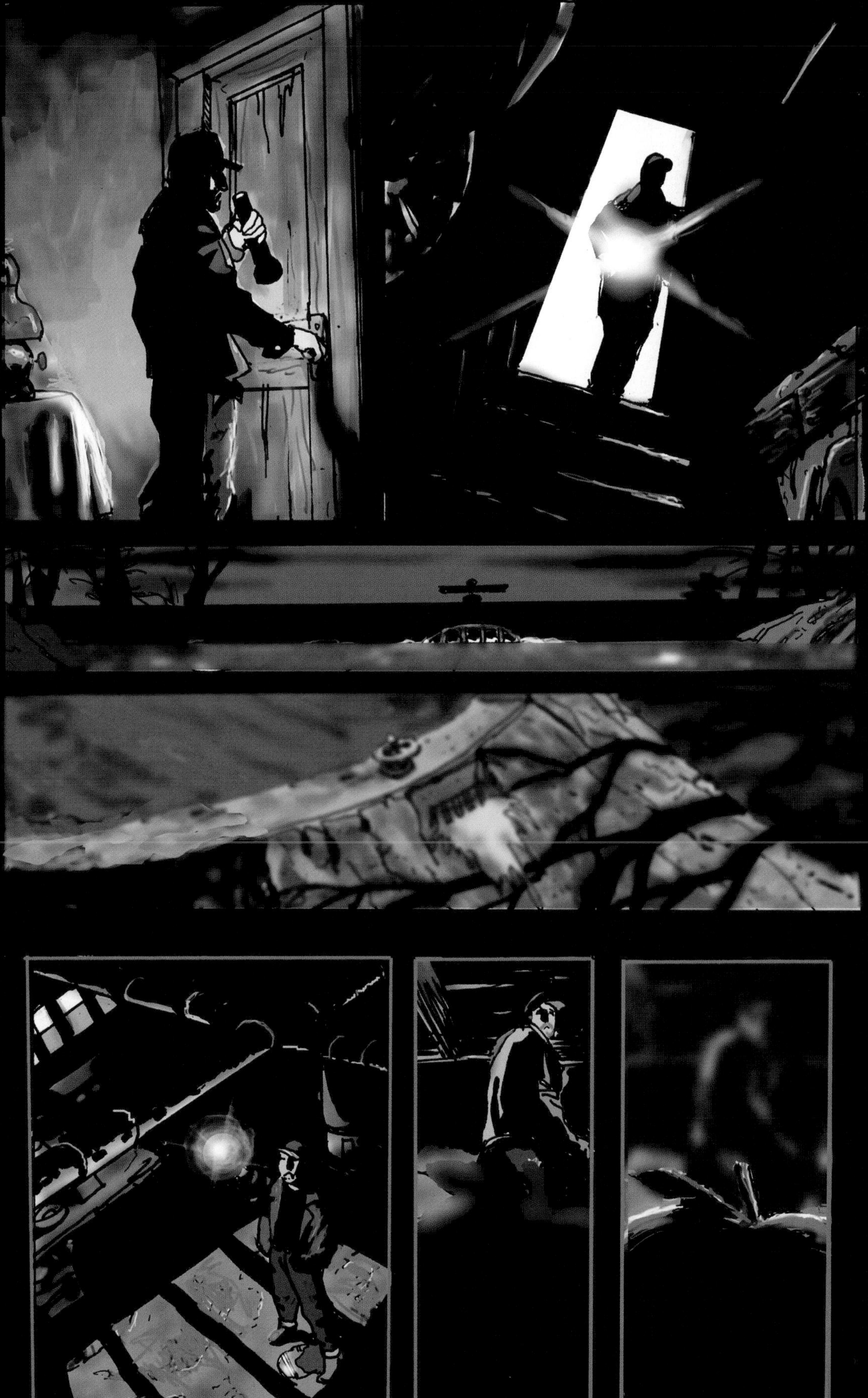

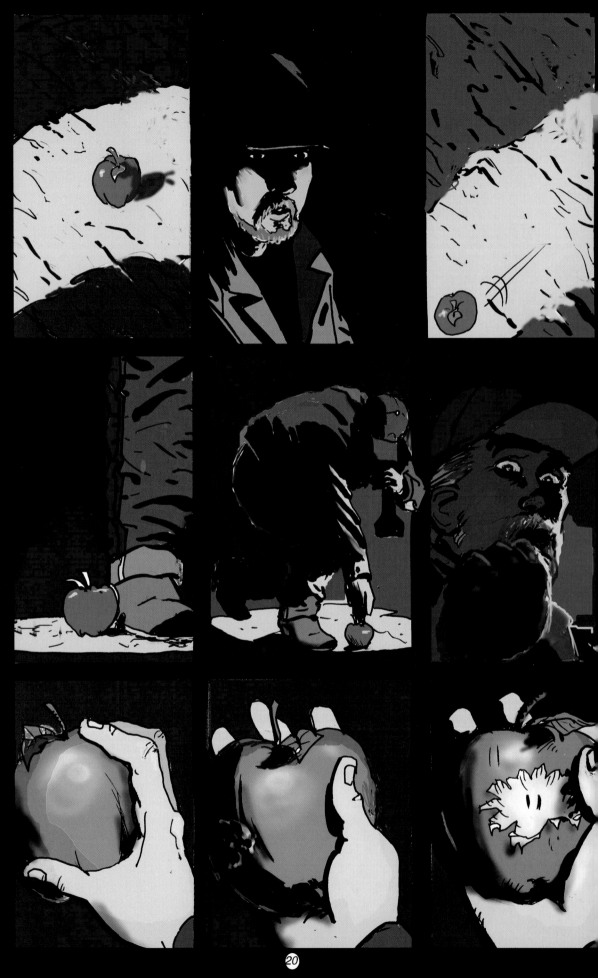

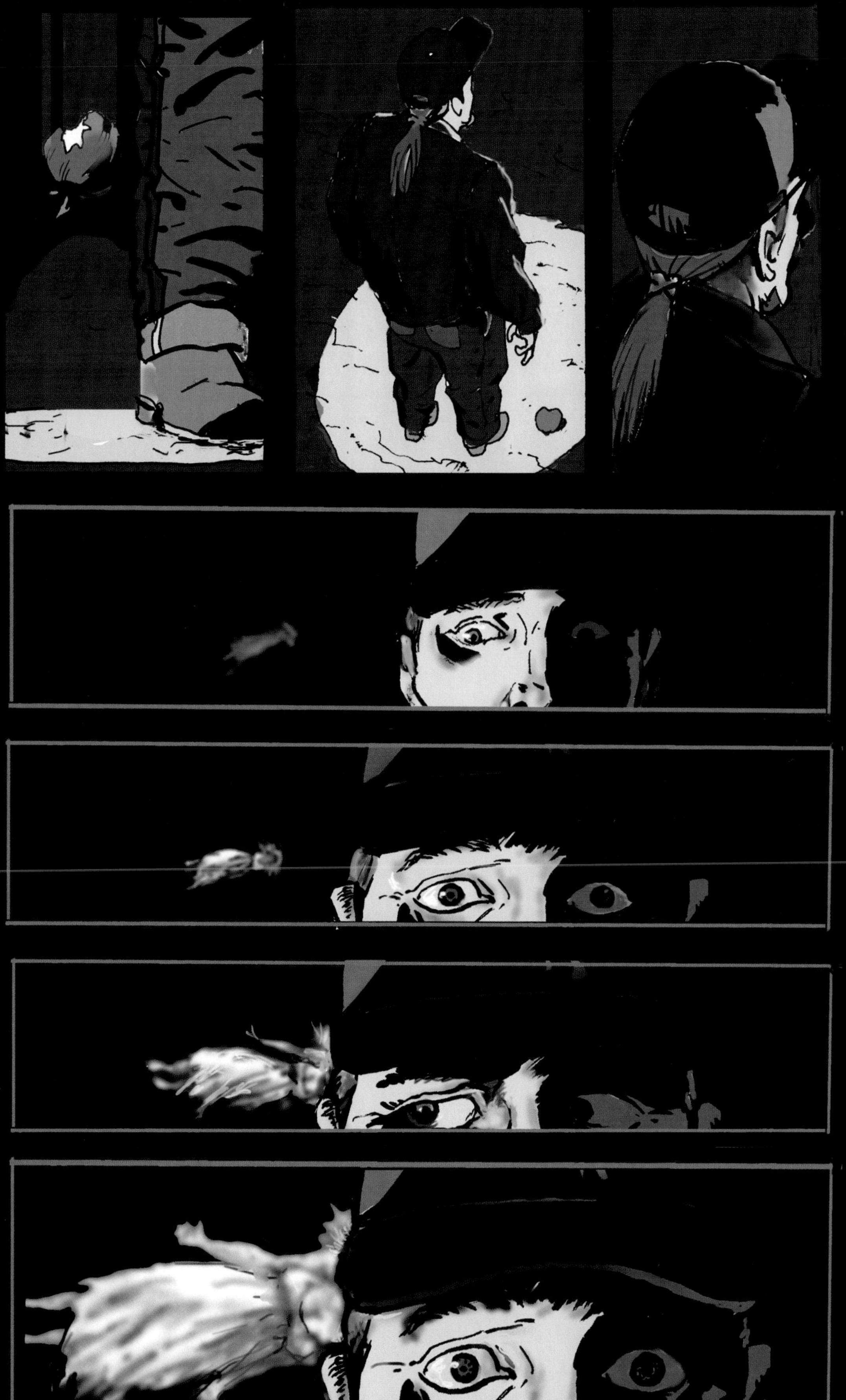

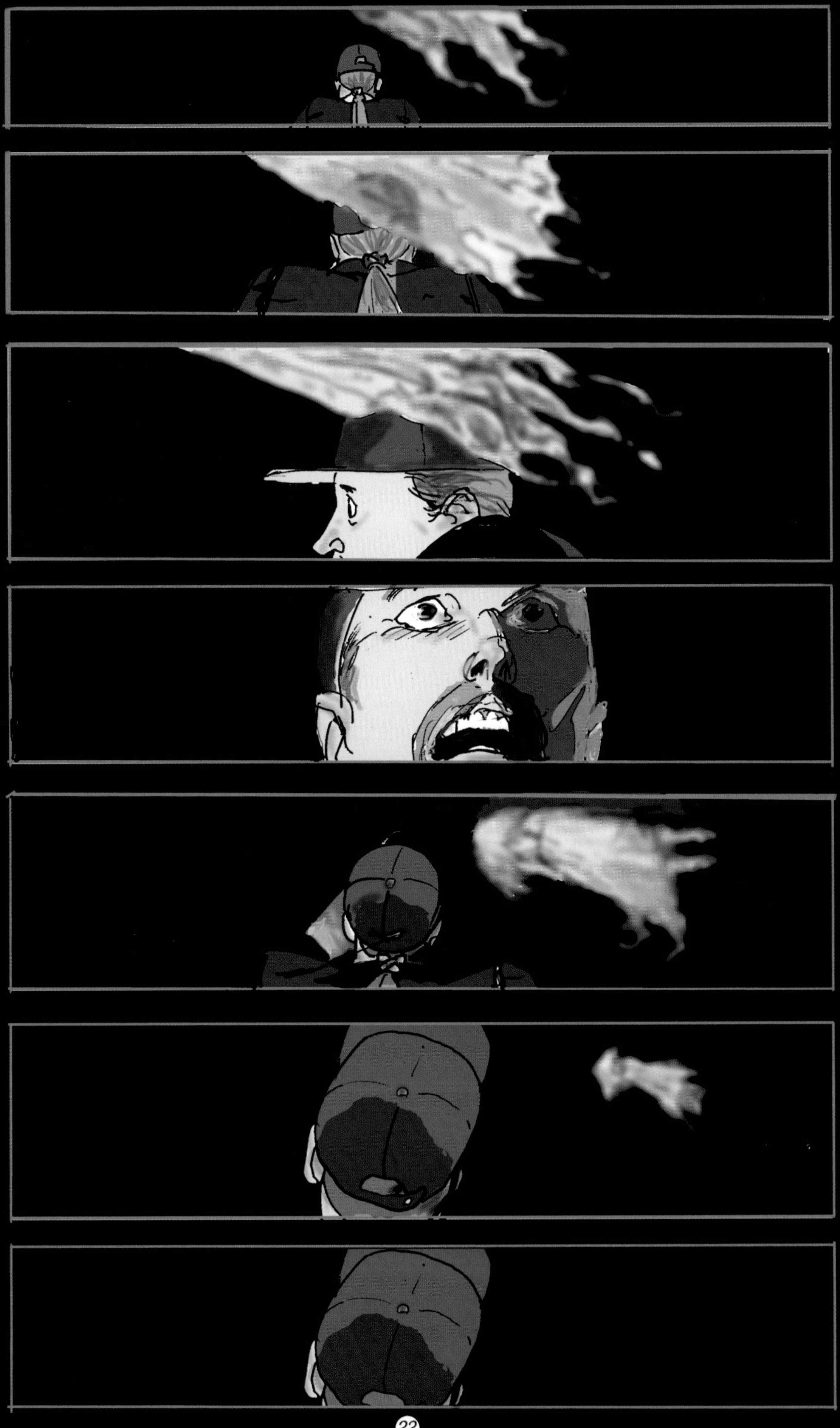

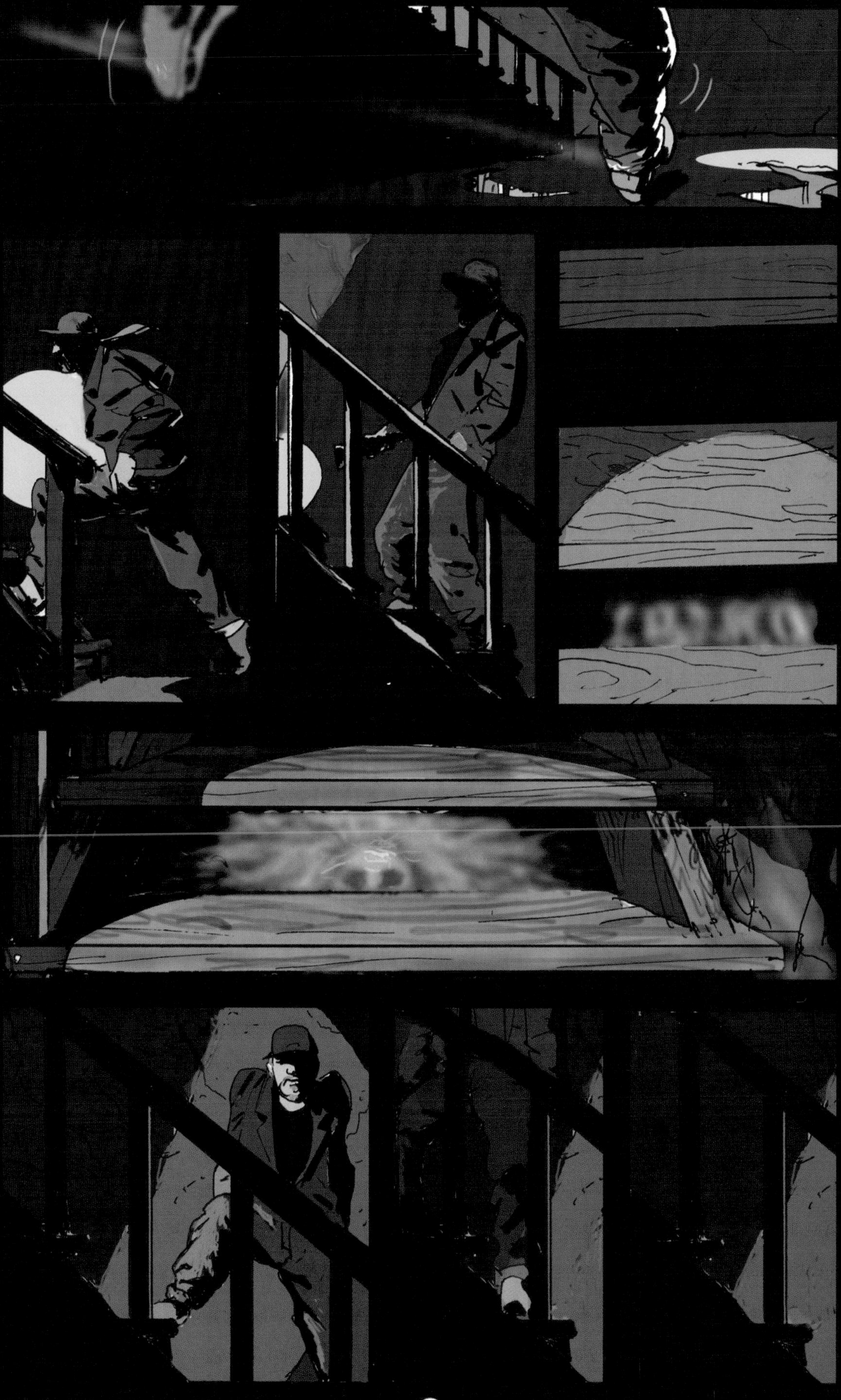

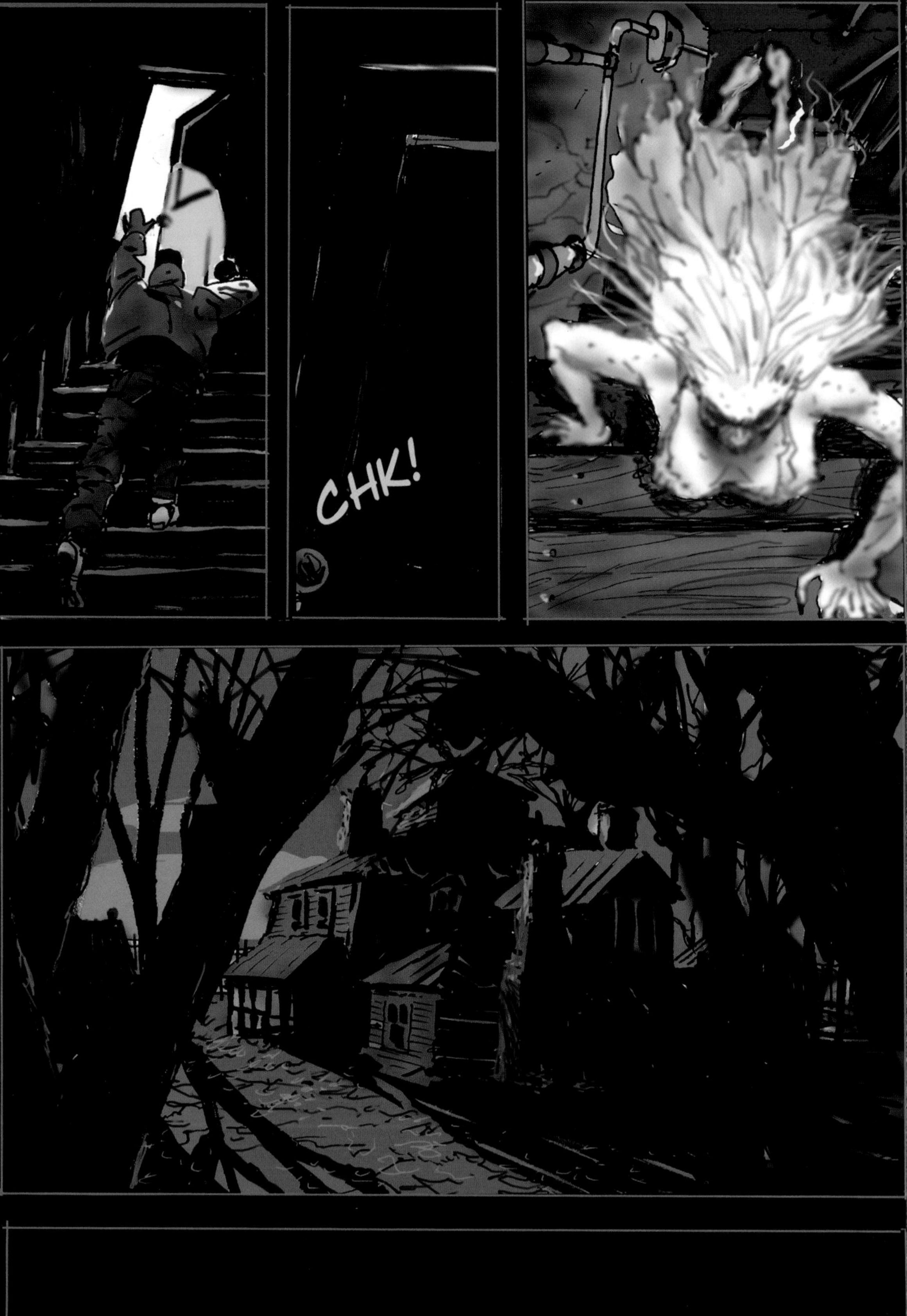
CHK!

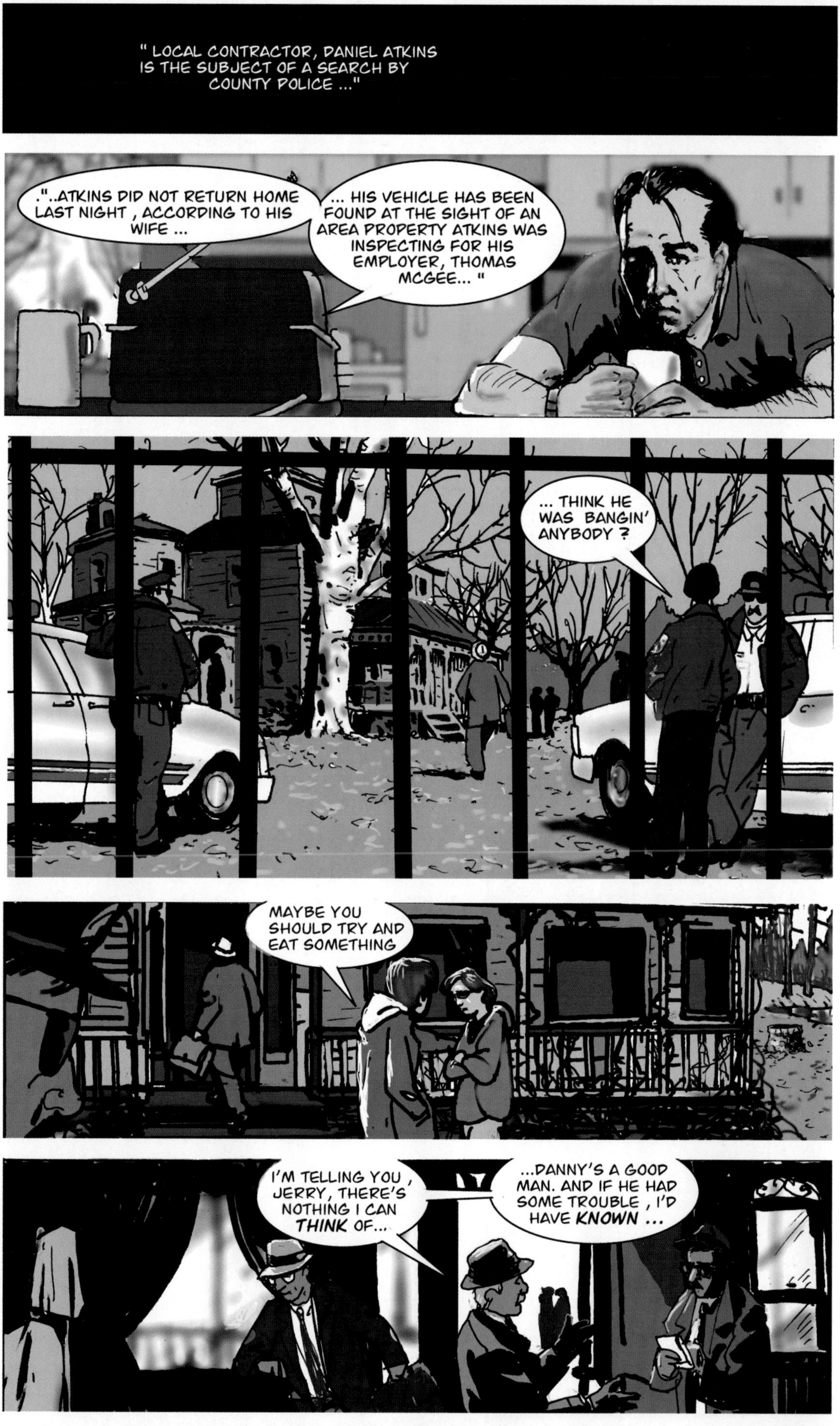
" LOCAL CONTRACTOR, DANIEL ATKINS IS THE SUBJECT OF A SEARCH BY COUNTY POLICE ..."
."..ATKINS DID NOT RETURN HOME LAST NIGHT , ACCORDING TO HIS WIFE ...
... HIS VEHICLE HAS BEEN FOUND AT THE SIGHT OF AN AREA PROPERTY ATKINS WAS INSPECTING FOR HIS EMPLOYER, THOMAS MCGEE... "
... THINK HE WAS BANGIN' ANYBODY ?
MAYBE YOU SHOULD TRY AND EAT SOMETHING
I'M TELLING YOU , JERRY, THERE'S NOTHING I CAN THINK OF...
...DANNY'S A GOOD MAN. AND IF HE HAD SOME TROUBLE , I'D HAVE KNOWN ...

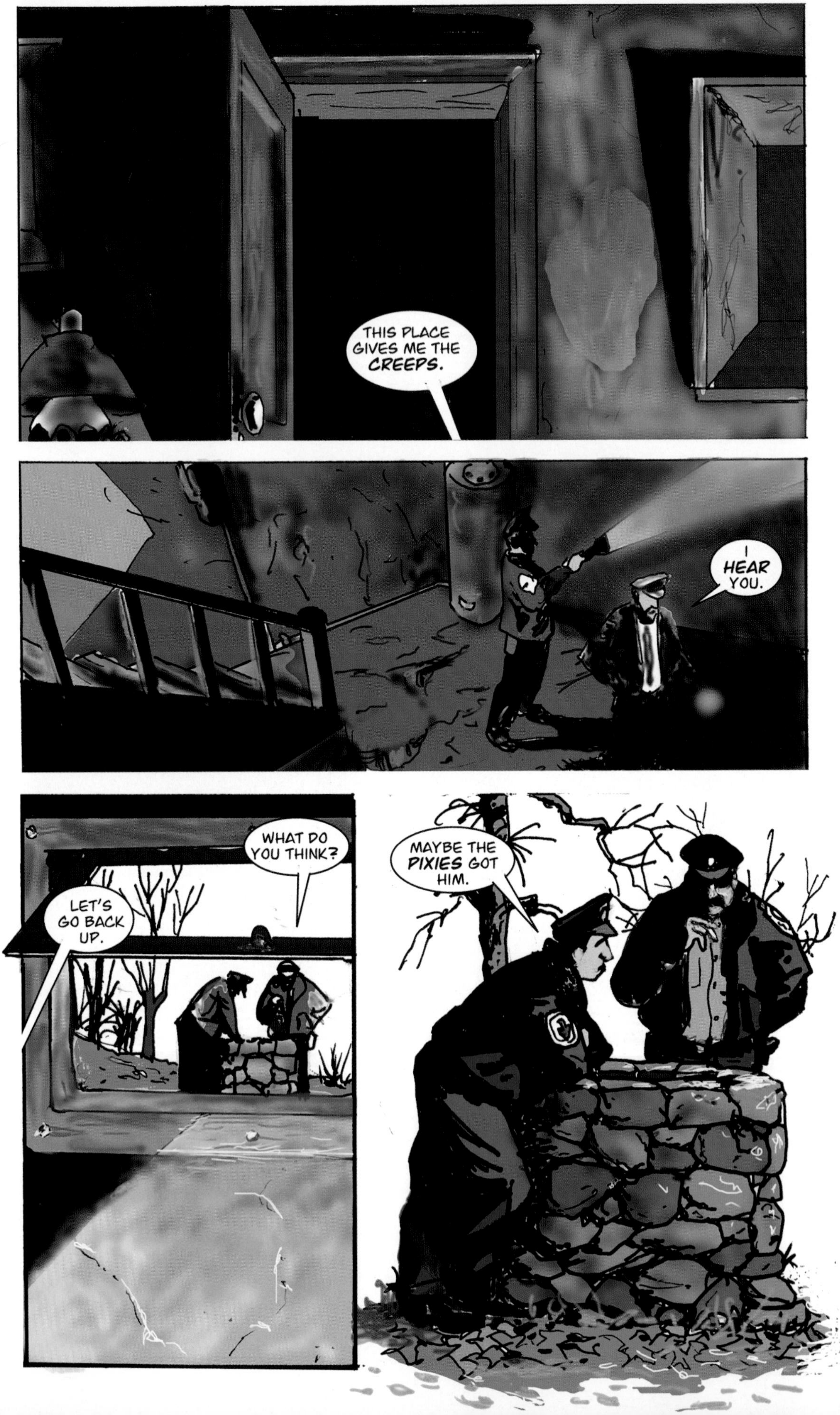
THIS PLACE GIVES ME THE CREEPS.
I HEAR YOU.
WHAT DO YOU THINK?
LET'S GO BACK UP.
MAYBE THE PIXIES GOT HIM.

OR MAYBE HE HOOKED UP WITH HIS " *GIRLFRIEND* " IN CLARKSVILLE.

YEAH, COULD BE ...

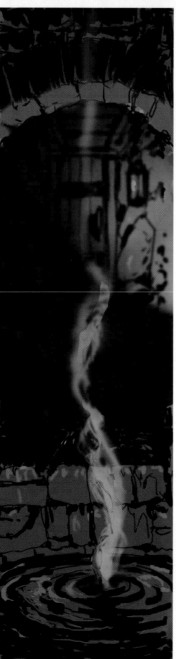

"IT'S BEEN A LONG TIME ..."

"...TOO LONG..."

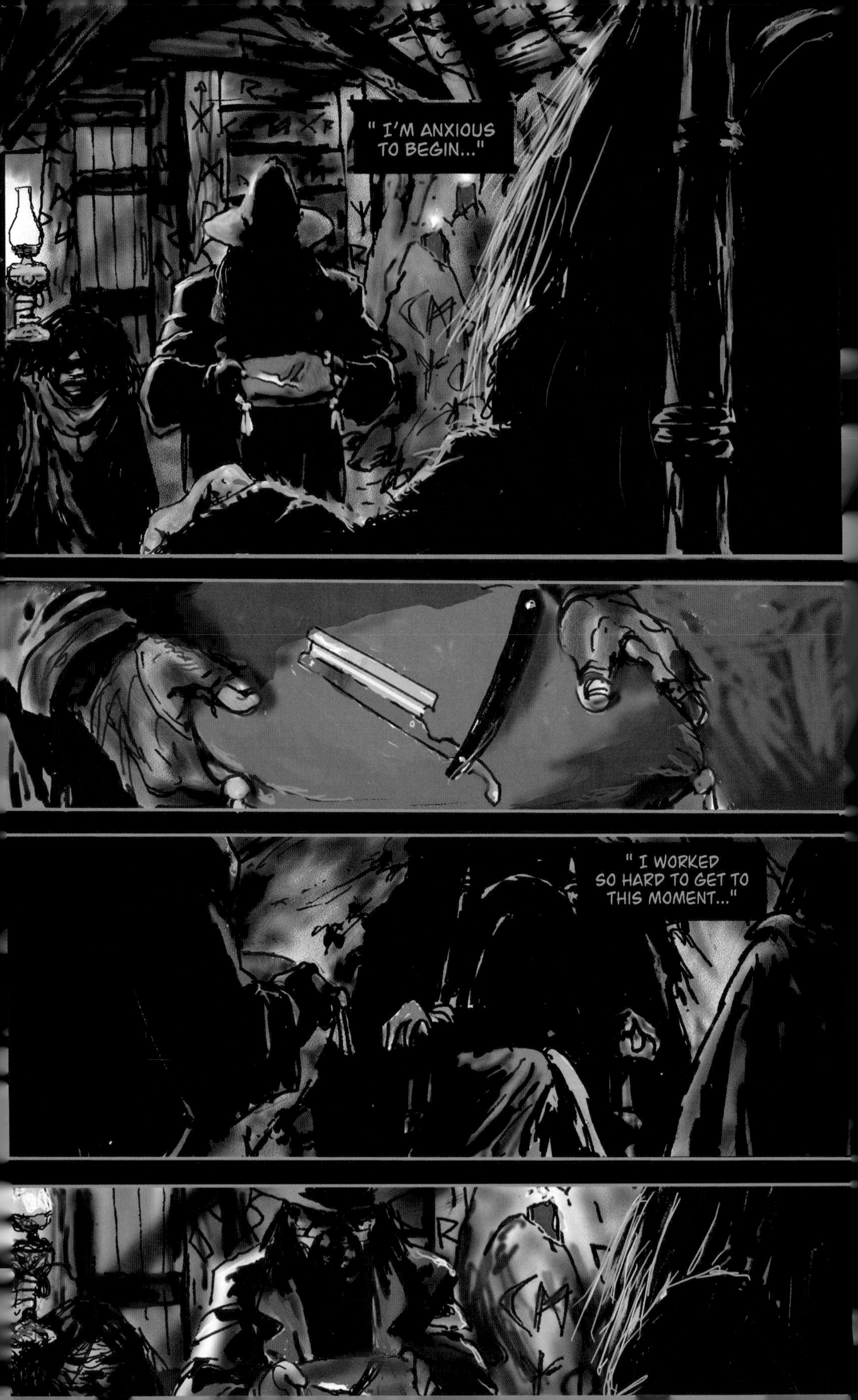
" I'M ANXIOUS TO BEGIN..."
" I WORKED SO HARD TO GET TO THIS MOMENT..."

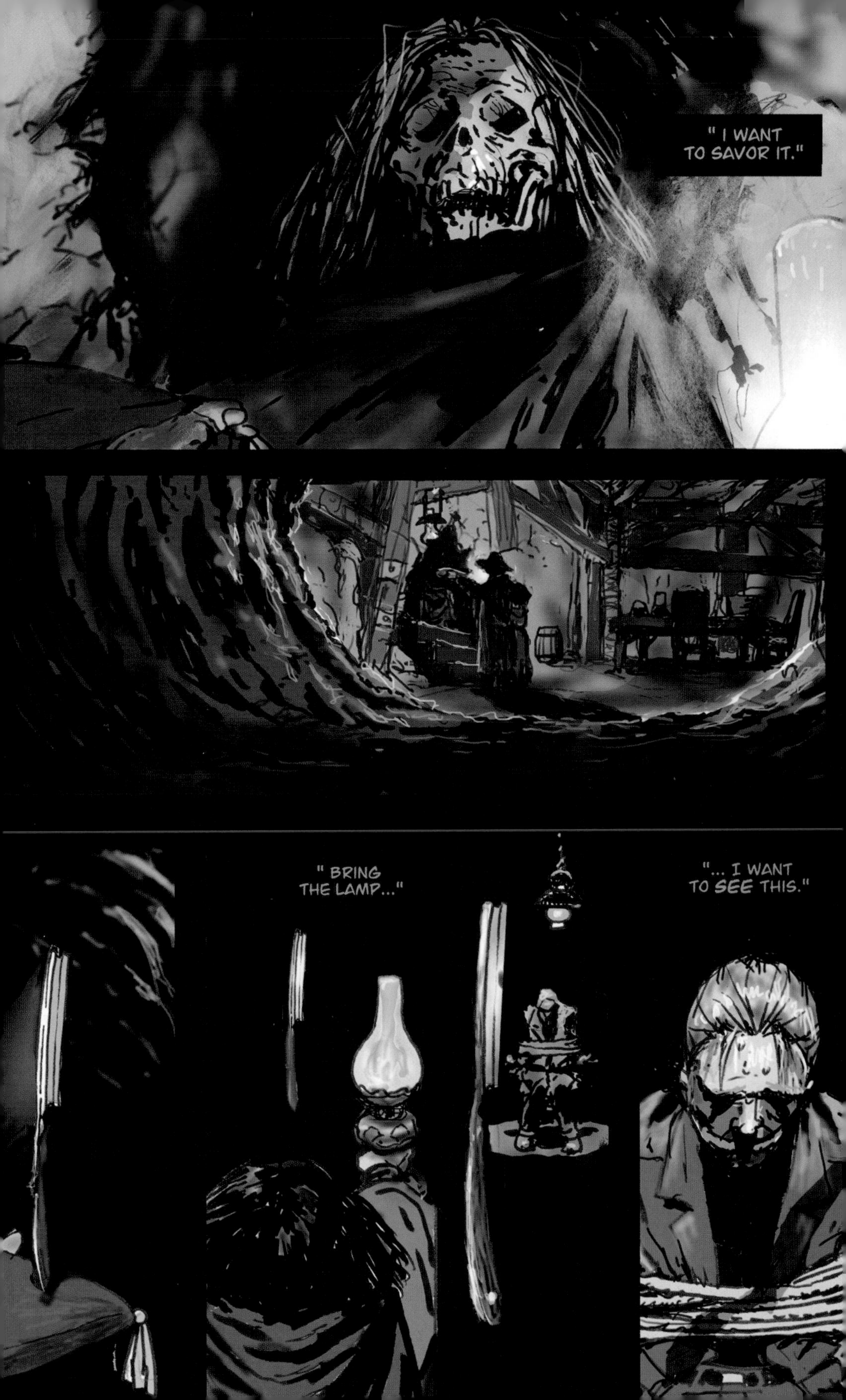
" I WANT
TO SAVOR IT."
" BRING
THE LAMP..."
"... I WANT
TO SEE THIS."

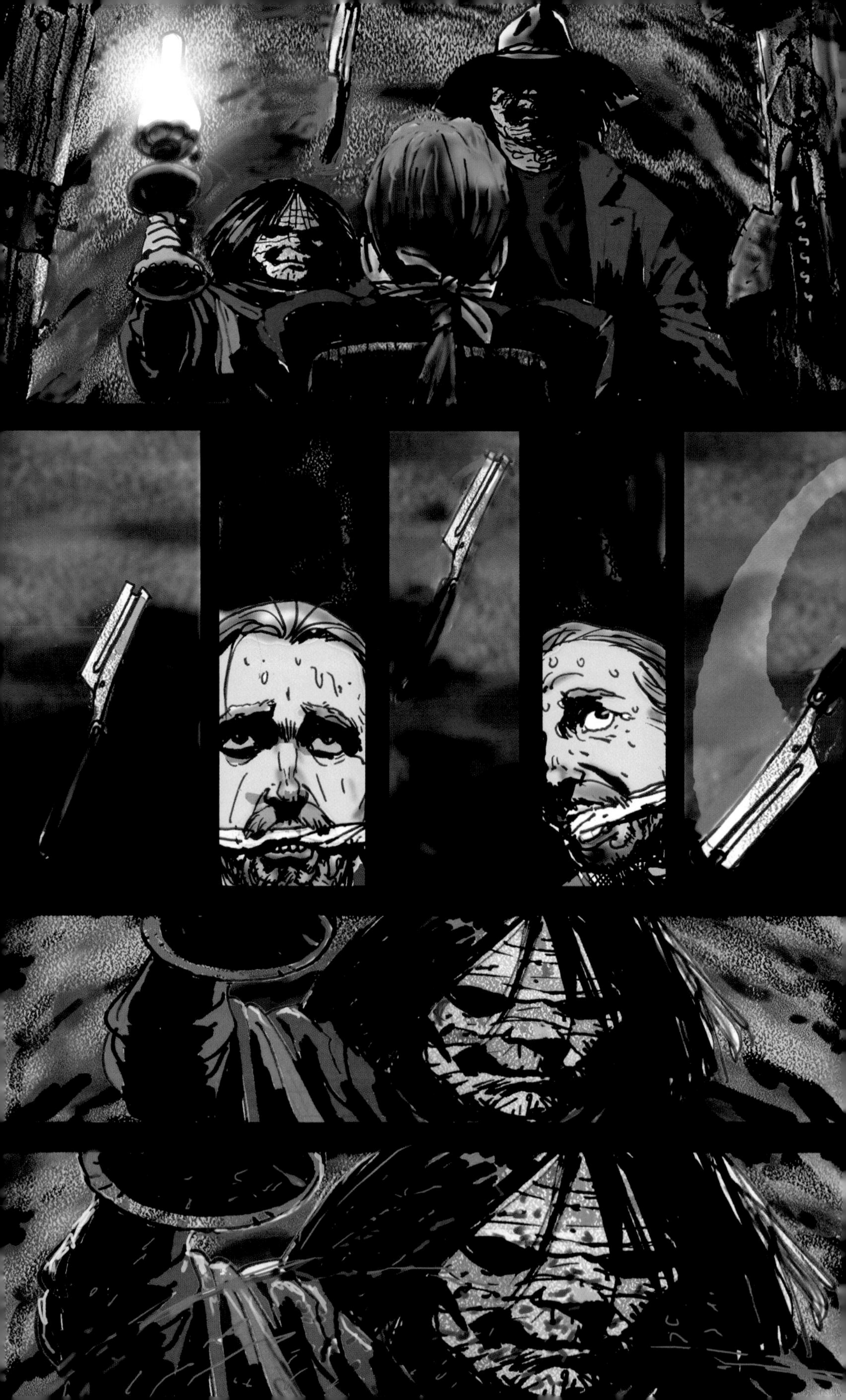

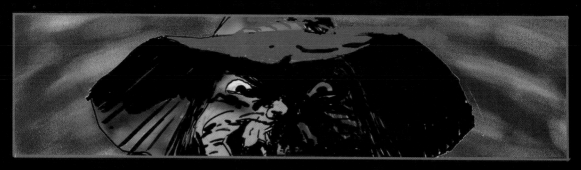

"SO VERY
HARD."

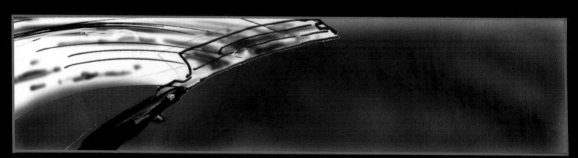

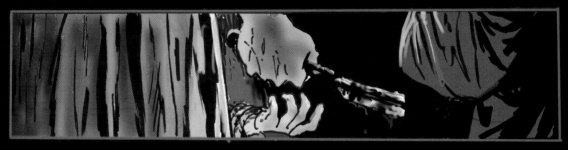

"AND IT FEELS SO
VERY GOOD."

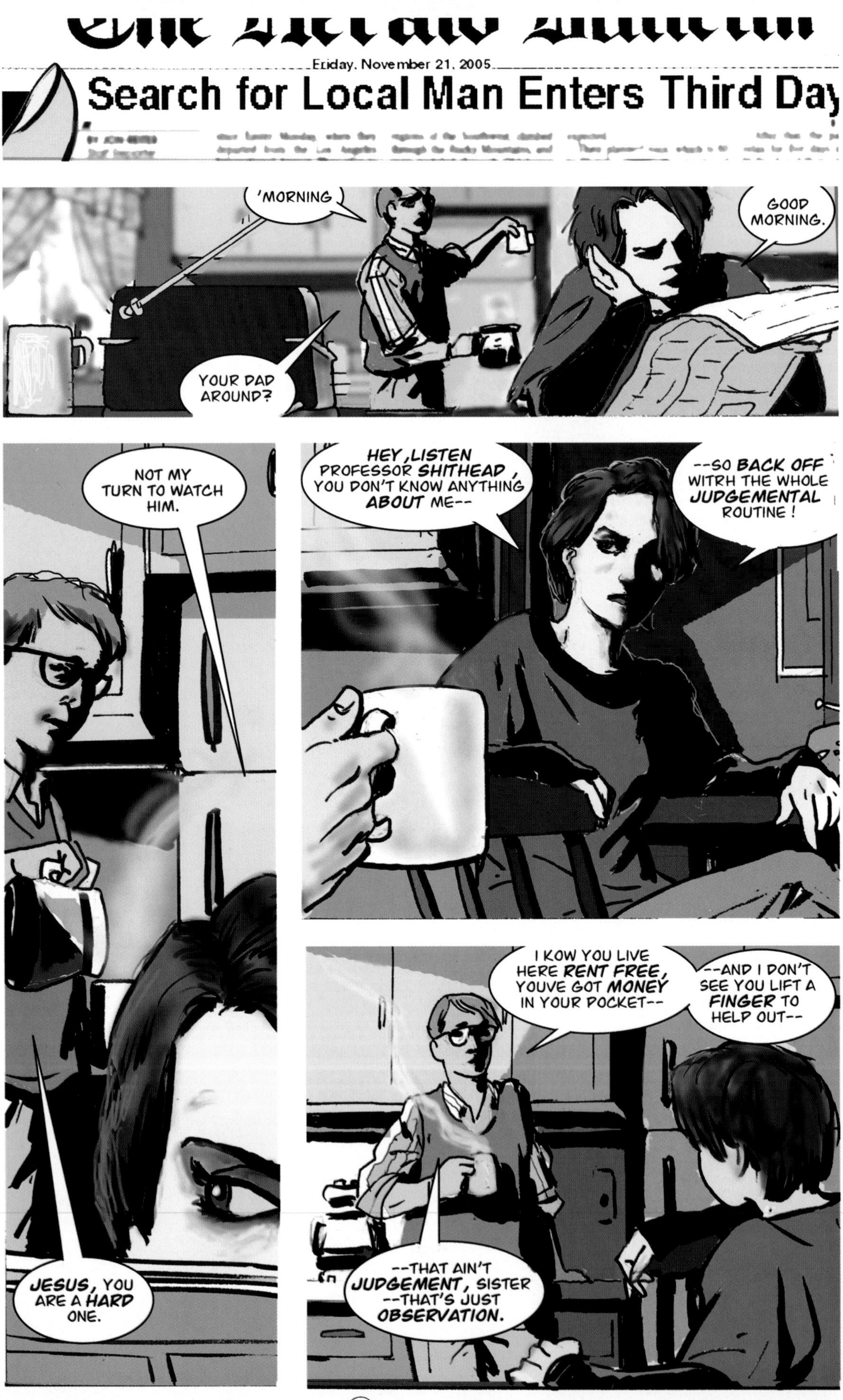
Friday, November 21, 2005
Search for Local Man Enters Third Day
'MORNING
GOOD MORNING.
YOUR DAD AROUND?
NOT MY TURN TO WATCH HIM.
JESUS, YOU ARE A HARD ONE.
HEY, LISTEN PROFESSOR SHITHEAD, YOU DON'T KNOW ANYTHING ABOUT ME--
--SO BACK OFF WITRH THE WHOLE JUDGEMENTAL ROUTINE!
I KOW YOU LIVE HERE RENT FREE, YOUVE GOT MONEY IN YOUR POCKET--
--AND I DON'T SEE YOU LIFT A FINGER TO HELP OUT--
--THAT AIN'T JUDGEMENT, SISTER --THAT'S JUST OBSERVATION.

OBSERVE THIS !!

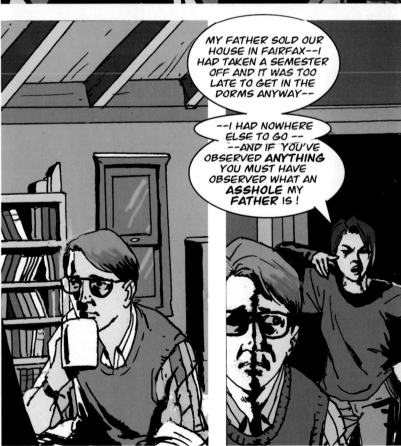

MY FATHER SOLD OUR HOUSE IN FAIRFAX--I HAD TAKEN A SEMESTER OFF AND IT WAS TOO LATE TO GET IN THE DORMS ANYWAY--

--I HAD NOWHERE ELSE TO GO -- --AND IF YOU'VE OBSERVED **ANYTHING** YOU MUST HAVE OBSERVED WHAT AN **ASSHOLE** MY FATHER IS !

IT'S NOT YOUR FATHER'S FAULT YOUR MOTHER IS DEAD, MOLLY...

...IT WAS AN ACCIDENT.

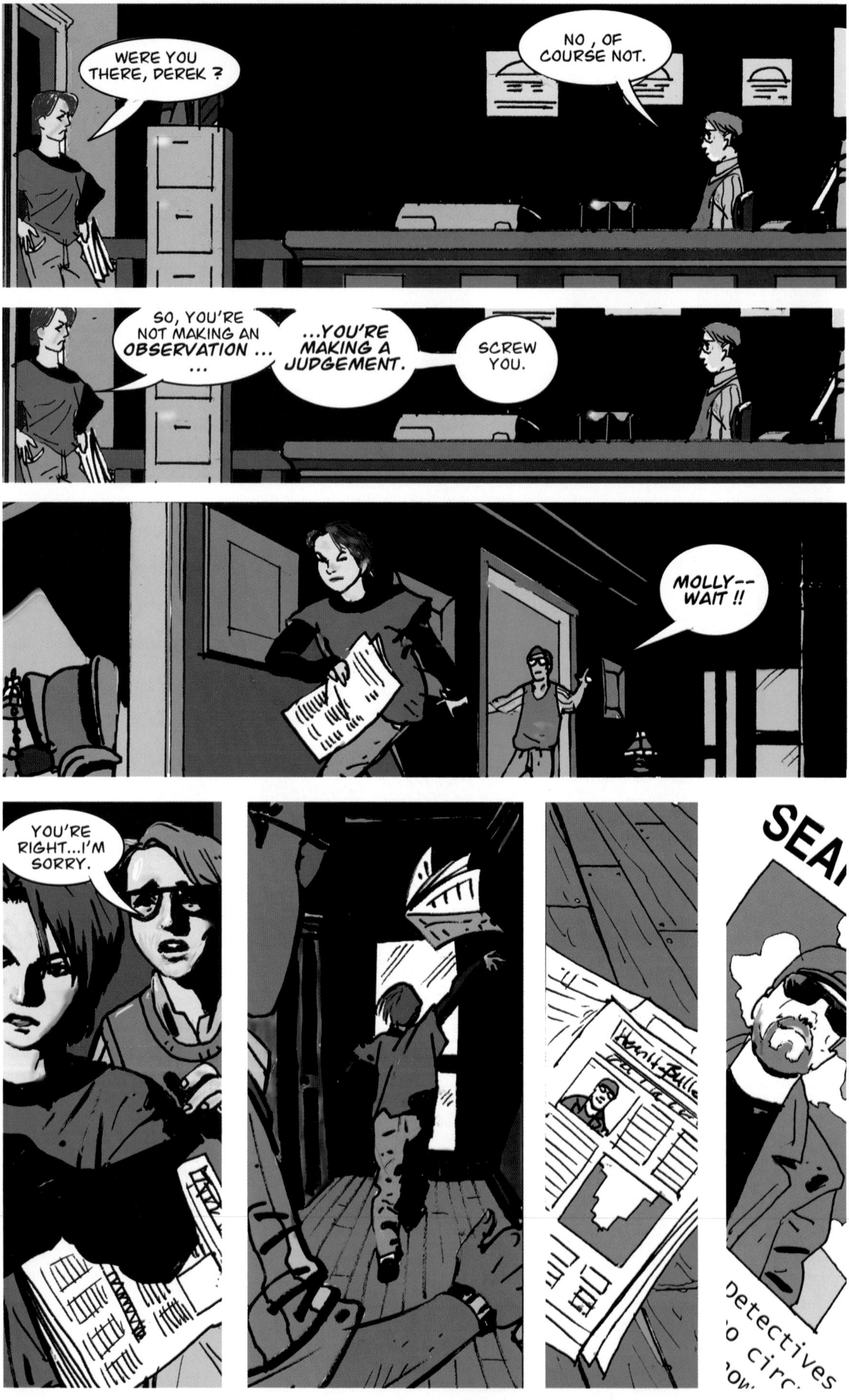
WERE YOU THERE, DEREK ?
NO , OF COURSE NOT.
SO, YOU'RE NOT MAKING AN OBSERVATION ... ...
...YOU'RE MAKING A JUDGEMENT.
SCREW YOU.
MOLLY-- WAIT !!
YOU'RE RIGHT...I'M SORRY.

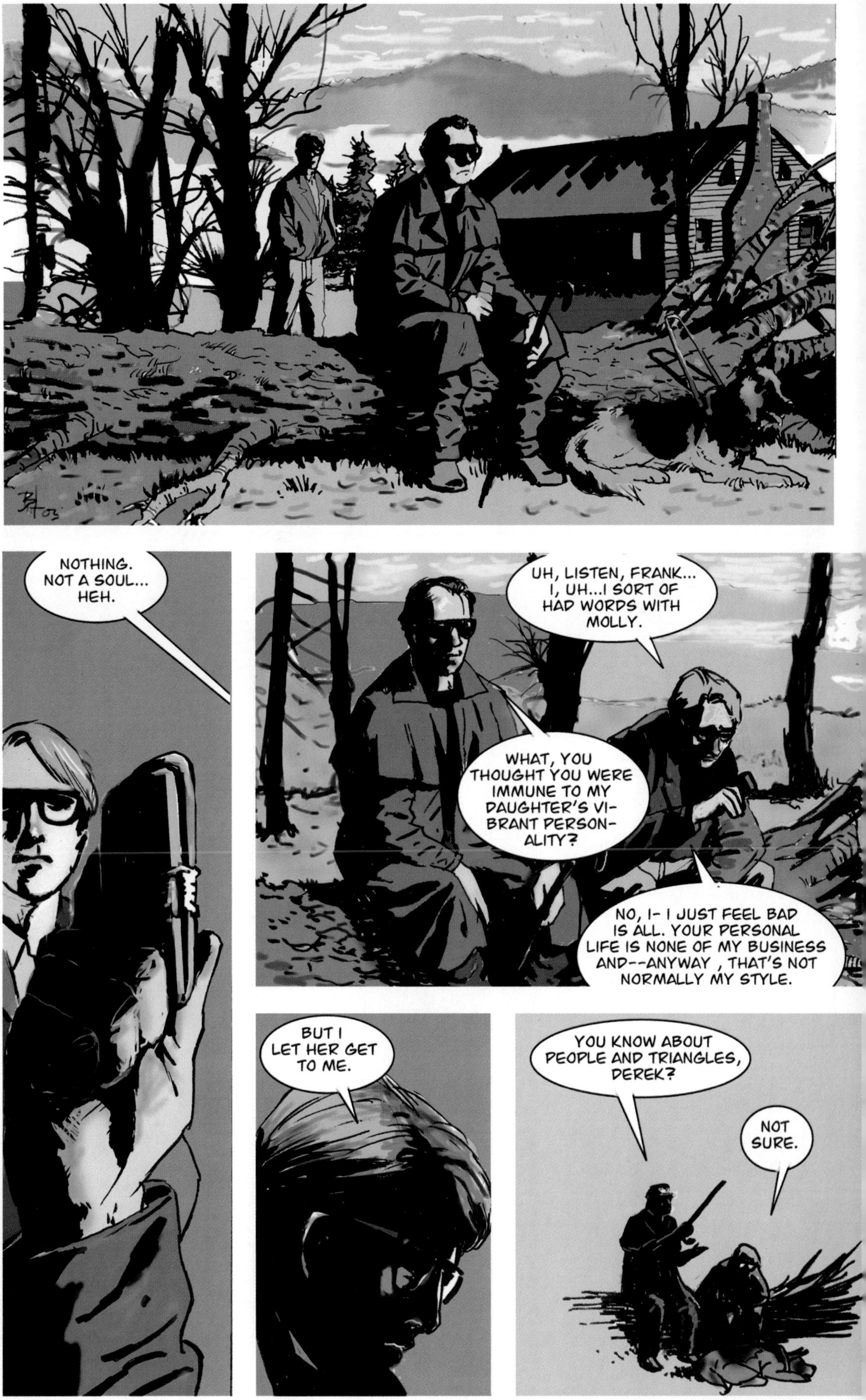
NOTHING.
NOT A SOUL...
HEH.
UH, LISTEN, FRANK...
I, UH...I SORT OF
HAD WORDS WITH
MOLLY.
WHAT, YOU
THOUGHT YOU WERE
IMMUNE TO MY
DAUGHTER'S VI-
BRANT PERSON-
ALITY?
NO, I- I JUST FEEL BAD
IS ALL. YOUR PERSONAL
LIFE IS NONE OF MY BUSINESS
AND--ANYWAY , THAT'S NOT
NORMALLY MY STYLE.
BUT I
LET HER GET
TO ME.
YOU KNOW ABOUT
PEOPLE AND TRIANGLES,
DEREK?
NOT
SURE.

IT'S LIKE THIS. PEOPLE FORM TRIANGLES IN ALL THEIR RELATION- SHIPS...

...THOSE TRIANGLES RESULT IN ALLIANCES AND ENEMIES AND STRIFE AND PREGNANCIES AND ALL OF LIFE'S DRAMA...

...AND USUALLY THE TRIANGLES RESULT IN TWO SIDES GANGING UP ON THE OTHER--AND THEN IT CAN SHIFT AND SO ON, ACCORD- ING TO CHANGING CIRCUM- STANCES...

WHEN LESLIE DIED MOLLY AND I LOST A PART OF THE TRIANGLE. SO, WE'RE OUT OF BALANCE. MAKE SENSE ?

YEAH, ACTUALLY IT DOES.

I THOUGHT SO, TOO, WHEN I HEARD SOME SHRINK TALKING ABOUT IT, LAST NIGHT, ON THE RADIO...

I'M HUNGRY, I'M GOING TO GET SOMETHING TO EAT.

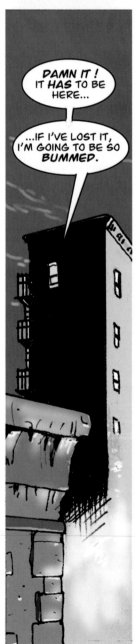

DAMN IT ! IT HAS TO BE HERE...

...IF I'VE LOST IT, I'M GOING TO BE SO BUMMED.

IF THE PIXIES GOT IT YOU'LL NEVER GET IT BACK.

WHAT ARE YOU TALK- ING ABOUT?

YOU HAVEN'T HEARD OF THE PIXIES? THEY'RE THESE MAGIC, LITTLE PEOPLE WHO LIVE IN THE WOODS AROUND HERE.

THEY'RE ALWAYS STEALING THINGS. USUALLY FOOD OR CLOTHES...BUT SOMETHING BRIGHT AND SHINY LIKE AN EAR- RING WOULD PROBABLY--

CHAD!! WILL YOU SHUT UP WITH THE TOLKEIN CRAP AND HELP ME FIND IT??

I'LL BUY YOU ANOTHER ONE.

YOU CAN'T BUY ANOTHER ONE!! I NEED THAT ONE ! IT WAS-- MAYBE I LOST IT AT HOME. TAKE ME HOME.

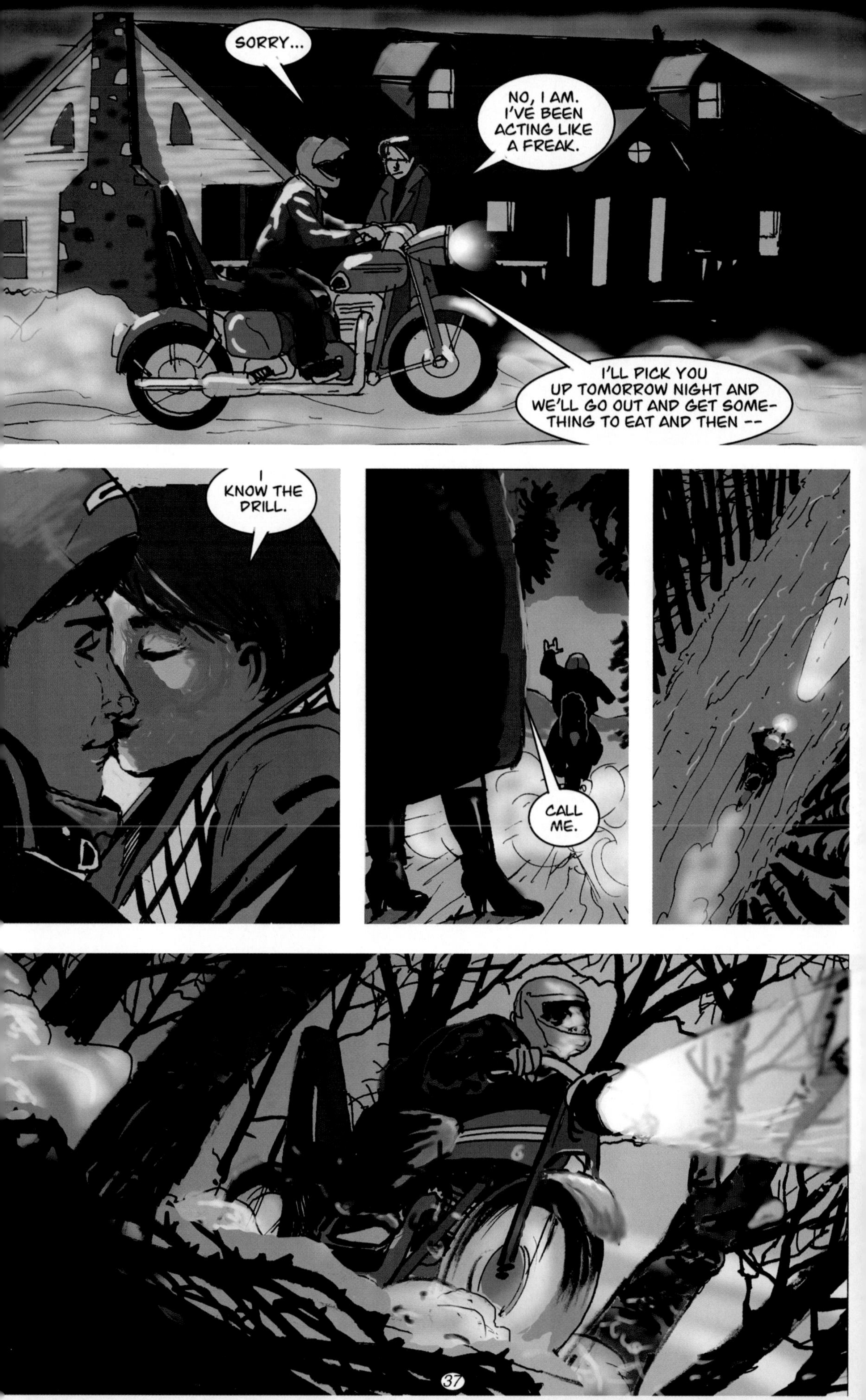
SORRY...
NO, I AM. I'VE BEEN ACTING LIKE A FREAK.
I'LL PICK YOU UP TOMORROW NIGHT AND WE'LL GO OUT AND GET SOME-THING TO EAT AND THEN --
I KNOW THE DRILL.
CALL ME.

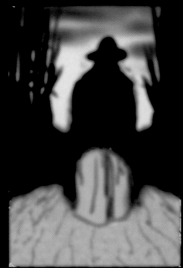

JESUS--!!

HEY !!

WHAT THE HELL
WERE YOU--?!!

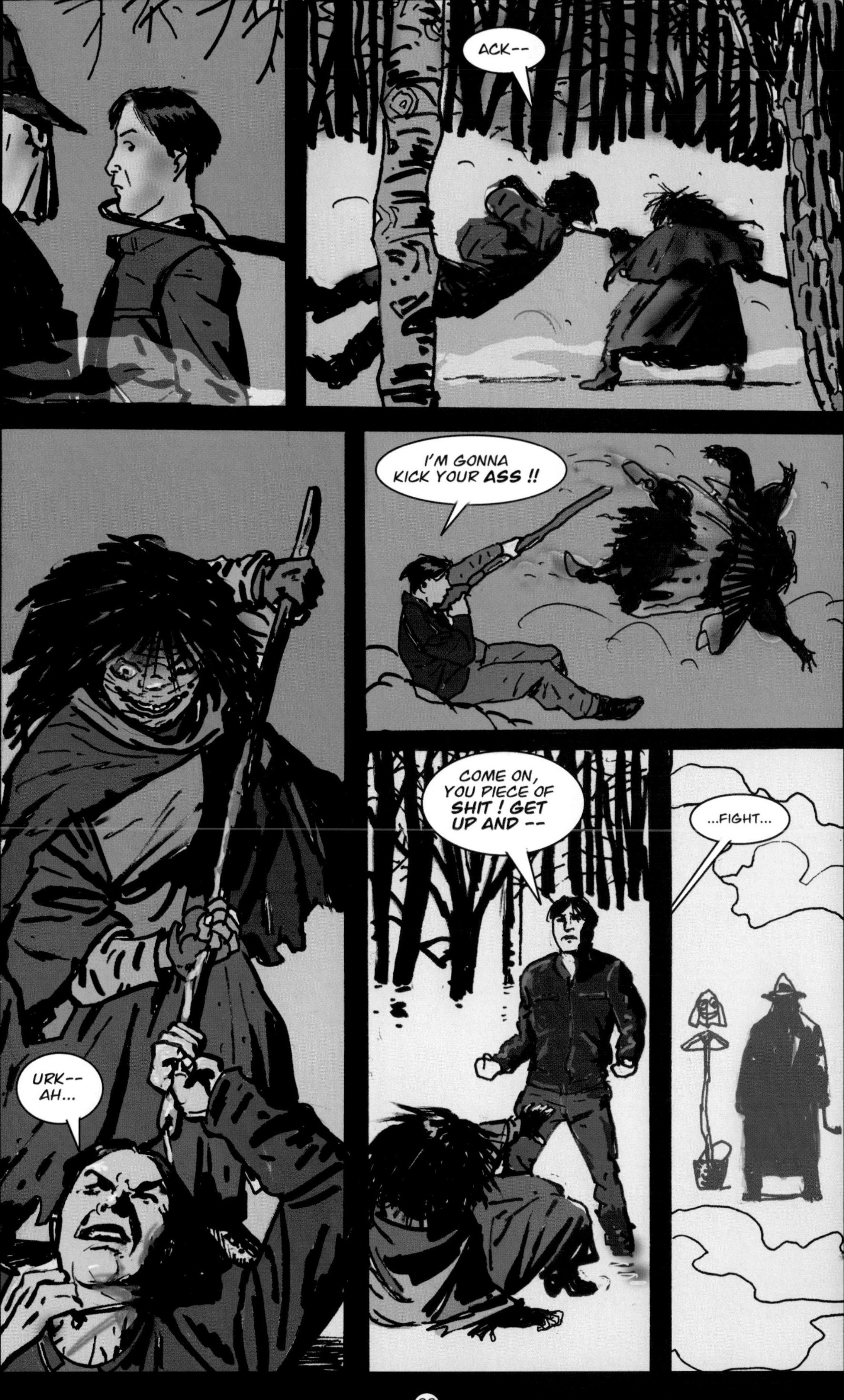
ACK--
I'M GONNA KICK YOUR ASS !!
URK-- AH...
COME ON, YOU PIECE OF SHIT ! GET UP AND --
...FIGHT...

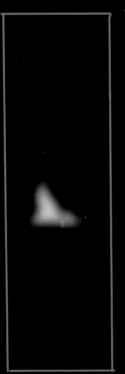

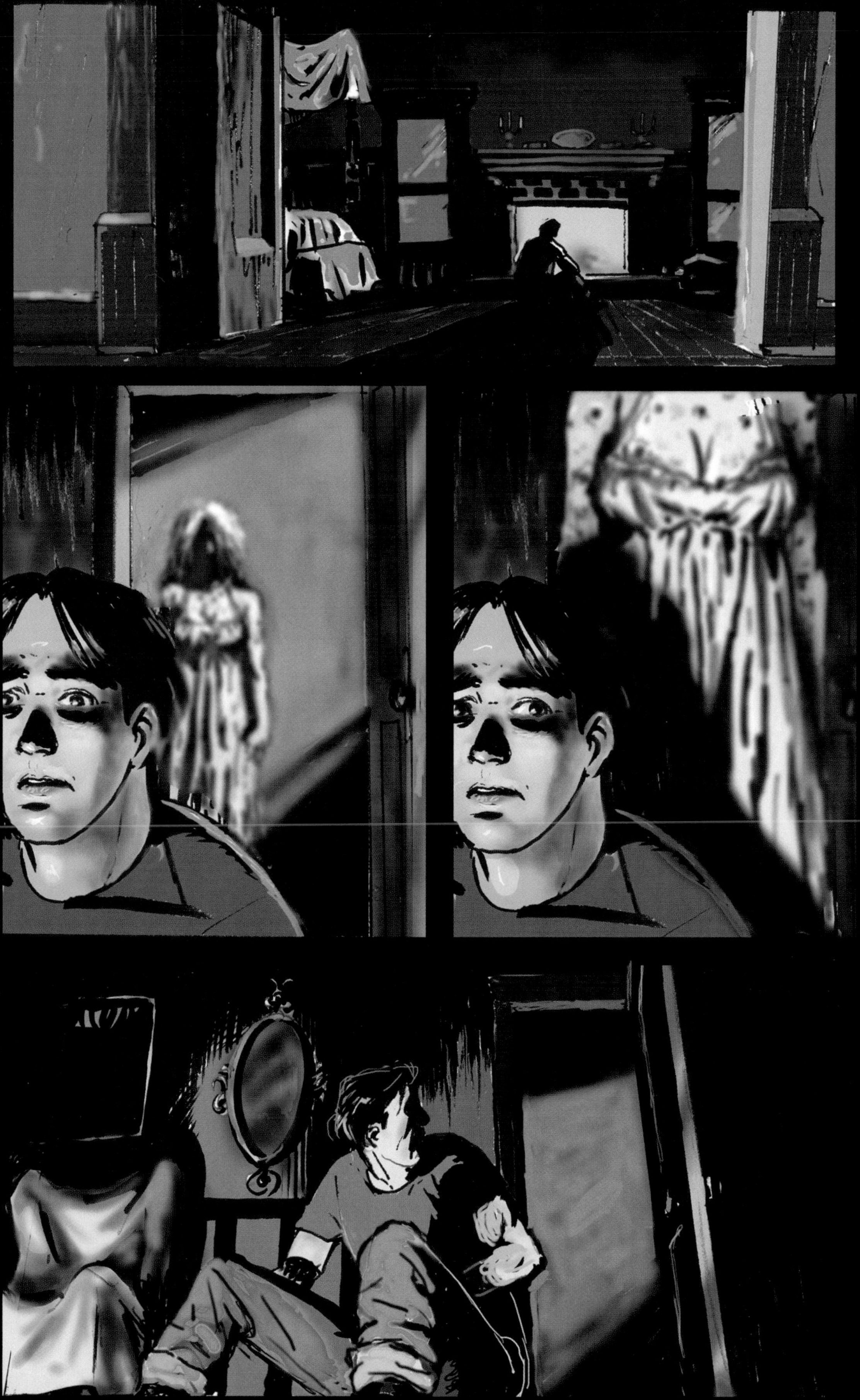

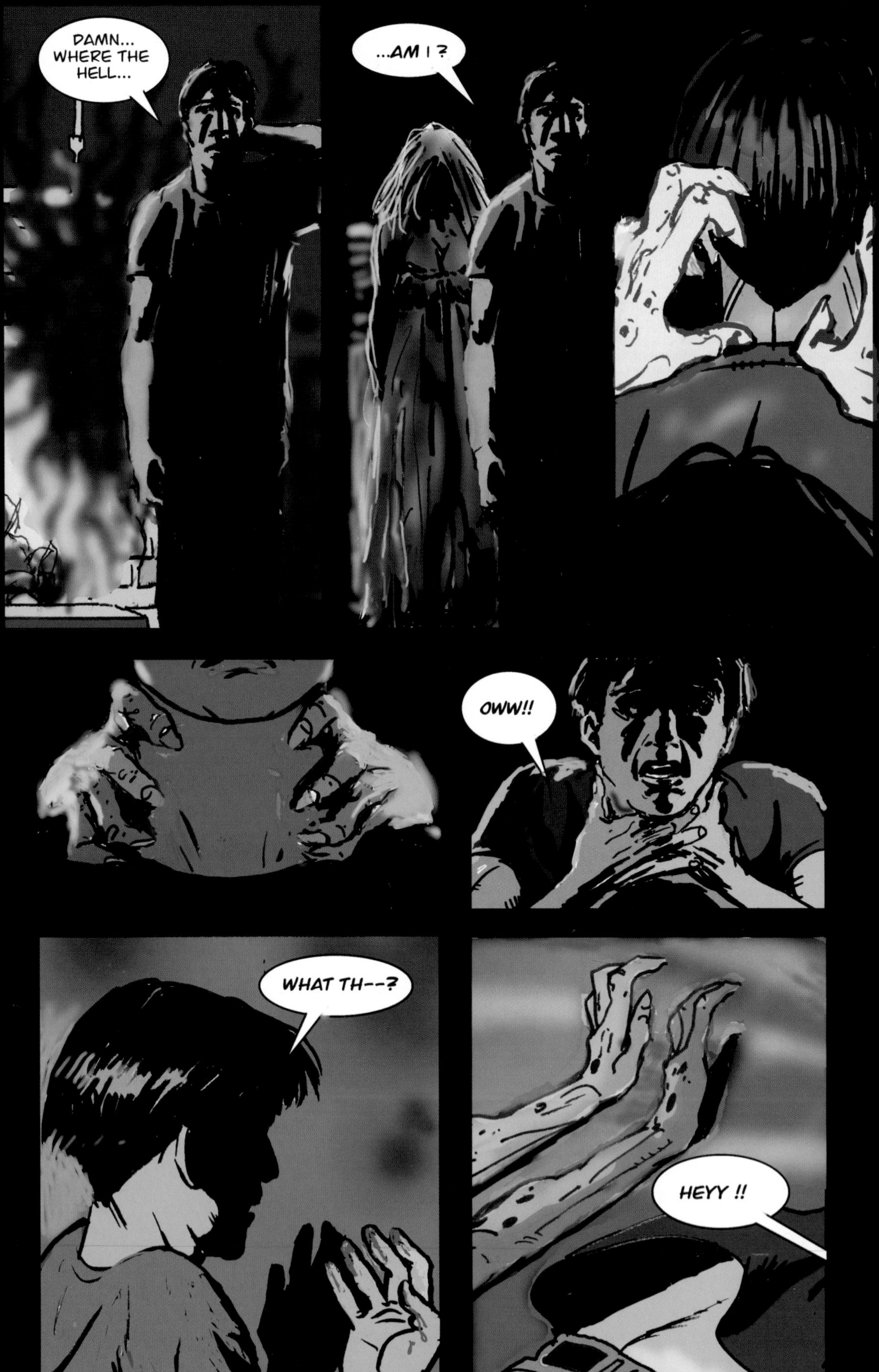
DAMN... WHERE THE HELL...
...AM I ?
OWW!!
WHAT TH--?
HEYY !!

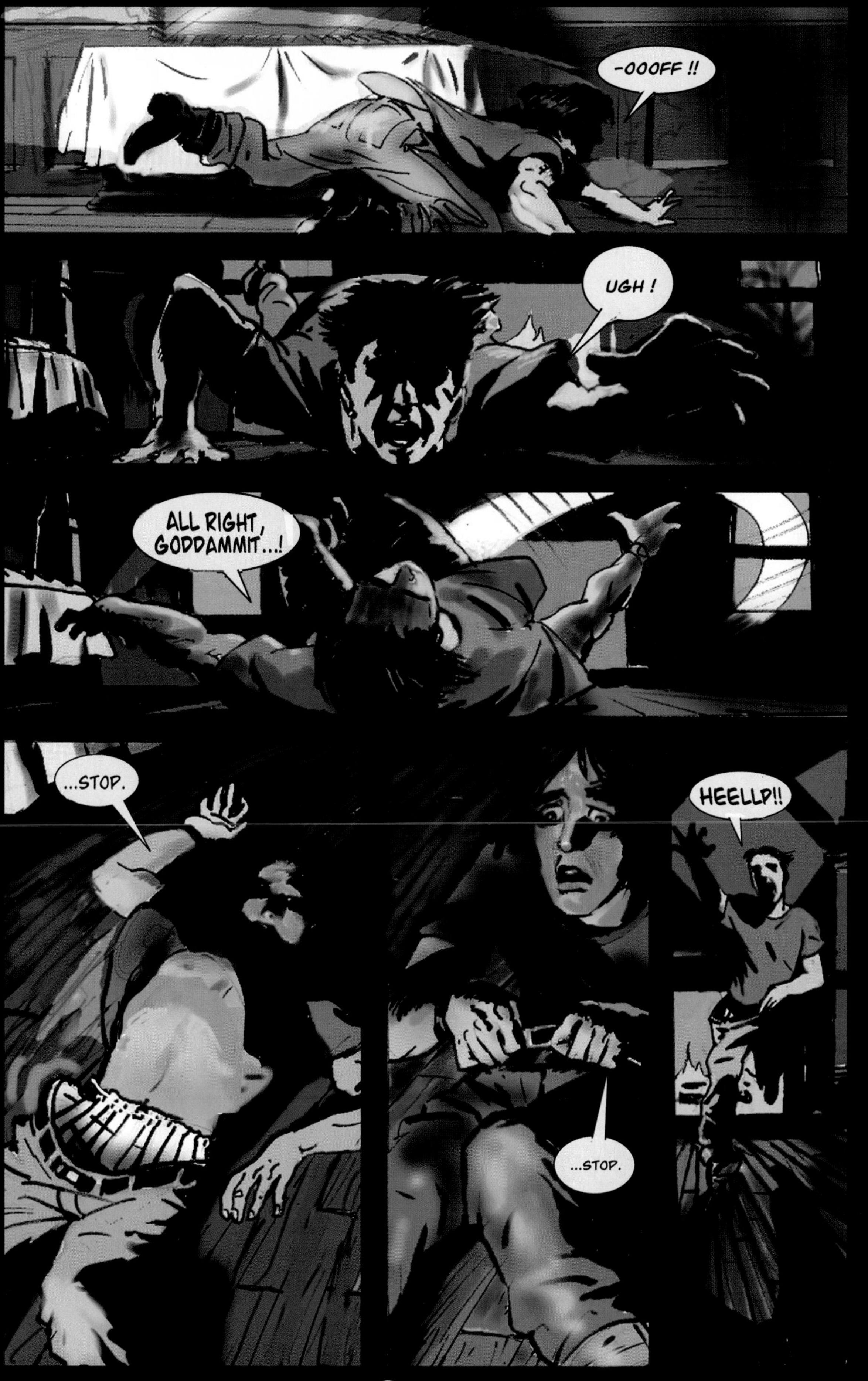
-OOOFF !!
UGH !
ALL RIGHT, GODDAMMIT...!
...STOP.
...STOP.
HEELLP!!

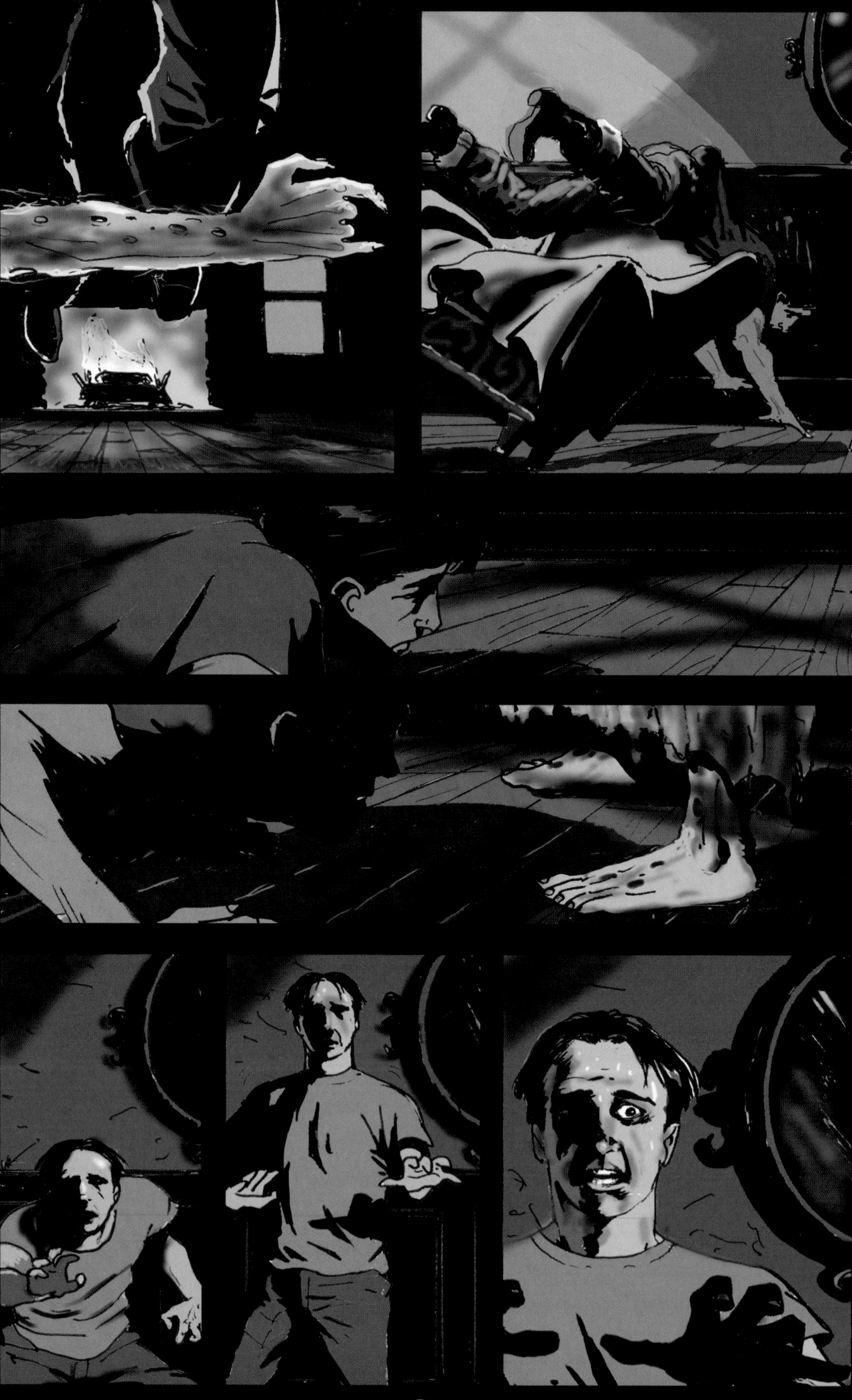

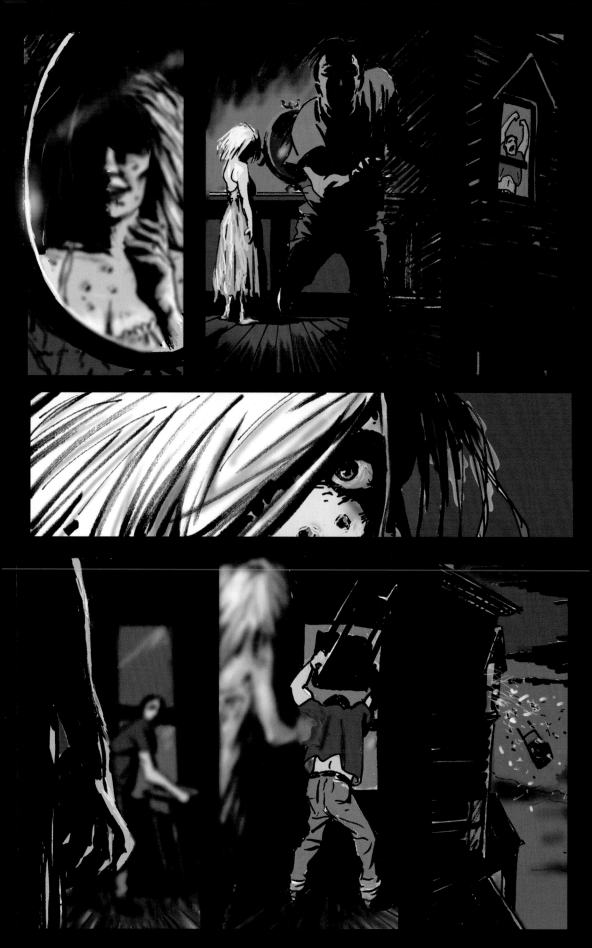

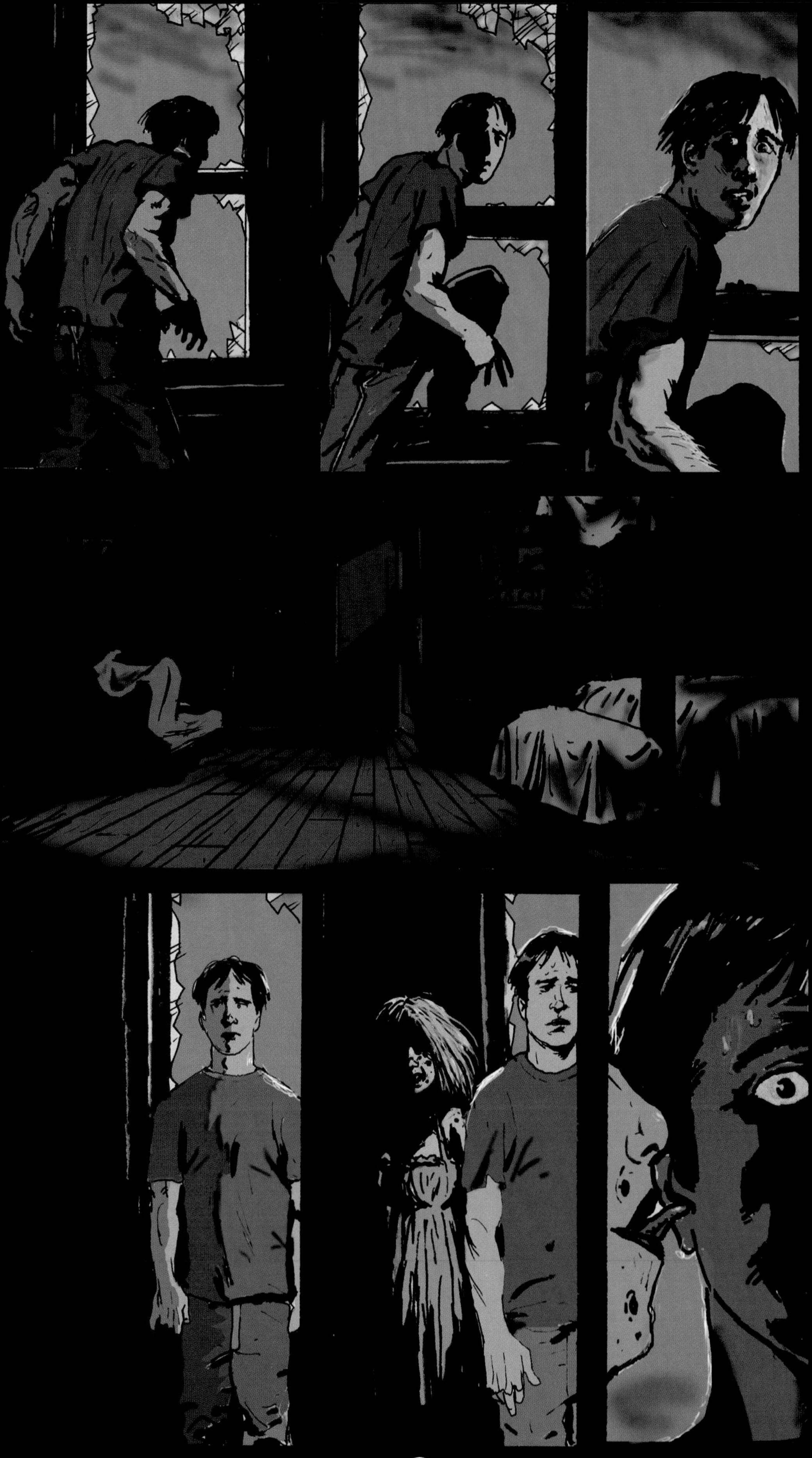

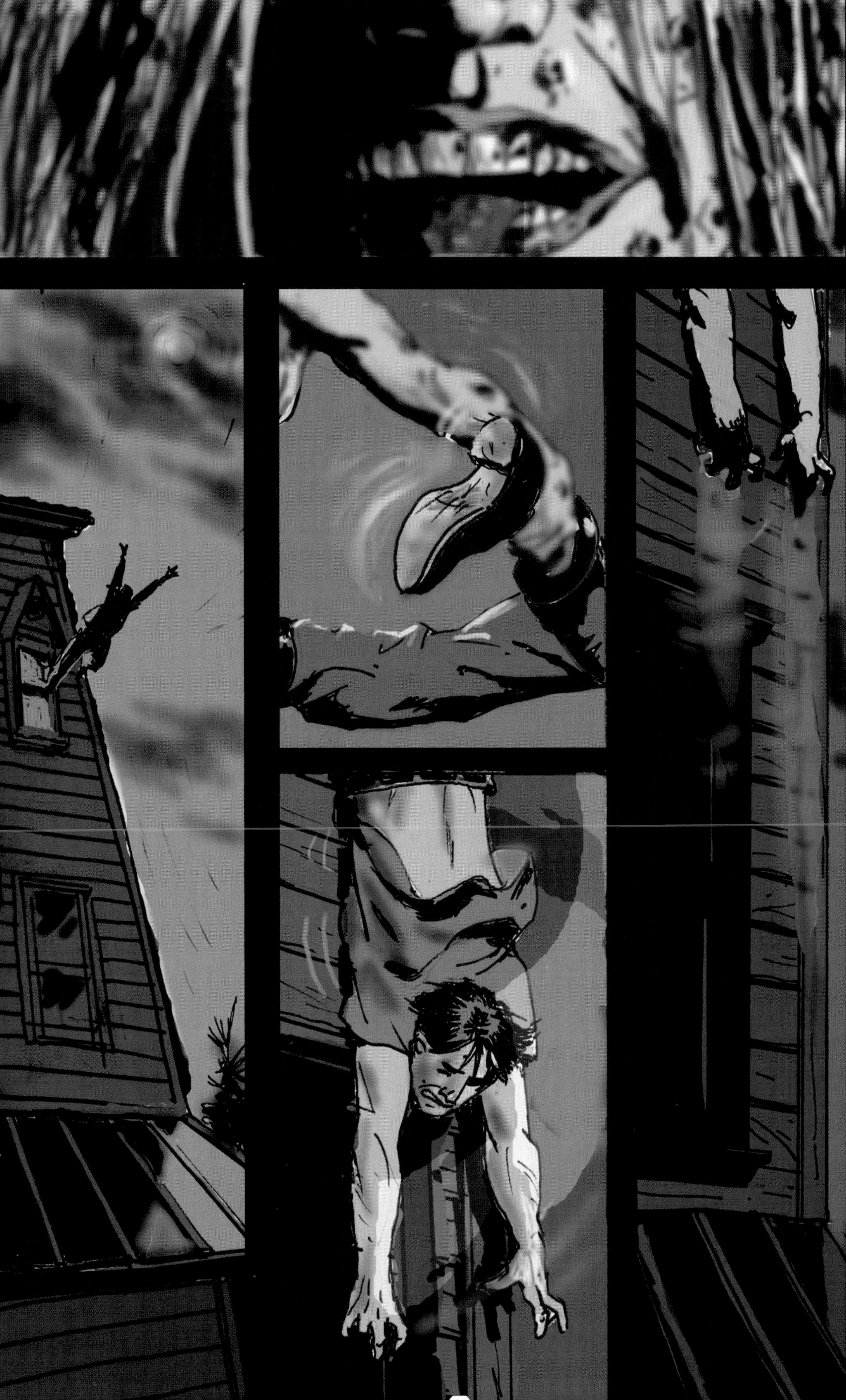

PRL 32.55677

ENTR'ACTE

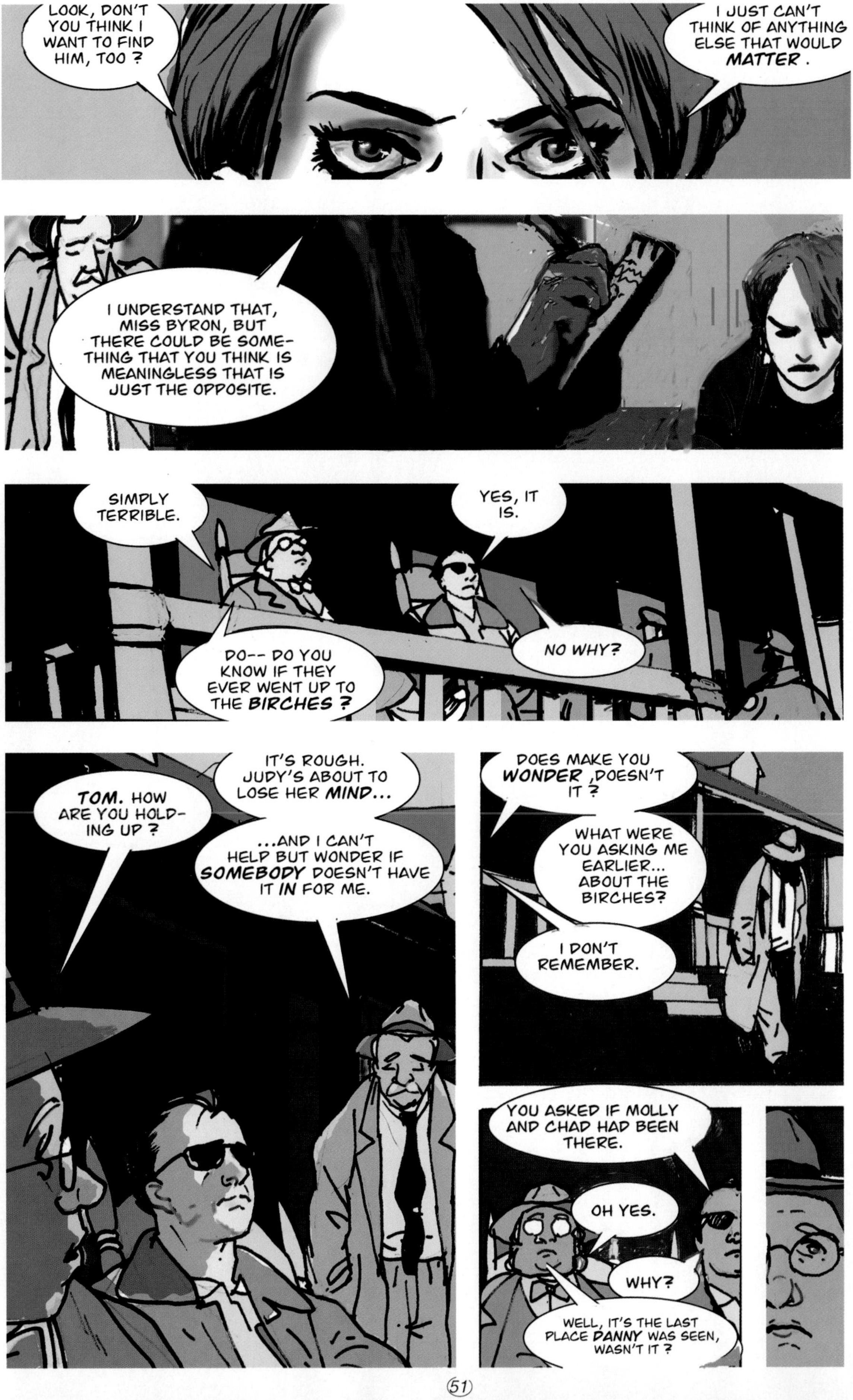
LOOK, DON'T YOU THINK I WANT TO FIND HIM, TOO?
I JUST CAN'T THINK OF ANYTHING ELSE THAT WOULD MATTER.
I UNDERSTAND THAT, MISS BYRON, BUT THERE COULD BE SOMETHING THAT YOU THINK IS MEANINGLESS THAT IS JUST THE OPPOSITE.
SIMPLY TERRIBLE.
YES, IT IS.
DO-- DO YOU KNOW IF THEY EVER WENT UP TO THE BIRCHES?
NO WHY?
TOM. HOW ARE YOU HOLDING UP?
IT'S ROUGH. JUDY'S ABOUT TO LOSE HER MIND...
...AND I CAN'T HELP BUT WONDER IF SOMEBODY DOESN'T HAVE IT IN FOR ME.
DOES MAKE YOU WONDER ,DOESN'T IT?
WHAT WERE YOU ASKING ME EARLIER... ABOUT THE BIRCHES?
I DON'T REMEMBER.
YOU ASKED IF MOLLY AND CHAD HAD BEEN THERE.
OH YES.
WHY?
WELL, IT'S THE LAST PLACE DANNY WAS SEEN, WASN'T IT?

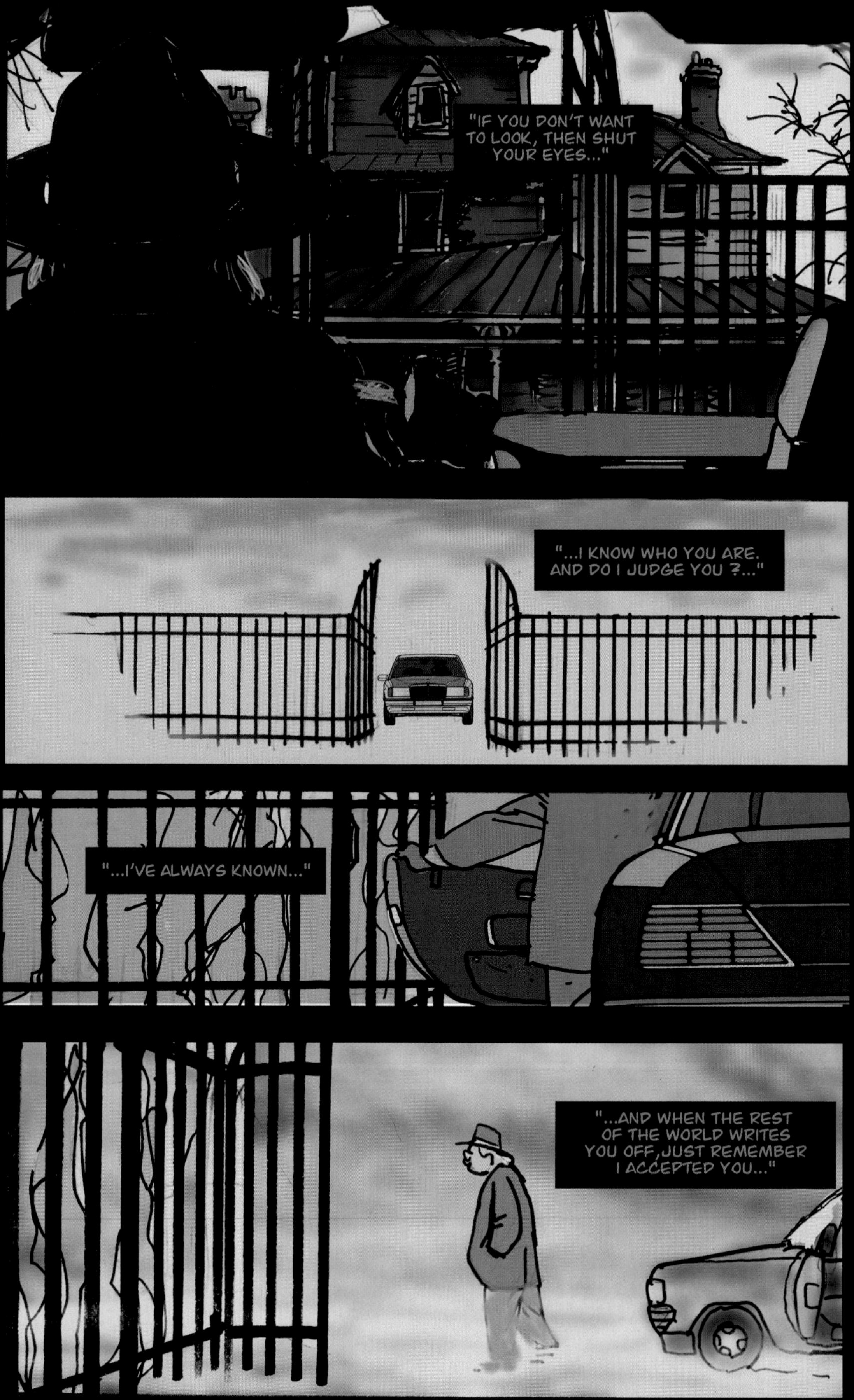
"IF YOU DON'T WANT TO LOOK, THEN SHUT YOUR EYES..."
"...I KNOW WHO YOU ARE. AND DO I JUDGE YOU ?..."
"...I'VE ALWAYS KNOWN..."
"...AND WHEN THE REST OF THE WORLD WRITES YOU OFF, JUST REMEMBER I ACCEPTED YOU..."

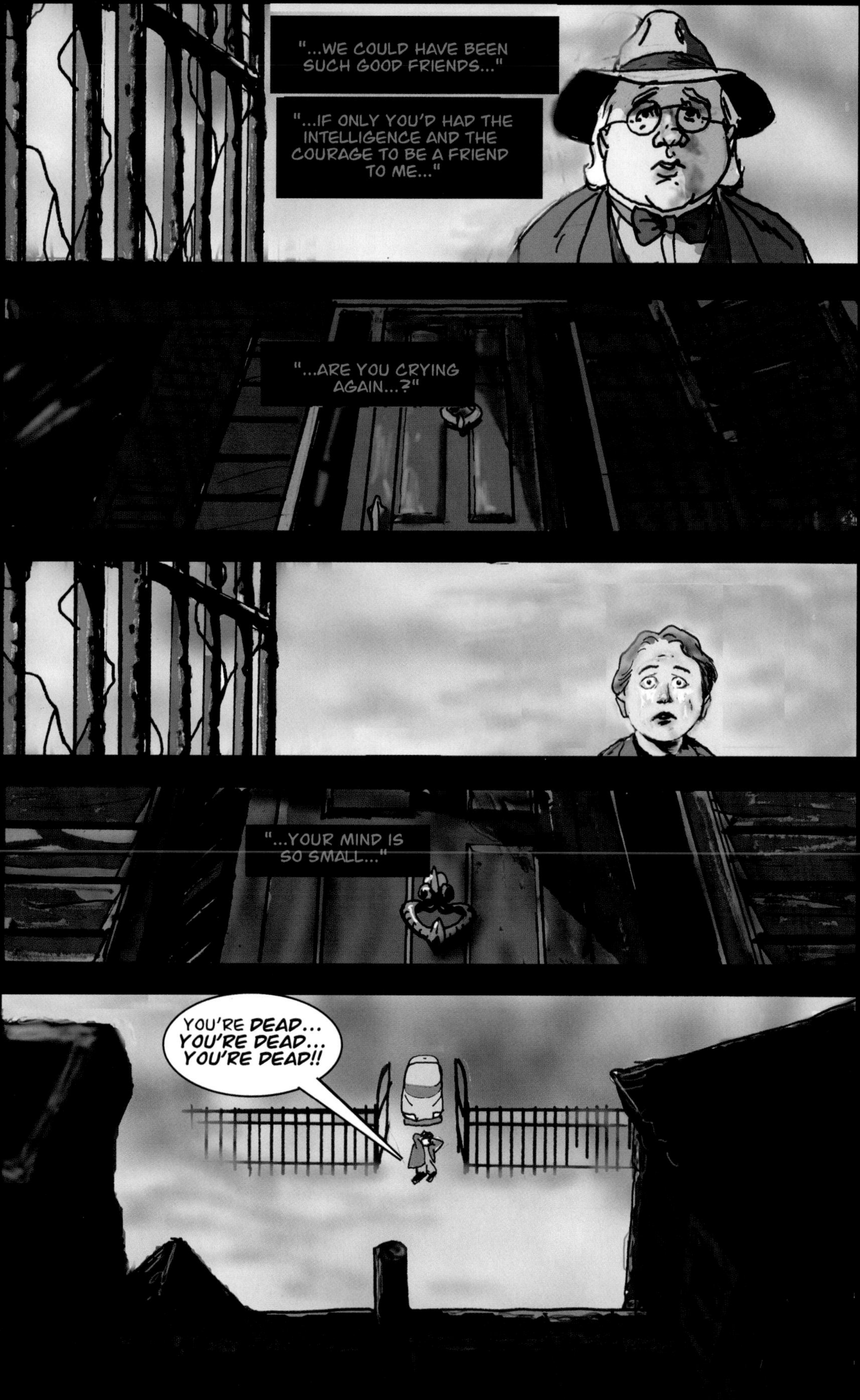
"...WE COULD HAVE BEEN SUCH GOOD FRIENDS..."
"...IF ONLY YOU'D HAD THE INTELLIGENCE AND THE COURAGE TO BE A FRIEND TO ME..."
"...ARE YOU CRYING AGAIN...?"
"...YOUR MIND IS SO SMALL..."
YOU'RE **DEAD**... *YOU'RE DEAD... YOU'RE DEAD!!*

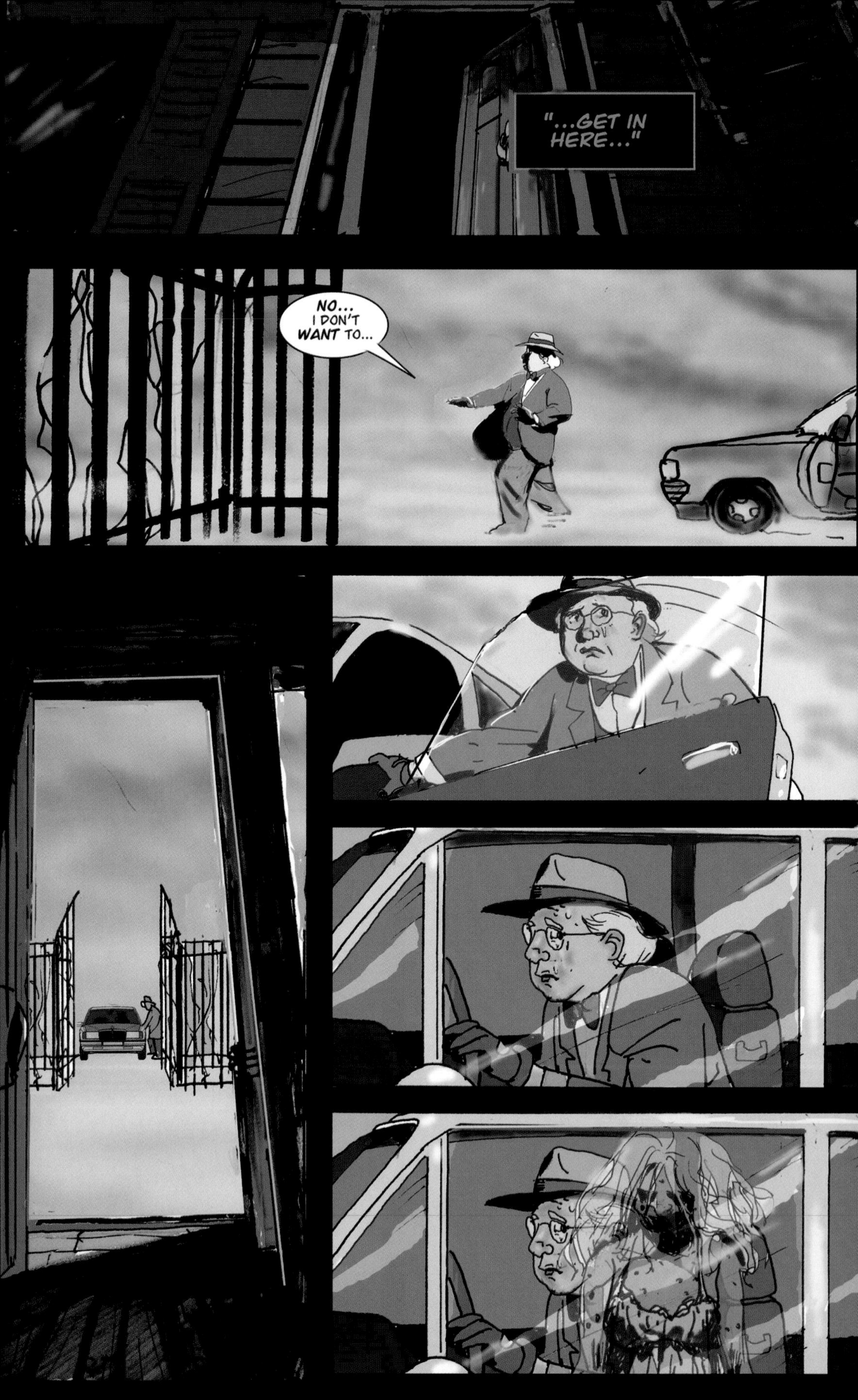
"...GET IN HERE..."
NO... I DON'T WANT TO...

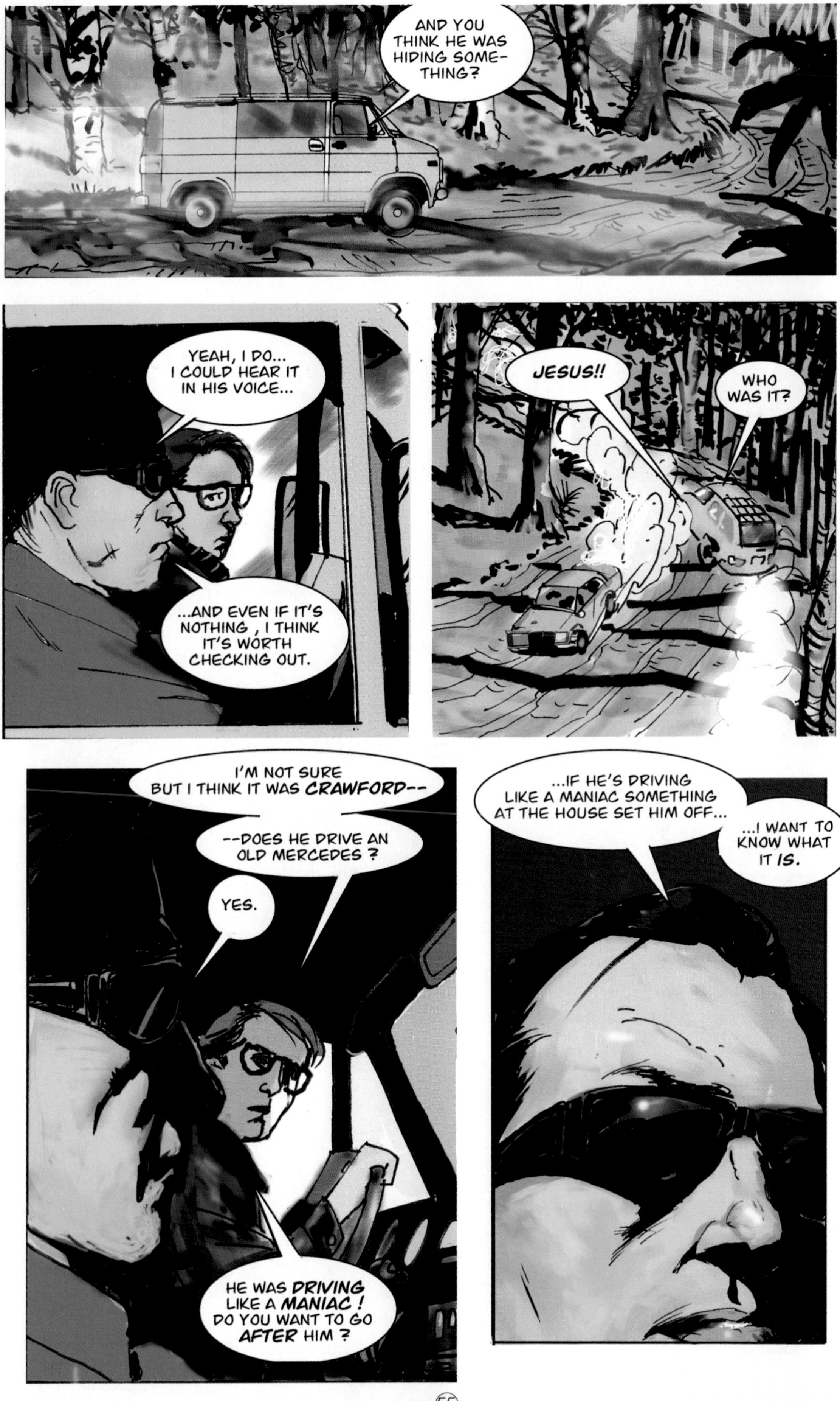
AND YOU THINK HE WAS HIDING SOME-THING?
YEAH, I DO... I COULD HEAR IT IN HIS VOICE...
...AND EVEN IF IT'S NOTHING , I THINK IT'S WORTH CHECKING OUT.
JESUS!!
WHO WAS IT?
I'M NOT SURE BUT I THINK IT WAS CRAWFORD--
--DOES HE DRIVE AN OLD MERCEDES ?
YES.
HE WAS DRIVING LIKE A MANIAC ! DO YOU WANT TO GO AFTER HIM ?
...IF HE'S DRIVING LIKE A MANIAC SOMETHING AT THE HOUSE SET HIM OFF...
...I WANT TO KNOW WHAT IT IS.

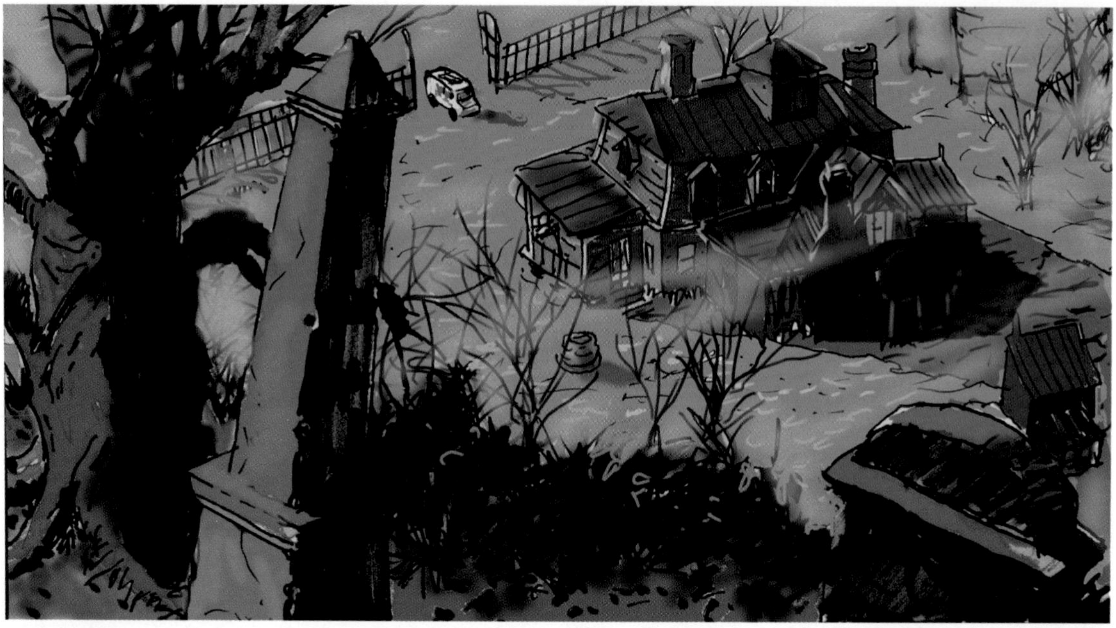

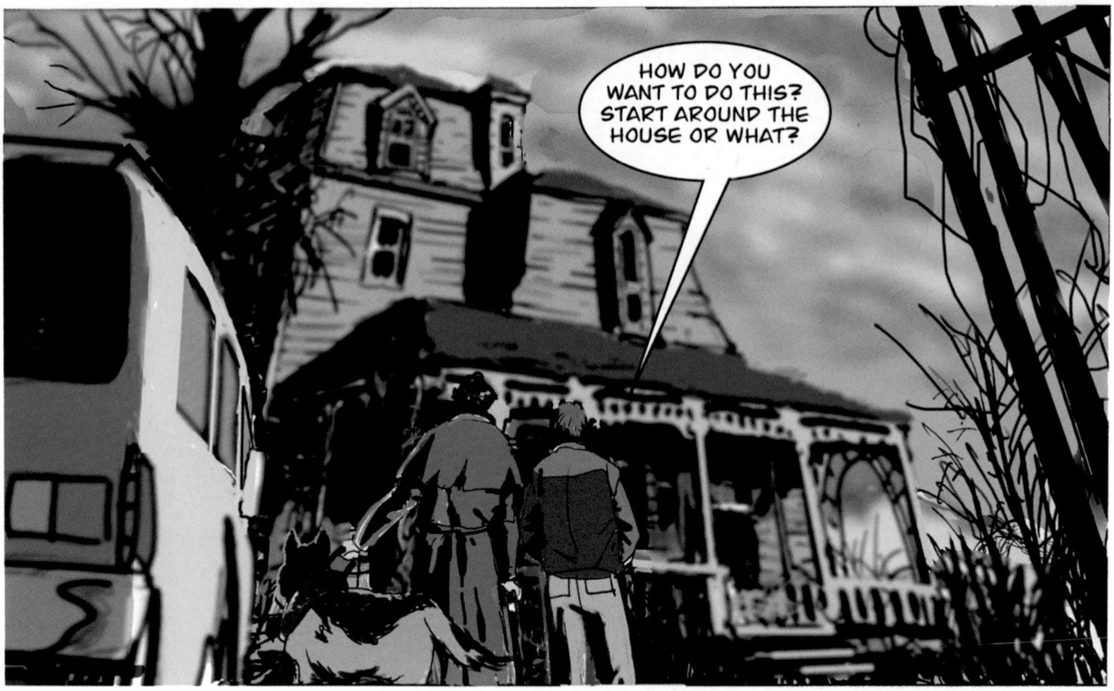
HOW DO YOU WANT TO DO THIS? START AROUND THE HOUSE OR WHAT?

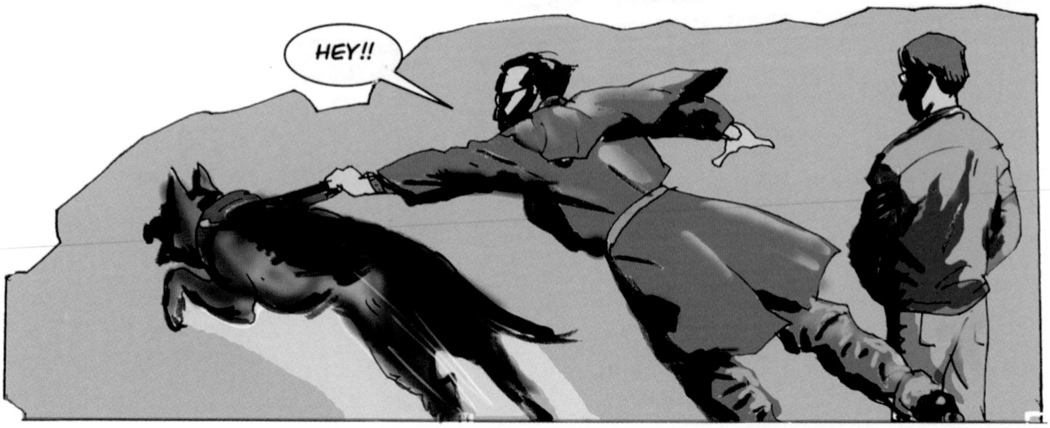
HEY!!

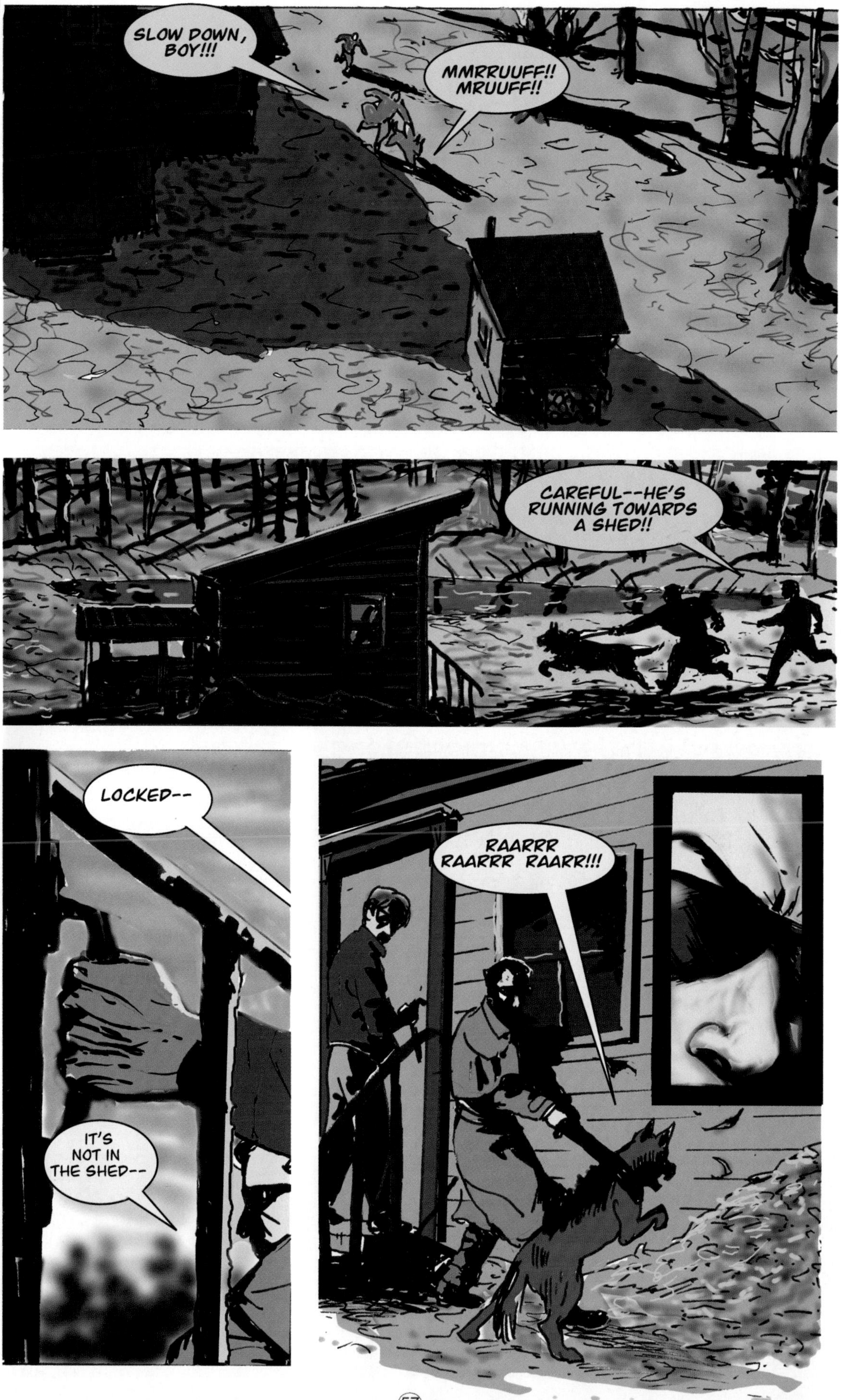
SLOW DOWN, BOY!!!
MMRRUUFF!! MRUUFF!!
CAREFUL--HE'S RUNNING TOWARDS A SHED!!
LOCKED--
IT'S NOT IN THE SHED--
RAARRR RAARRR RAARR!!!

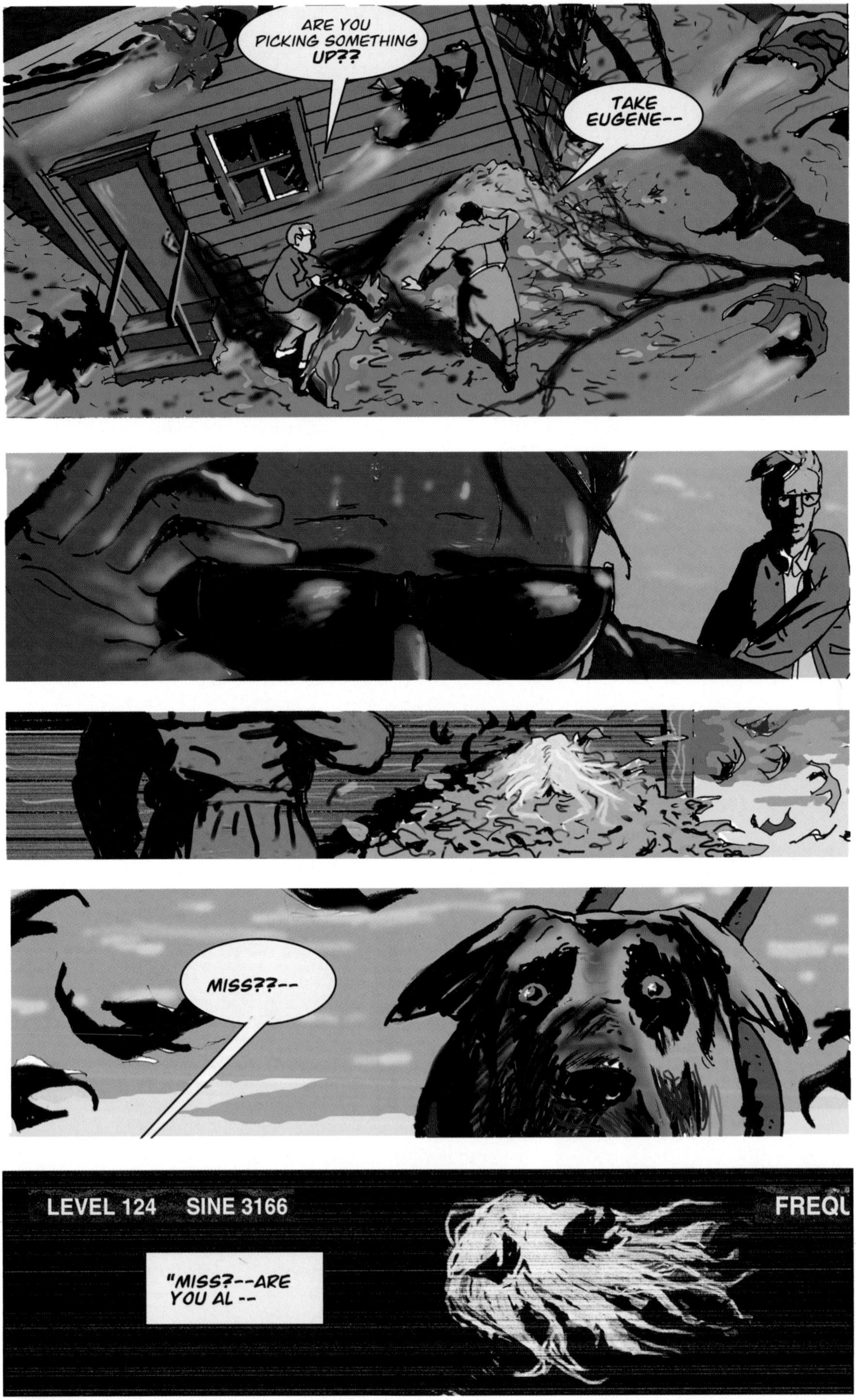
ARE YOU PICKING SOMETHING UP??
TAKE EUGENE--
MISS??--
LEVEL 124 SINE 3166
FREQU
"MISS?--ARE YOU AL --

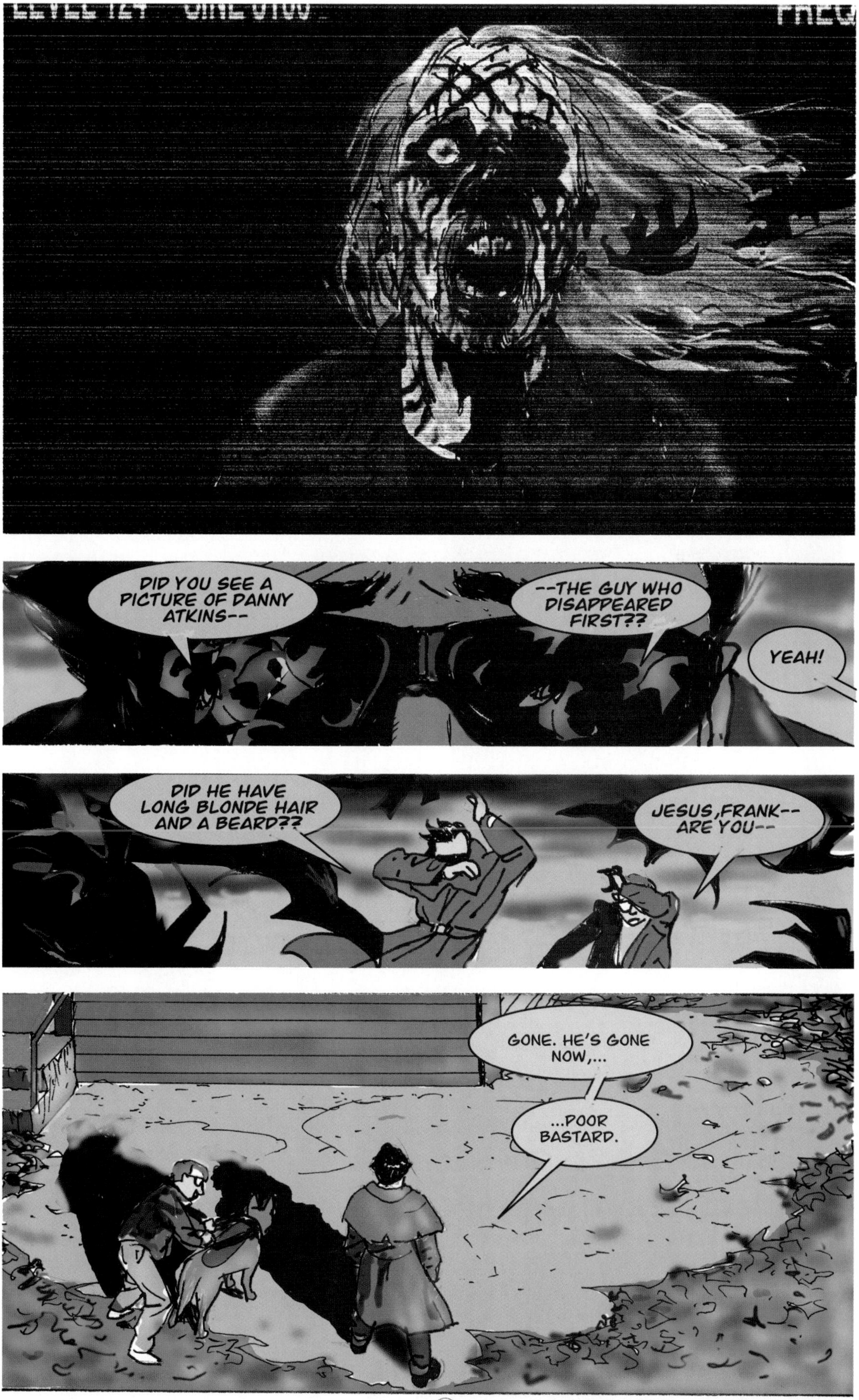
DID YOU SEE A PICTURE OF DANNY ATKINS--
--THE GUY WHO DISAPPEARED FIRST??
YEAH!
DID HE HAVE LONG BLONDE HAIR AND A BEARD??
JESUS, FRANK-- ARE YOU--
GONE. HE'S GONE NOW,...
...POOR BASTARD.

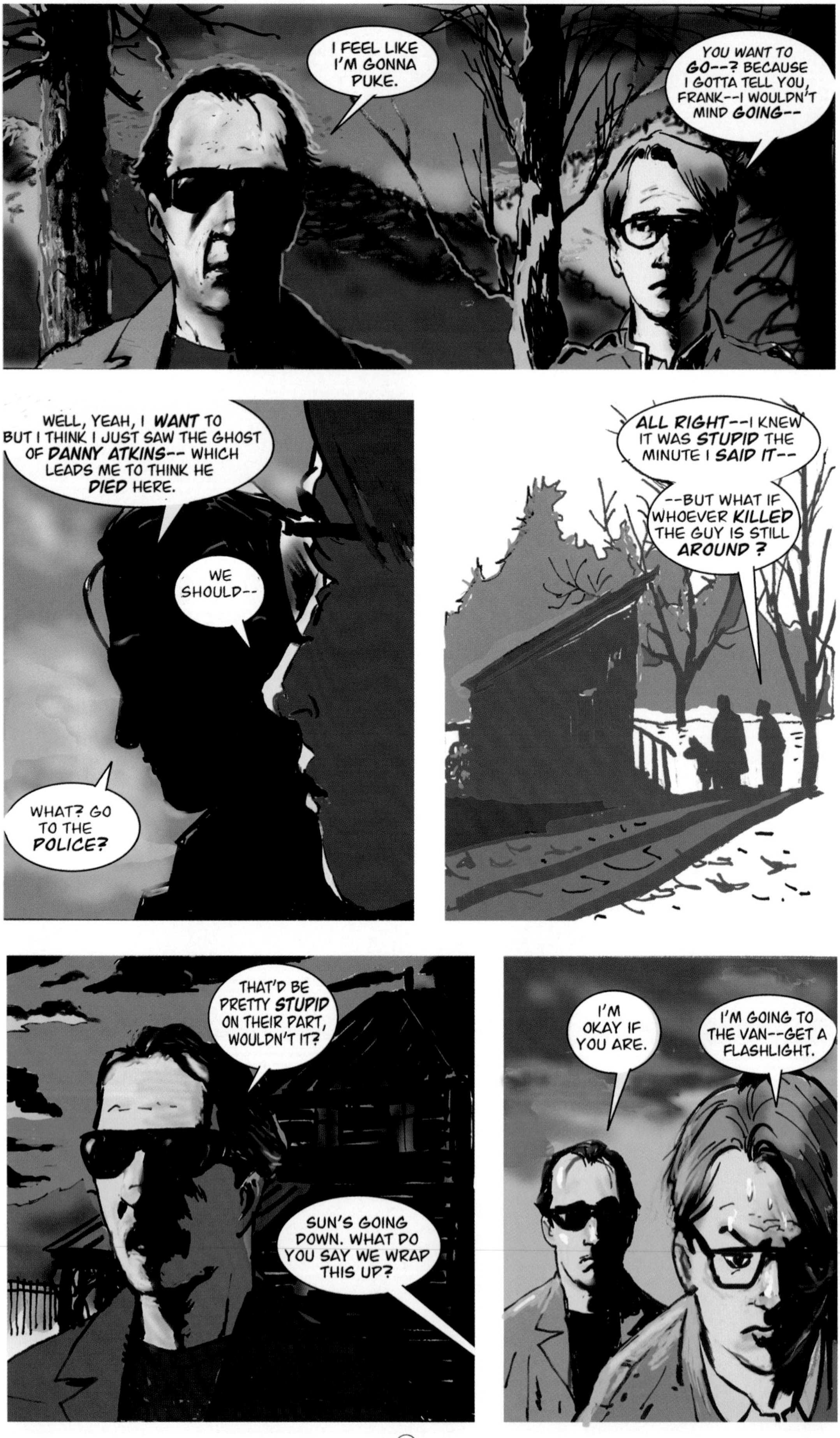
I FEEL LIKE I'M GONNA PUKE.
YOU WANT TO GO--? BECAUSE I GOTTA TELL YOU, FRANK--I WOULDN'T MIND GOING--
WELL, YEAH, I WANT TO BUT I THINK I JUST SAW THE GHOST OF DANNY ATKINS-- WHICH LEADS ME TO THINK HE DIED HERE.
WE SHOULD--
WHAT? GO TO THE POLICE?
ALL RIGHT--I KNEW IT WAS STUPID THE MINUTE I SAID IT--
--BUT WHAT IF WHOEVER KILLED THE GUY IS STILL AROUND?
THAT'D BE PRETTY STUPID ON THEIR PART, WOULDN'T IT?
SUN'S GOING DOWN. WHAT DO YOU SAY WE WRAP THIS UP?
I'M OKAY IF YOU ARE.
I'M GOING TO THE VAN--GET A FLASHLIGHT.

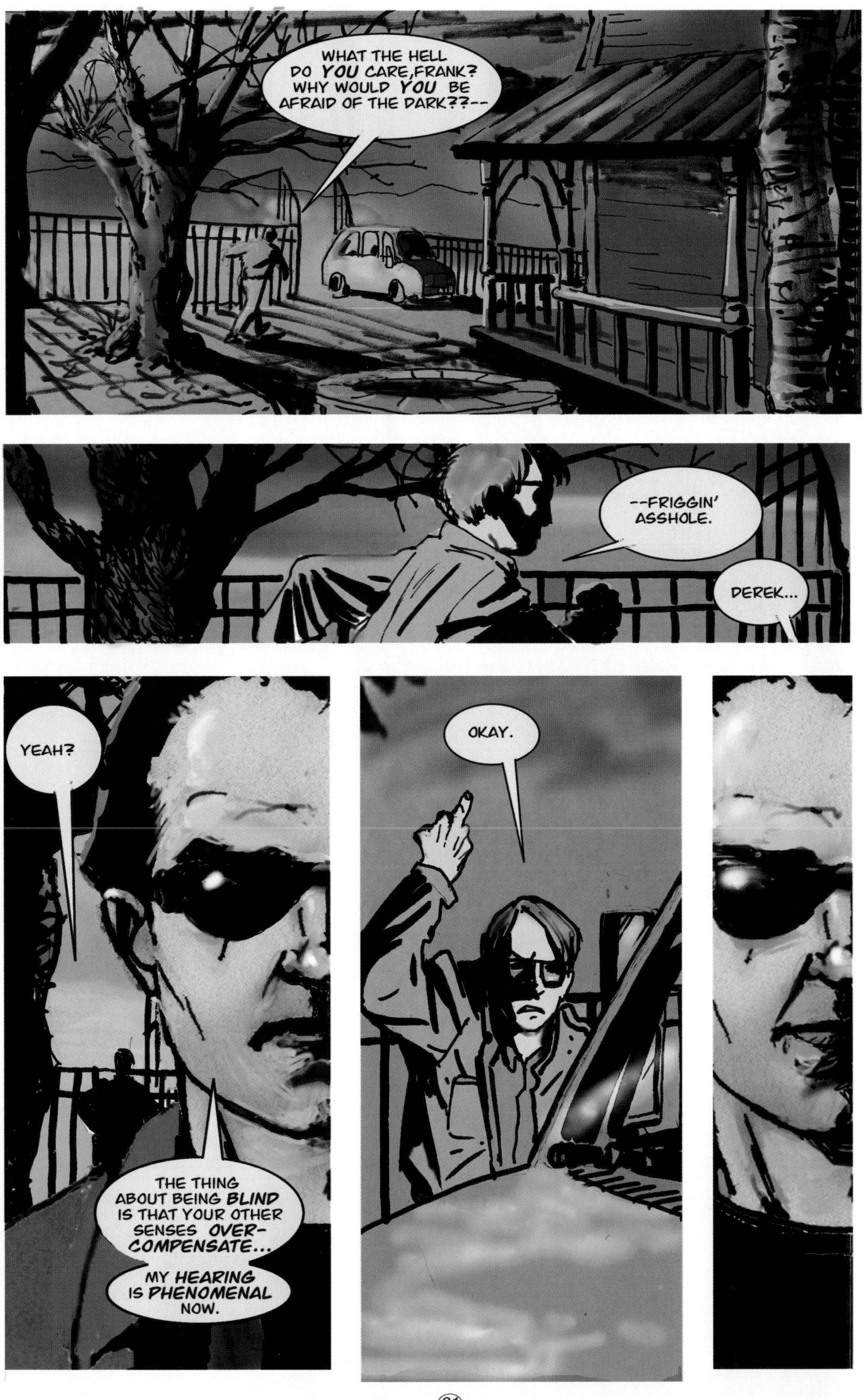
WHAT THE HELL DO YOU CARE, FRANK? WHY WOULD YOU BE AFRAID OF THE DARK??--
--FRIGGIN' ASSHOLE.
DEREK...
YEAH?
THE THING ABOUT BEING BLIND IS THAT YOUR OTHER SENSES OVER-COMPENSATE...
MY HEARING IS PHENOMENAL NOW.
OKAY.

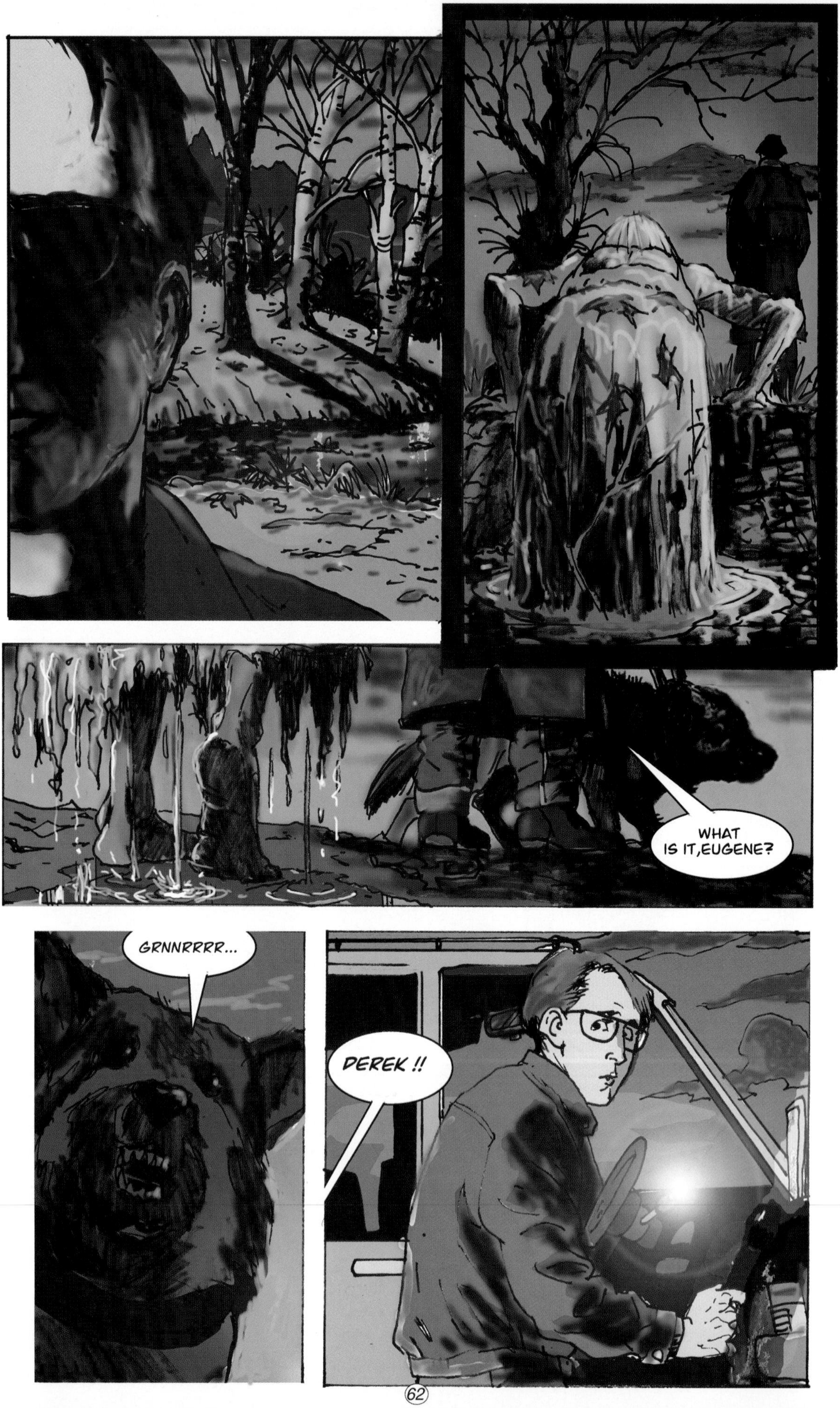
WHAT IS IT,EUGENE?
GRNNRRRR...
DEREK !!

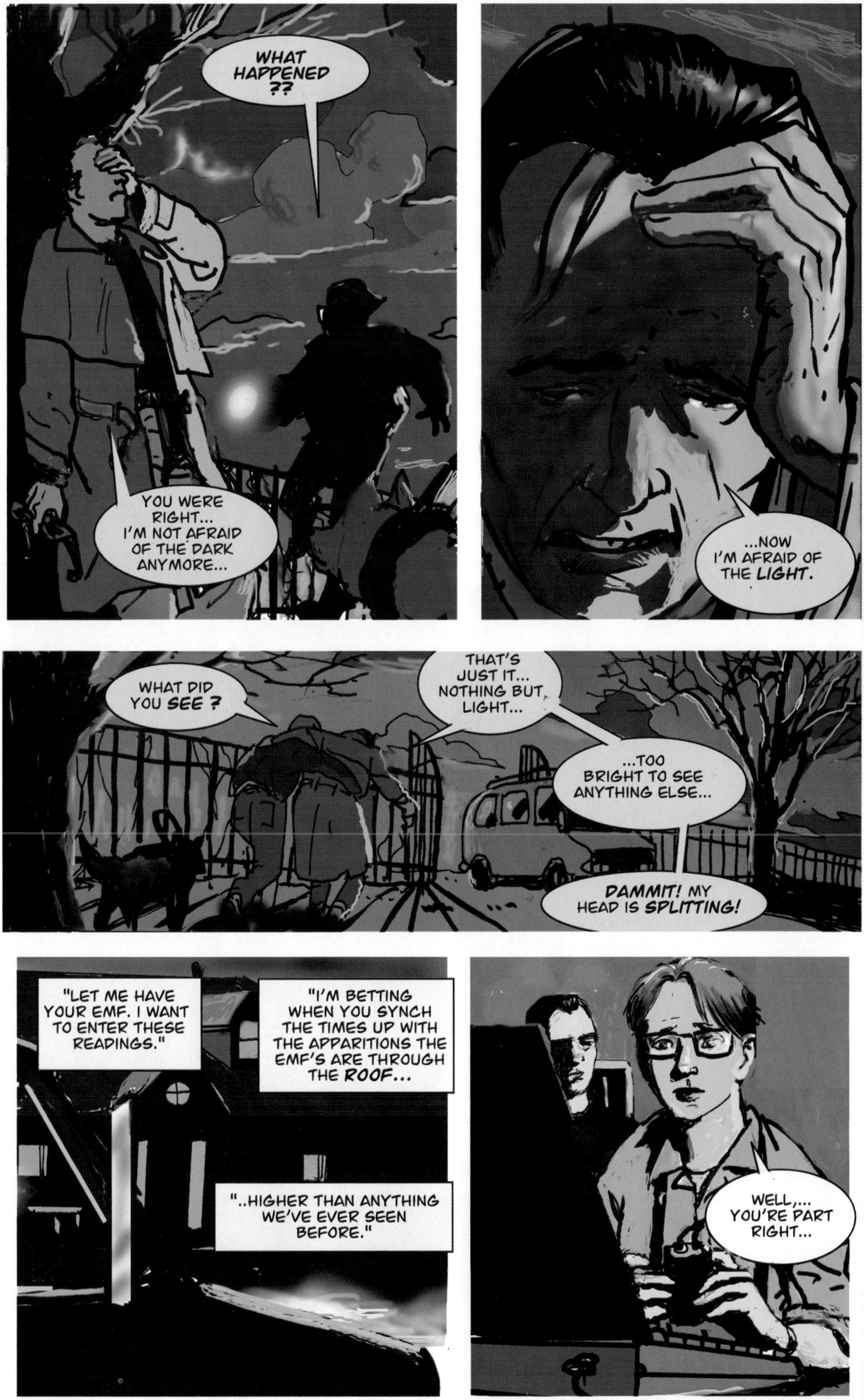

WHAT HAPPENED ??
YOU WERE RIGHT... I'M NOT AFRAID OF THE DARK ANYMORE...
...NOW I'M AFRAID OF THE LIGHT.
WHAT DID YOU SEE ?
THAT'S JUST IT... NOTHING BUT LIGHT...
...TOO BRIGHT TO SEE ANYTHING ELSE...
DAMMIT! MY HEAD IS SPLITTING!
"LET ME HAVE YOUR EMF. I WANT TO ENTER THESE READINGS."
"I'M BETTING WHEN YOU SYNCH THE TIMES UP WITH THE APPARITIONS THE EMF'S ARE THROUGH THE ROOF...
"..HIGHER THAN ANYTHING WE'VE EVER SEEN BEFORE."
WELL,... YOU'RE PART RIGHT...

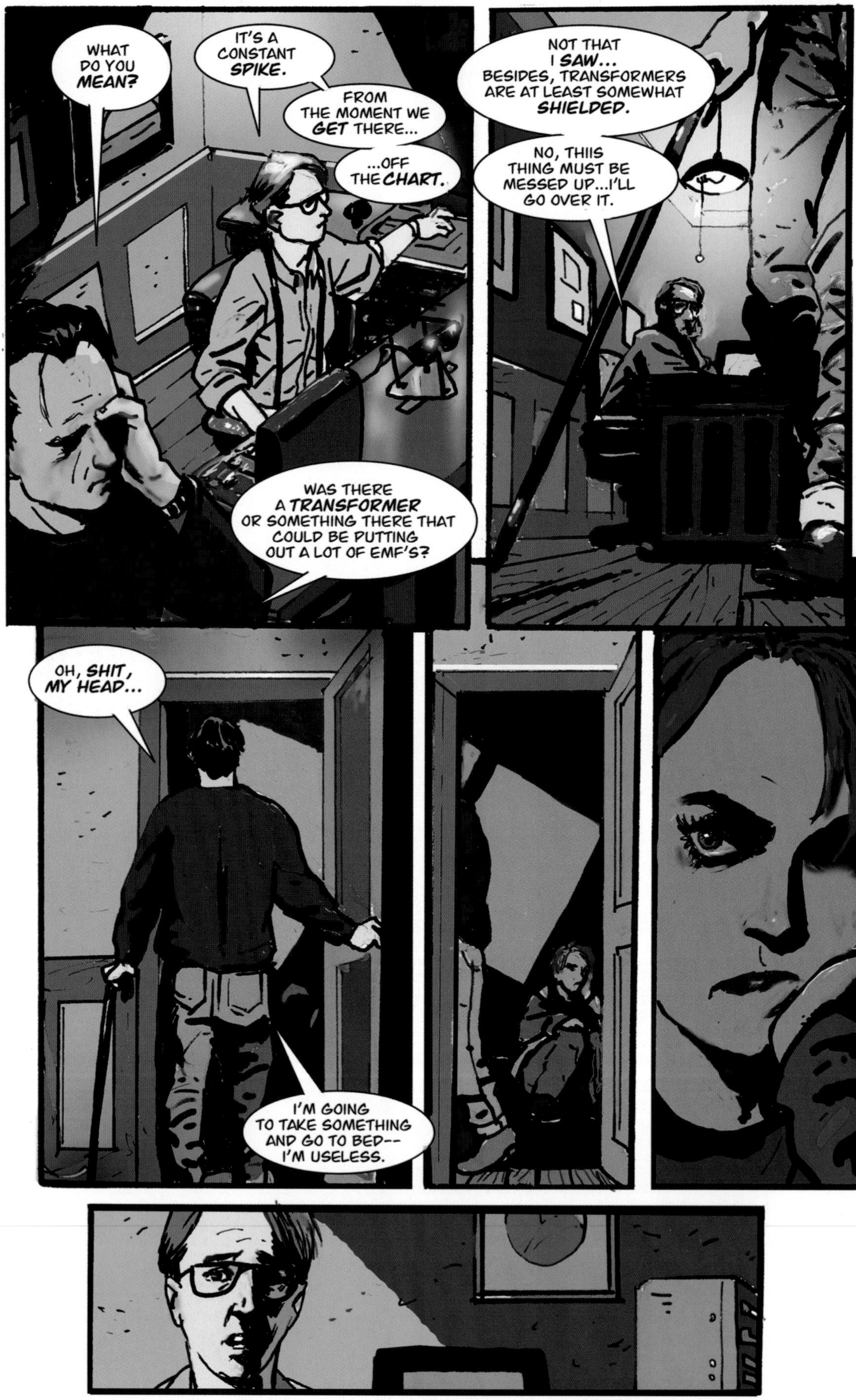
WHAT DO YOU MEAN?
IT'S A CONSTANT SPIKE.
FROM THE MOMENT WE GET THERE...
...OFF THE CHART.
WAS THERE A TRANSFORMER OR SOMETHING THERE THAT COULD BE PUTTING OUT A LOT OF EMF'S?
NOT THAT I SAW... BESIDES, TRANSFORMERS ARE AT LEAST SOMEWHAT SHIELDED.
NO, THIIS THING MUST BE MESSED UP...I'LL GO OVER IT.
OH, SHIT, MY HEAD...
I'M GOING TO TAKE SOMETHING AND GO TO BED-- I'M USELESS.

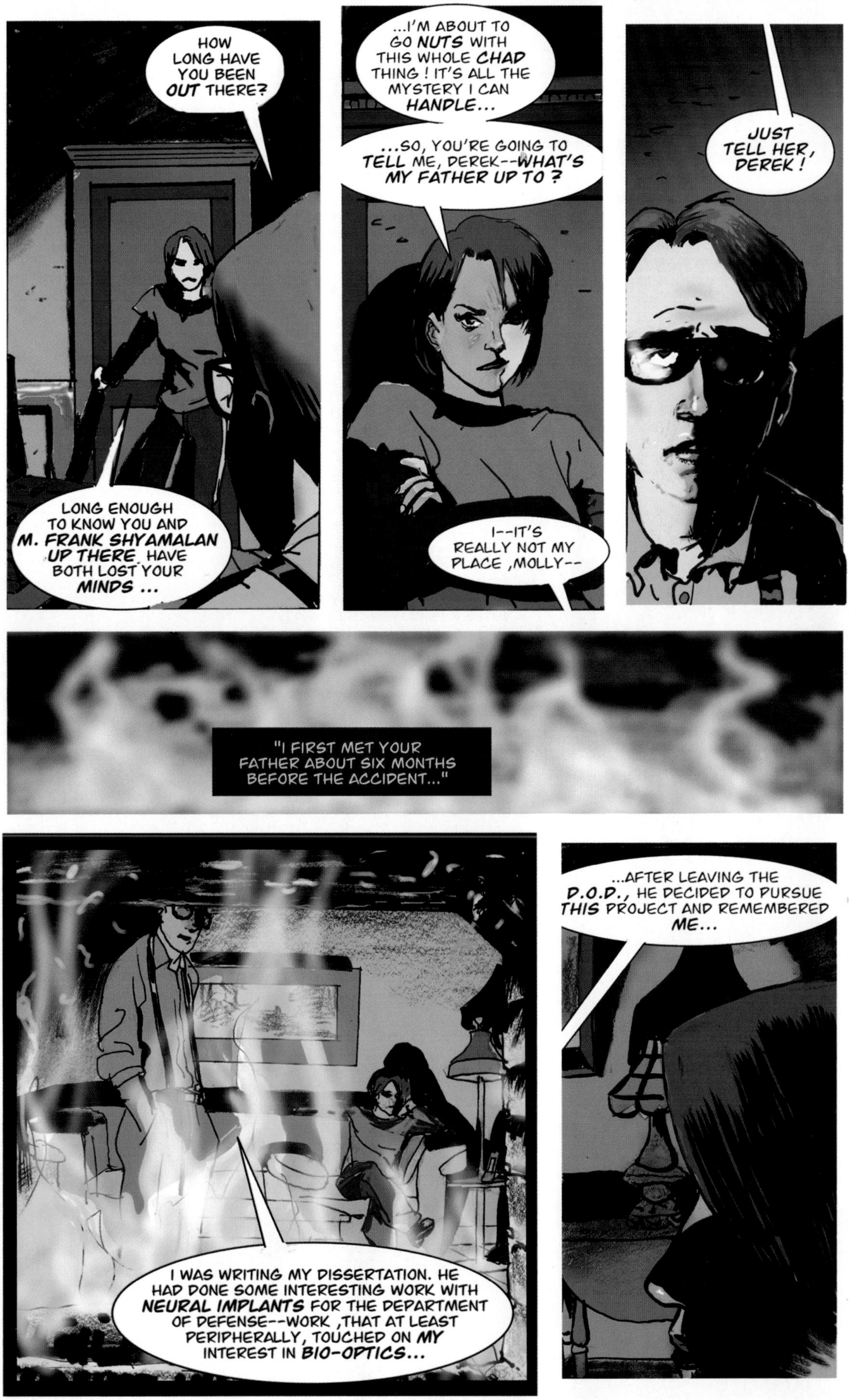
HOW LONG HAVE YOU BEEN OUT THERE?
LONG ENOUGH TO KNOW YOU AND M. FRANK SHYAMALAN UP THERE HAVE BOTH LOST YOUR MINDS ...
...I'M ABOUT TO GO NUTS WITH THIS WHOLE CHAD THING ! IT'S ALL THE MYSTERY I CAN HANDLE...
...SO, YOU'RE GOING TO TELL ME, DEREK--WHAT'S MY FATHER UP TO ?
I--IT'S REALLY NOT MY PLACE ,MOLLY--
JUST TELL HER, DEREK !
"I FIRST MET YOUR FATHER ABOUT SIX MONTHS BEFORE THE ACCIDENT..."
I WAS WRITING MY DISSERTATION. HE HAD DONE SOME INTERESTING WORK WITH NEURAL IMPLANTS FOR THE DEPARTMENT OF DEFENSE--WORK ,THAT AT LEAST PERIPHERALLY, TOUCHED ON MY INTEREST IN BIO-OPTICS...
...AFTER LEAVING THE D.O.D., HE DECIDED TO PURSUE THIS PROJECT AND REMEMBERED ME...

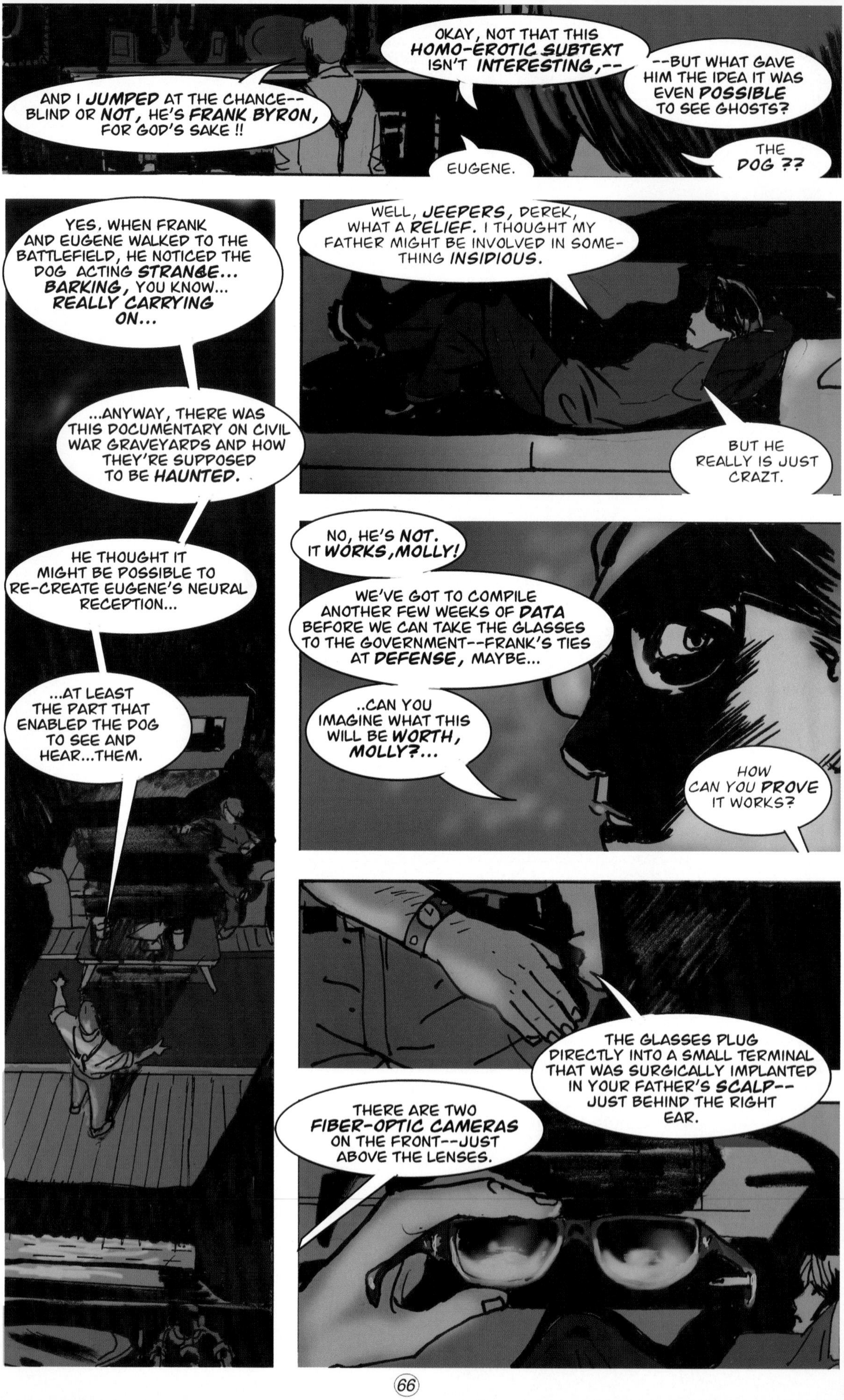
AND I JUMPED AT THE CHANCE-- BLIND OR NOT, HE'S FRANK BYRON, FOR GOD'S SAKE !!
OKAY, NOT THAT THIS HOMO-EROTIC SUBTEXT ISN'T INTERESTING,--
--BUT WHAT GAVE HIM THE IDEA IT WAS EVEN POSSIBLE TO SEE GHOSTS?
EUGENE.
THE DOG ??
YES. WHEN FRANK AND EUGENE WALKED TO THE BATTLEFIELD, HE NOTICED THE DOG ACTING STRANGE... BARKING, YOU KNOW... REALLY CARRYING ON...
...ANYWAY, THERE WAS THIS DOCUMENTARY ON CIVIL WAR GRAVEYARDS AND HOW THEY'RE SUPPOSED TO BE HAUNTED.
HE THOUGHT IT MIGHT BE POSSIBLE TO RE-CREATE EUGENE'S NEURAL RECEPTION...
...AT LEAST THE PART THAT ENABLED THE DOG TO SEE AND HEAR...THEM.
WELL, JEEPERS, DEREK, WHAT A RELIEF. I THOUGHT MY FATHER MIGHT BE INVOLVED IN SOME-THING INSIDIOUS.
BUT HE REALLY IS JUST CRAZT.
NO, HE'S NOT. IT WORKS, MOLLY!
WE'VE GOT TO COMPILE ANOTHER FEW WEEKS OF DATA BEFORE WE CAN TAKE THE GLASSES TO THE GOVERNMENT--FRANK'S TIES AT DEFENSE, MAYBE...
..CAN YOU IMAGINE WHAT THIS WILL BE WORTH, MOLLY?...
HOW CAN YOU PROVE IT WORKS?
THE GLASSES PLUG DIRECTLY INTO A SMALL TERMINAL THAT WAS SURGICALLY IMPLANTED IN YOUR FATHER'S SCALP-- JUST BEHIND THE RIGHT EAR.
THERE ARE TWO FIBER-OPTIC CAMERAS ON THE FRONT--JUST ABOVE THE LENSES.

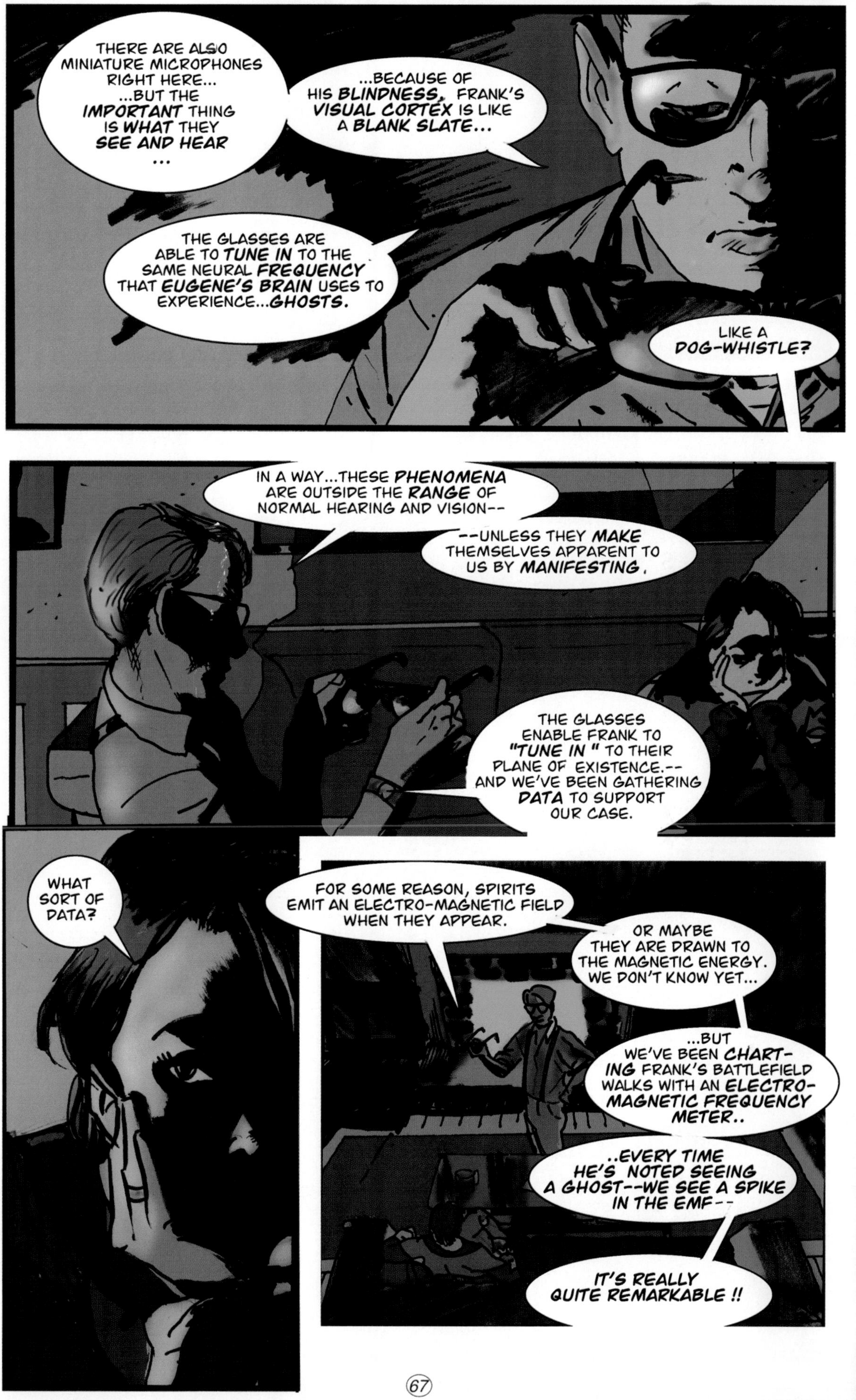
THERE ARE ALSO MINIATURE MICROPHONES RIGHT HERE... ...BUT THE IMPORTANT THING IS WHAT THEY SEE AND HEAR ...
...BECAUSE OF HIS BLINDNESS, FRANK'S VISUAL CORTEX IS LIKE A BLANK SLATE...
THE GLASSES ARE ABLE TO TUNE IN TO THE SAME NEURAL FREQUENCY THAT EUGENE'S BRAIN USES TO EXPERIENCE...GHOSTS.
LIKE A DOG-WHISTLE?
IN A WAY...THESE PHENOMENA ARE OUTSIDE THE RANGE OF NORMAL HEARING AND VISION--
--UNLESS THEY MAKE THEMSELVES APPARENT TO US BY MANIFESTING.
THE GLASSES ENABLE FRANK TO "TUNE IN" TO THEIR PLANE OF EXISTENCE.-- AND WE'VE BEEN GATHERING DATA TO SUPPORT OUR CASE.
WHAT SORT OF DATA?
FOR SOME REASON, SPIRITS EMIT AN ELECTRO-MAGNETIC FIELD WHEN THEY APPEAR.
OR MAYBE THEY ARE DRAWN TO THE MAGNETIC ENERGY. WE DON'T KNOW YET...
...BUT WE'VE BEEN CHARTING FRANK'S BATTLEFIELD WALKS WITH AN ELECTRO-MAGNETIC FREQUENCY METER..
..EVERY TIME HE'S NOTED SEEING A GHOST--WE SEE A SPIKE IN THE EMF--
IT'S REALLY QUITE REMARKABLE !!

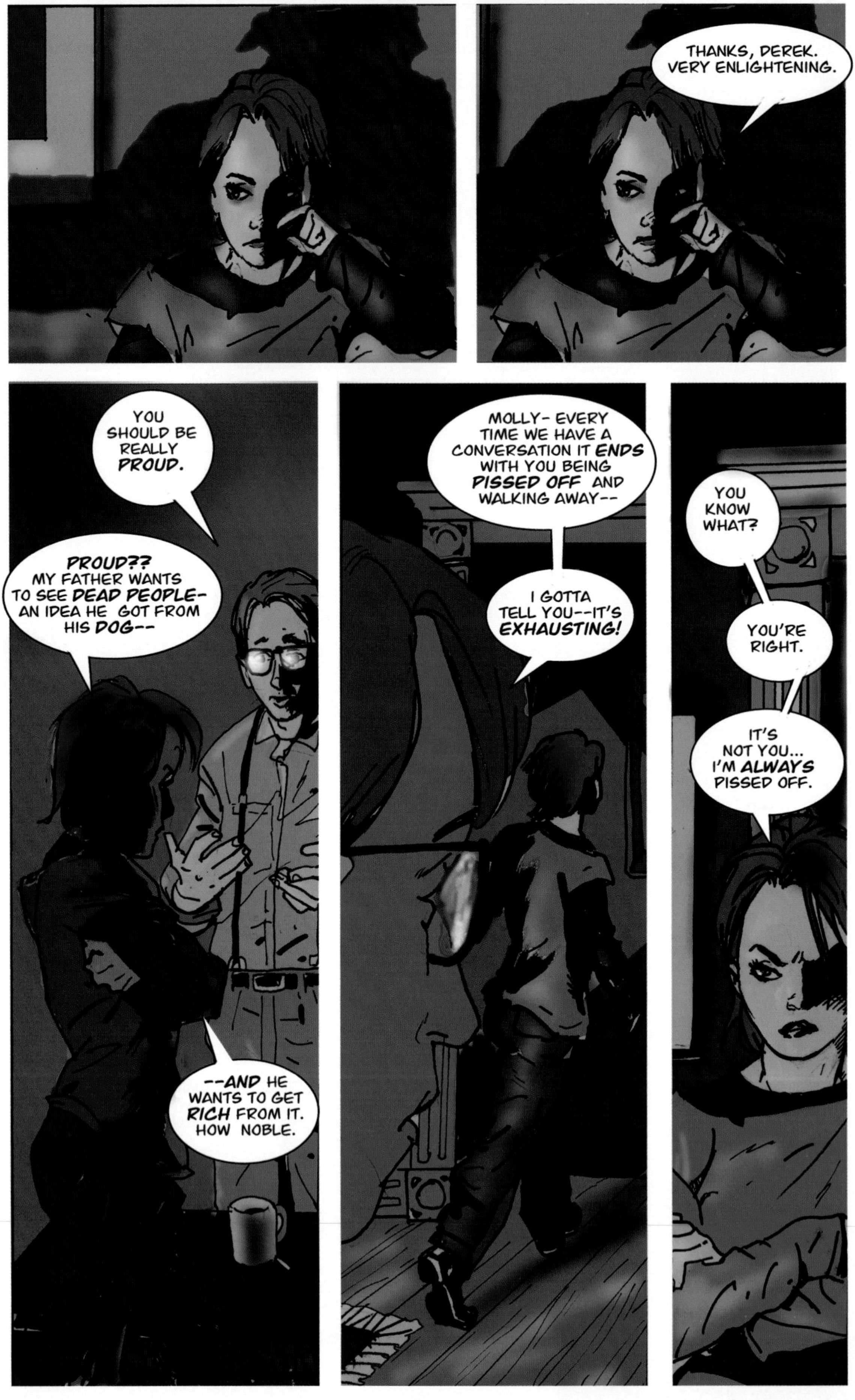
THANKS, DEREK. VERY ENLIGHTENING.
YOU SHOULD BE REALLY PROUD.
PROUD?? MY FATHER WANTS TO SEE DEAD PEOPLE- AN IDEA HE GOT FROM HIS DOG--
--AND HE WANTS TO GET RICH FROM IT. HOW NOBLE.
MOLLY- EVERY TIME WE HAVE A CONVERSATION IT ENDS WITH YOU BEING PISSED OFF AND WALKING AWAY--
I GOTTA TELL YOU--IT'S EXHAUSTING!
YOU KNOW WHAT?
YOU'RE RIGHT.
IT'S NOT YOU... I'M ALWAYS PISSED OFF.

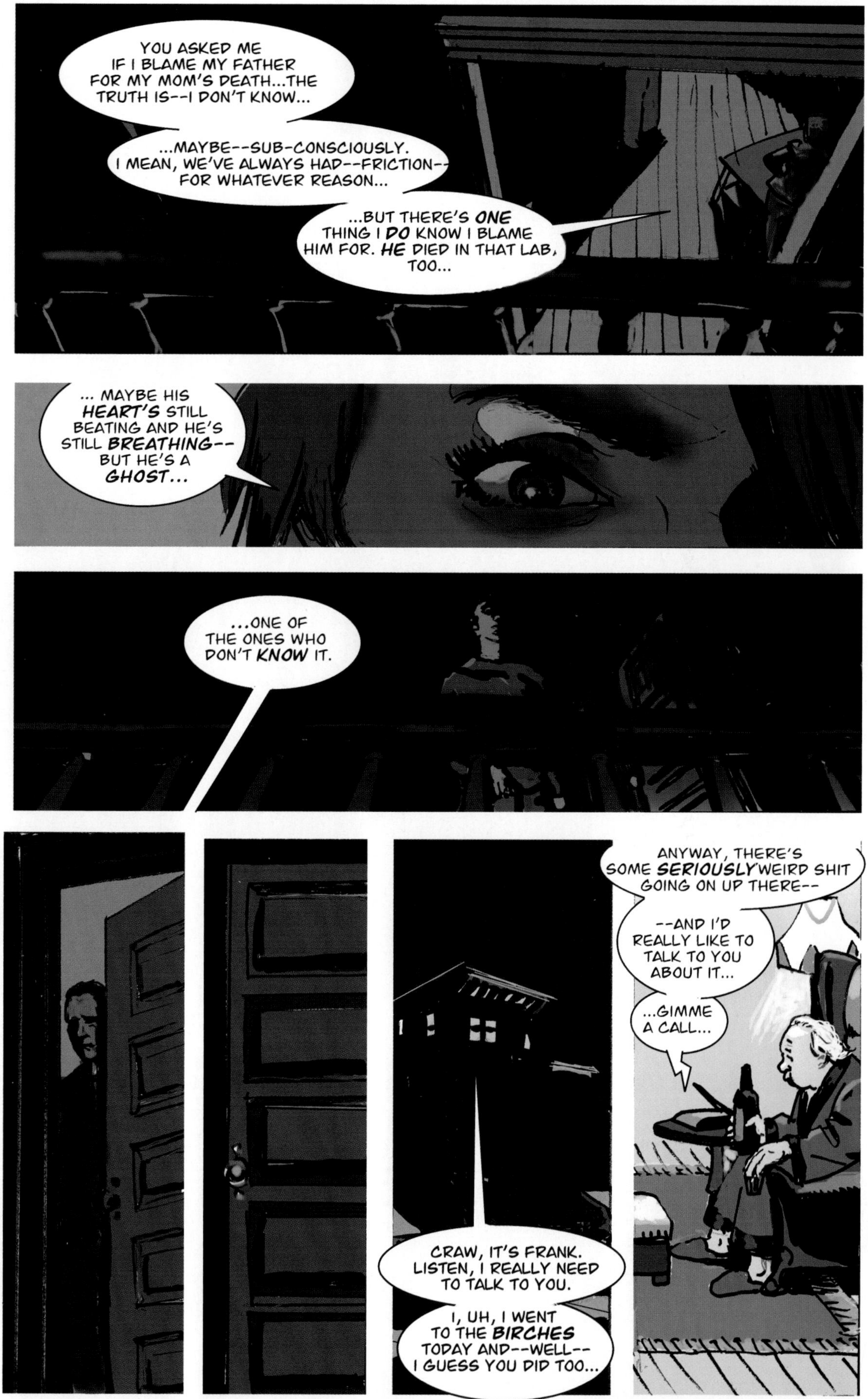
YOU ASKED ME IF I BLAME MY FATHER FOR MY MOM'S DEATH...THE TRUTH IS--I DON'T KNOW...
...MAYBE--SUB-CONSCIOUSLY. I MEAN, WE'VE ALWAYS HAD--FRICTION--FOR WHATEVER REASON...
...BUT THERE'S ONE THING I DO KNOW I BLAME HIM FOR. HE DIED IN THAT LAB, TOO...
... MAYBE HIS HEART'S STILL BEATING AND HE'S STILL BREATHING--BUT HE'S A GHOST...
...ONE OF THE ONES WHO DON'T KNOW IT.
CRAW, IT'S FRANK. LISTEN, I REALLY NEED TO TALK TO YOU.
I, UH, I WENT TO THE BIRCHES TODAY AND--WELL--I GUESS YOU DID TOO...
ANYWAY, THERE'S SOME SERIOUSLY WEIRD SHIT GOING ON UP THERE--
--AND I'D REALLY LIKE TO TALK TO YOU ABOUT IT...
...GIMME A CALL...

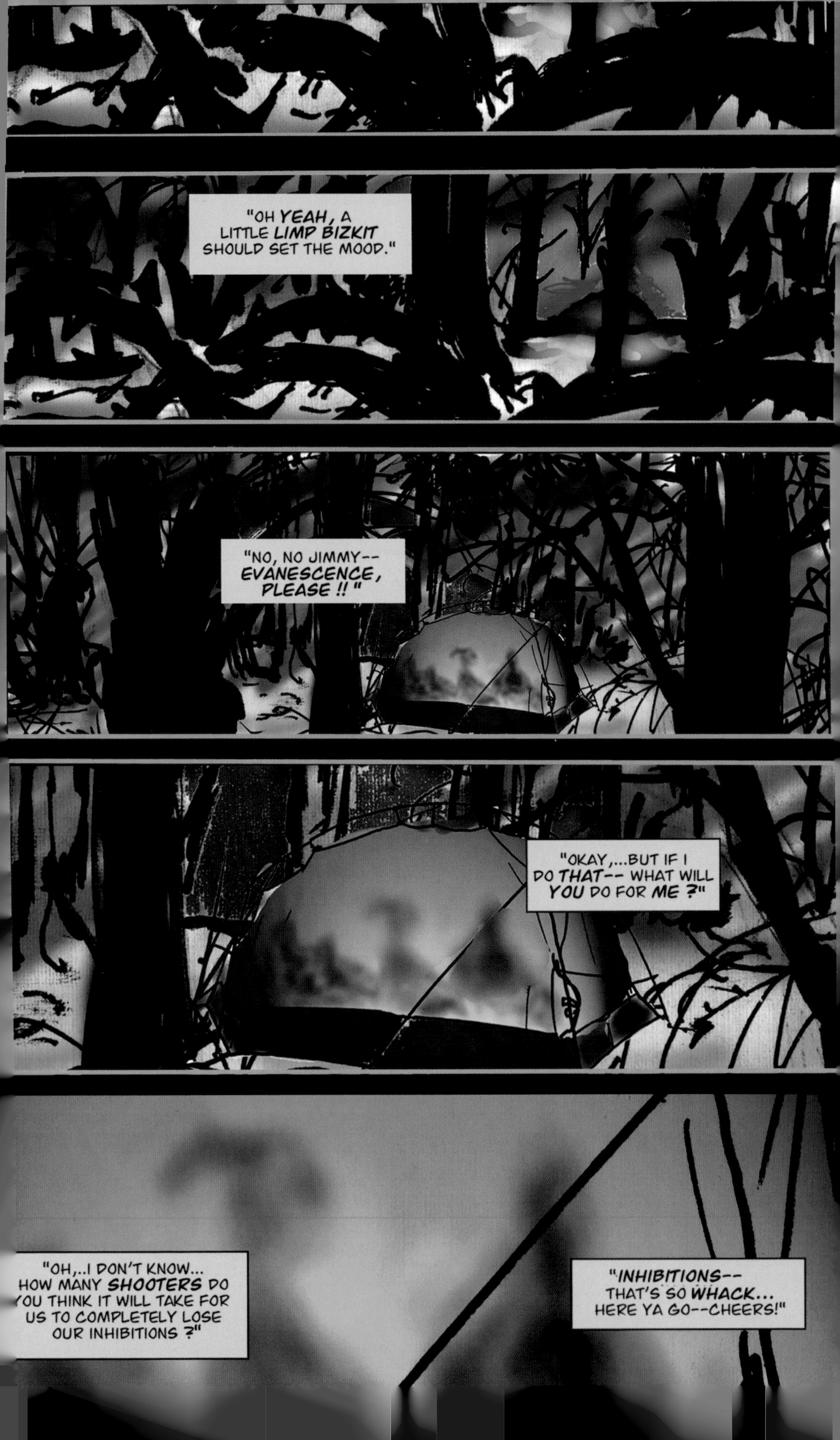
"OH YEAH, A LITTLE LIMP BIZKIT SHOULD SET THE MOOD."
"NO, NO JIMMY-- EVANESCENCE, PLEASE !! "
"OKAY,...BUT IF I DO THAT-- WHAT WILL YOU DO FOR ME ?"
"OH,..I DON'T KNOW... HOW MANY SHOOTERS DO YOU THINK IT WILL TAKE FOR US TO COMPLETELY LOSE OUR INHIBITIONS ?"
"INHIBITIONS-- THAT'S SO WHACK... HERE YA GO--CHEERS!"

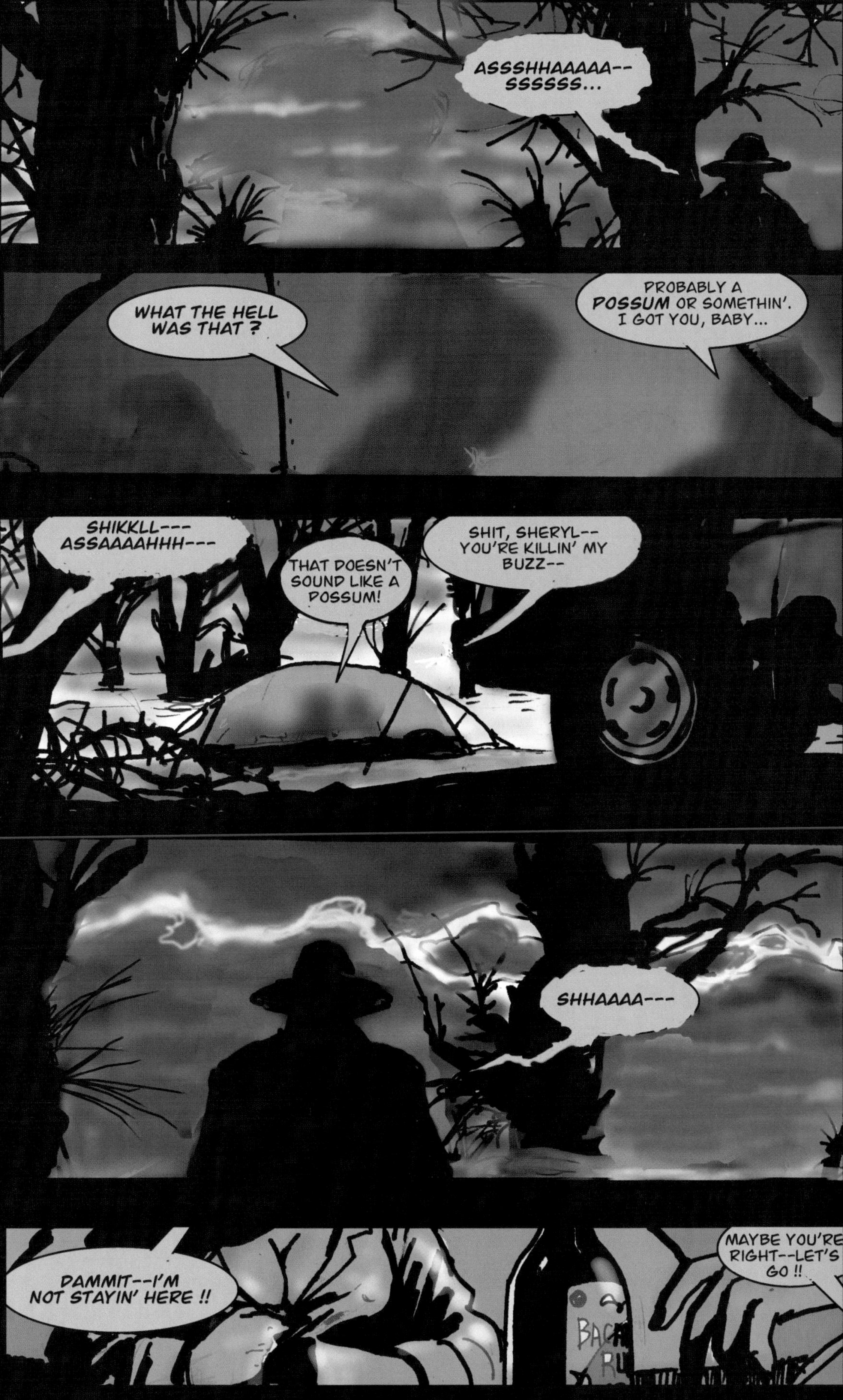
ASSSHHAAAAA--
SSSSSS...
WHAT THE HELL
WAS THAT ?
PROBABLY A
POSSUM OR SOMETHIN'.
I GOT YOU, BABY...
SHIKKLL---
ASSAAAAHHH---
THAT DOESN'T
SOUND LIKE A
POSSUM!
SHIT, SHERYL--
YOU'RE KILLIN' MY
BUZZ--
SHHAAAA---
DAMMIT--I'M
NOT STAYIN' HERE !!
MAYBE YOU'RE
RIGHT--LET'S
GO !!

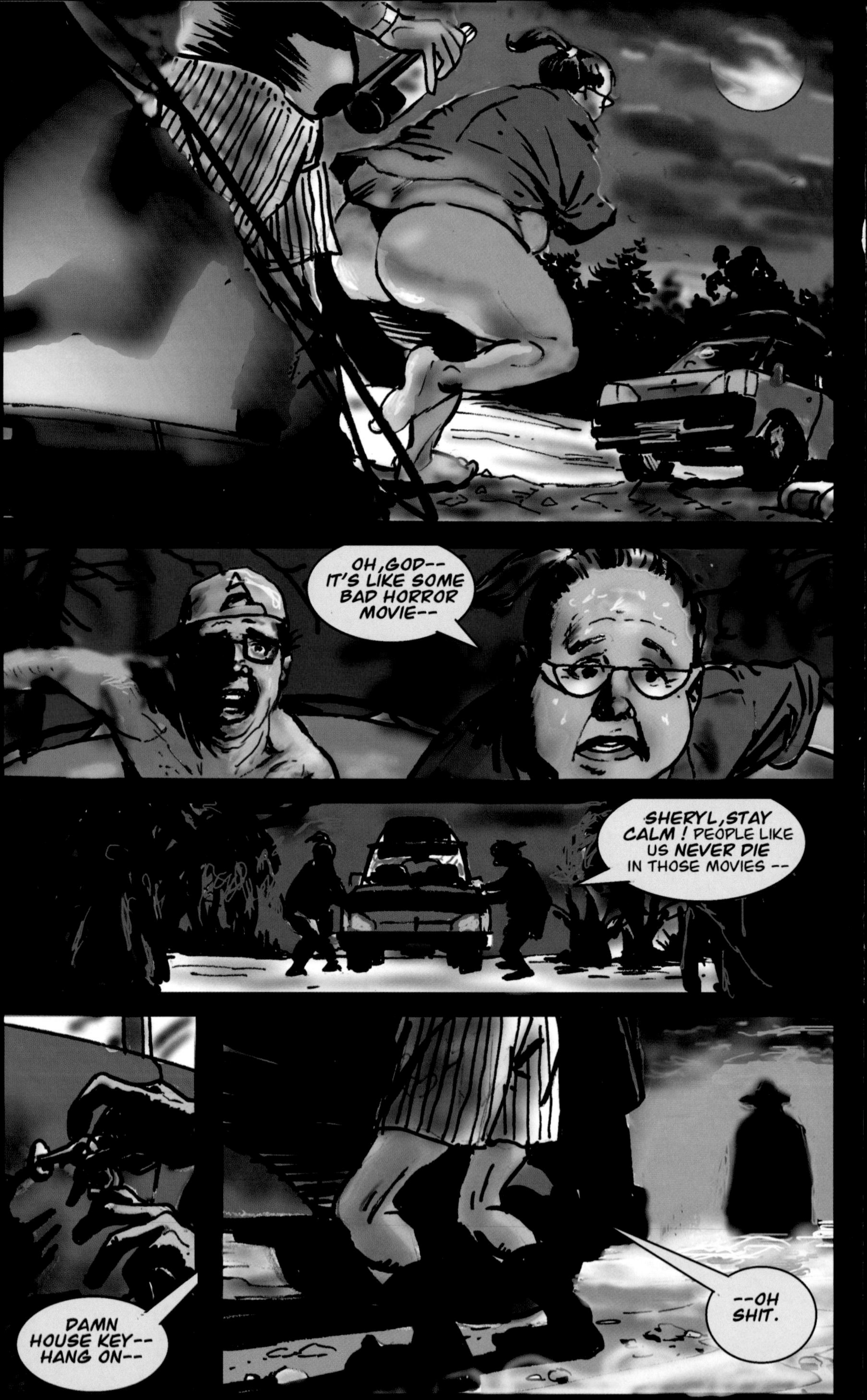
OH, GOD-- IT'S LIKE SOME BAD HORROR MOVIE--
SHERYL, STAY CALM! PEOPLE LIKE US NEVER DIE IN THOSE MOVIES --
DAMN HOUSE KEY-- HANG ON--
--OH SHIT.

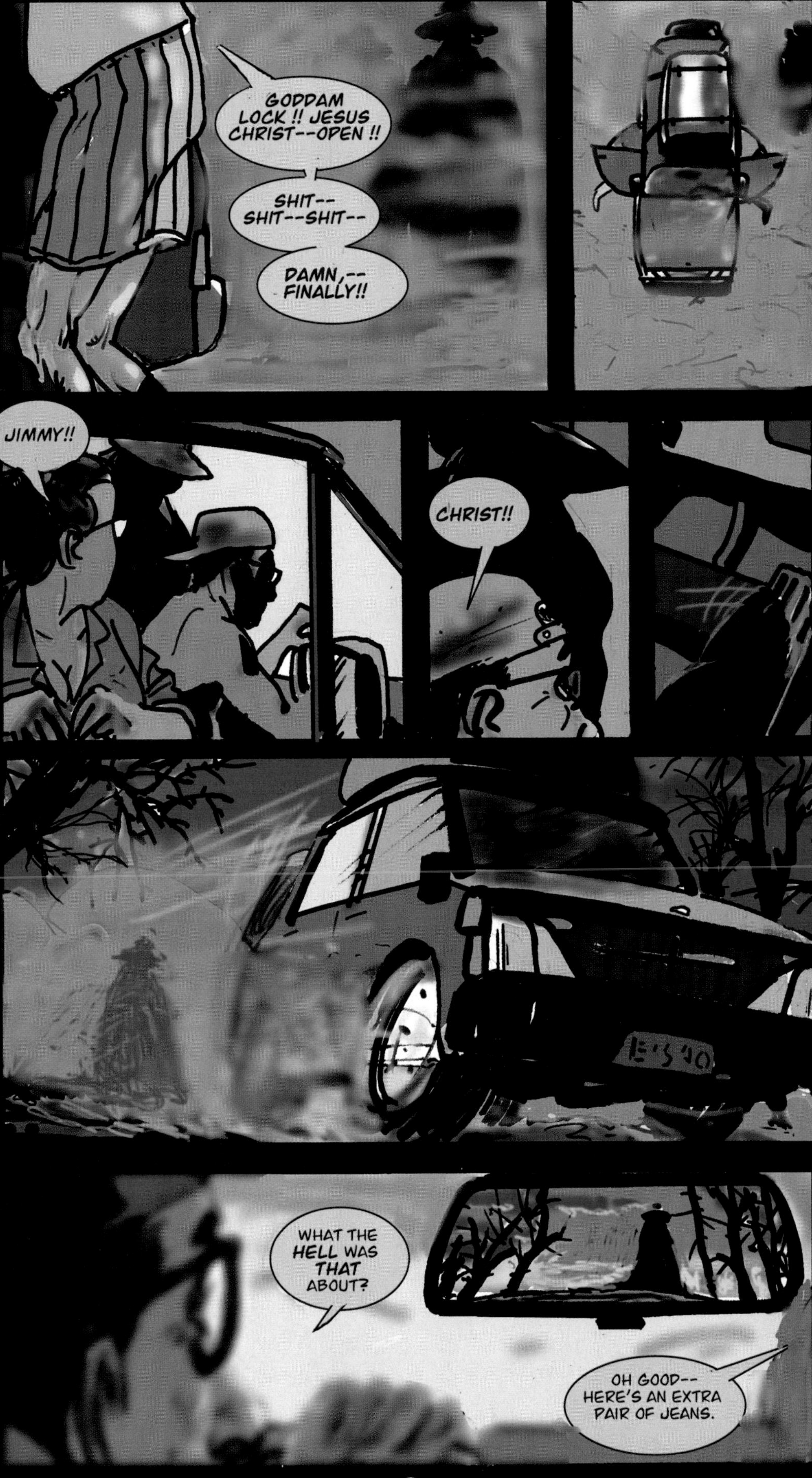
GODDAM LOCK !! JESUS CHRIST--OPEN !!
SHIT-- SHIT--SHIT--
DAMN,-- FINALLY!!
JIMMY!!
CHRIST!!
WHAT THE HELL WAS THAT ABOUT?
OH GOOD-- HERE'S AN EXTRA PAIR OF JEANS.

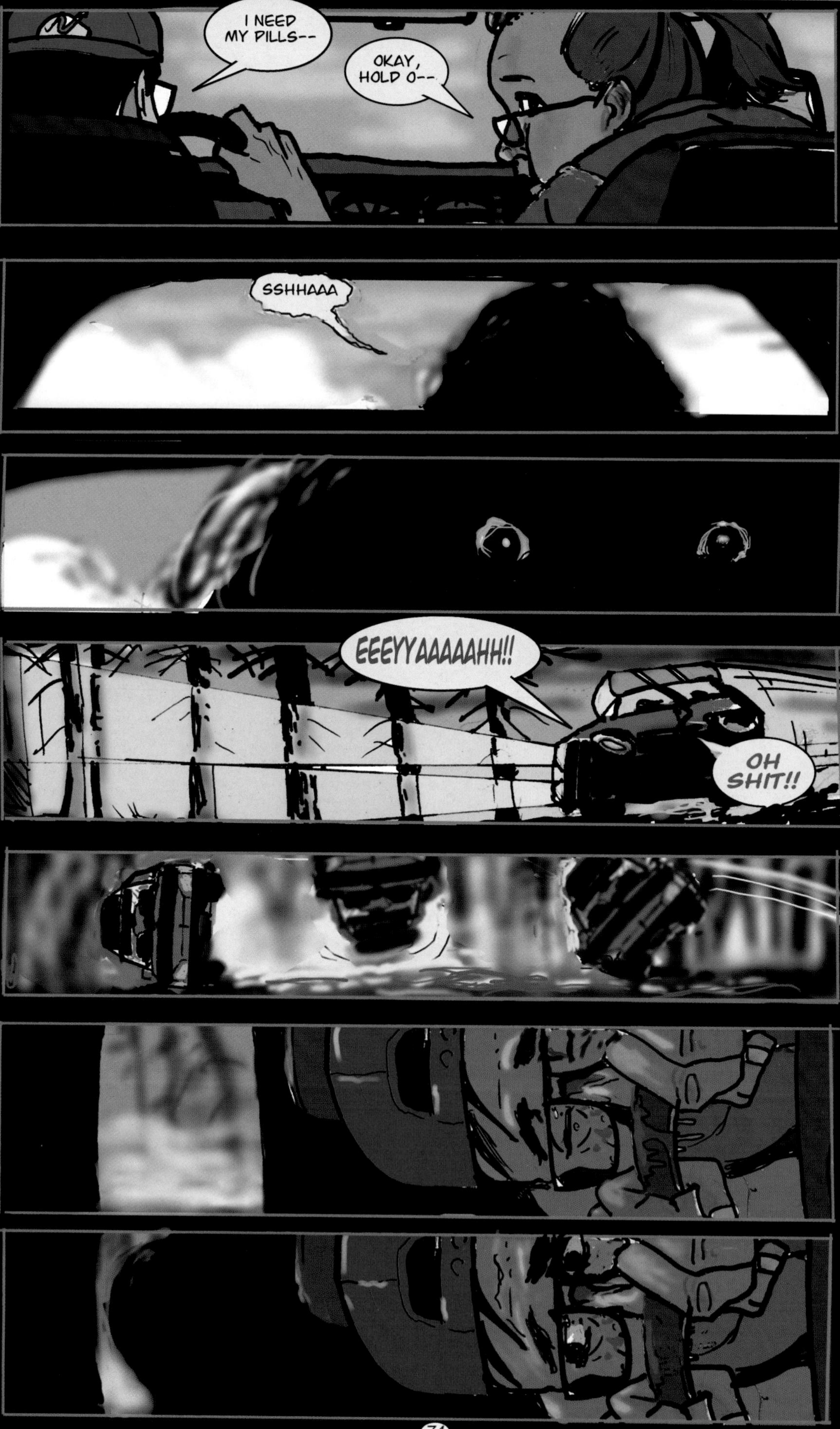

I NEED MY PILLS--
OKAY, HOLD O--
SSHHAAA
EEEYYAAAAAHH!!
OH SHIT!!

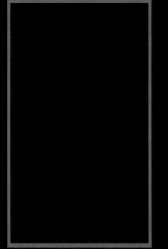

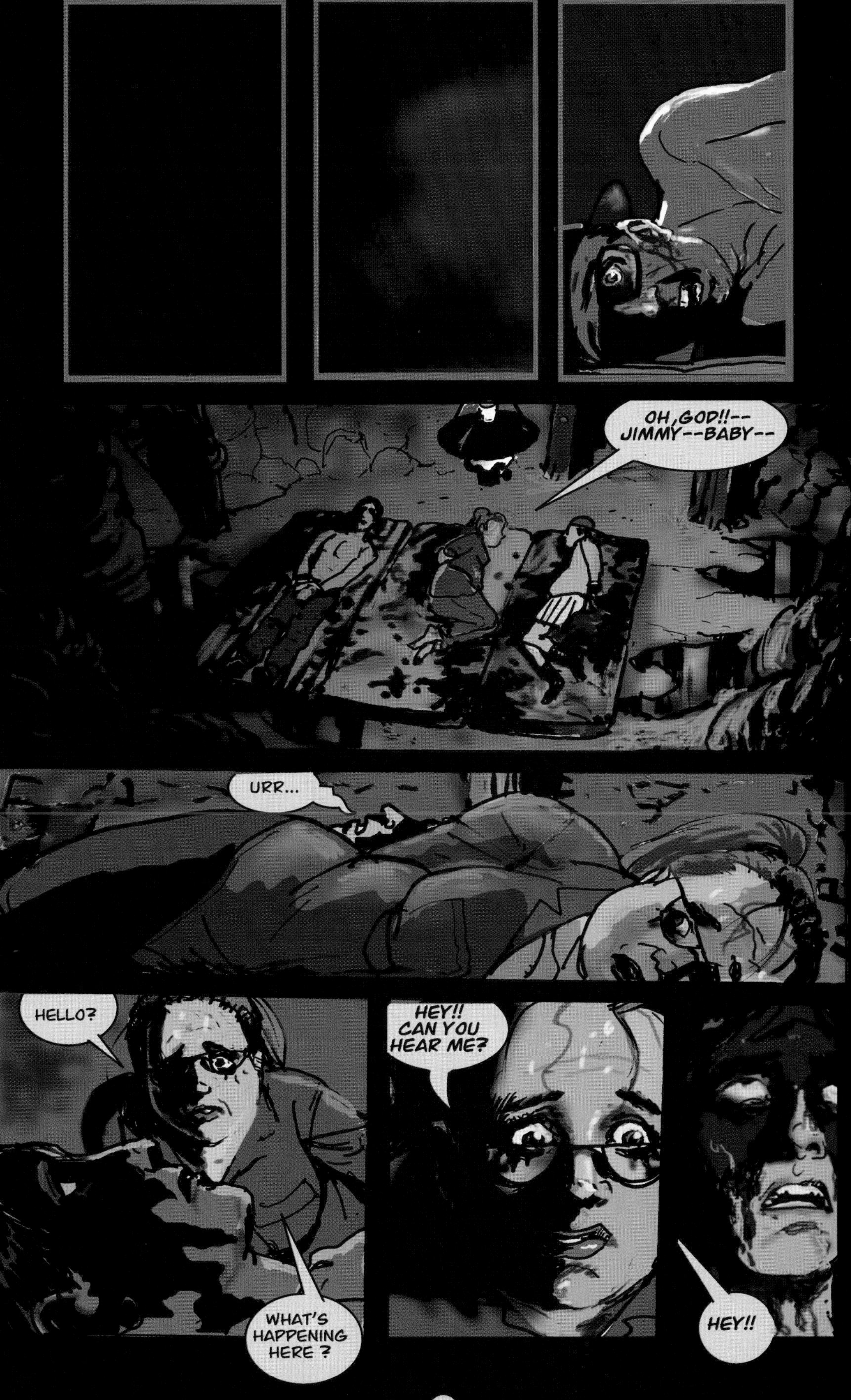
OH, GOD!!-- JIMMY--BABY--
URR...
HELLO?
WHAT'S HAPPENING HERE ?
HEY!! CAN YOU HEAR ME?
HEY!!

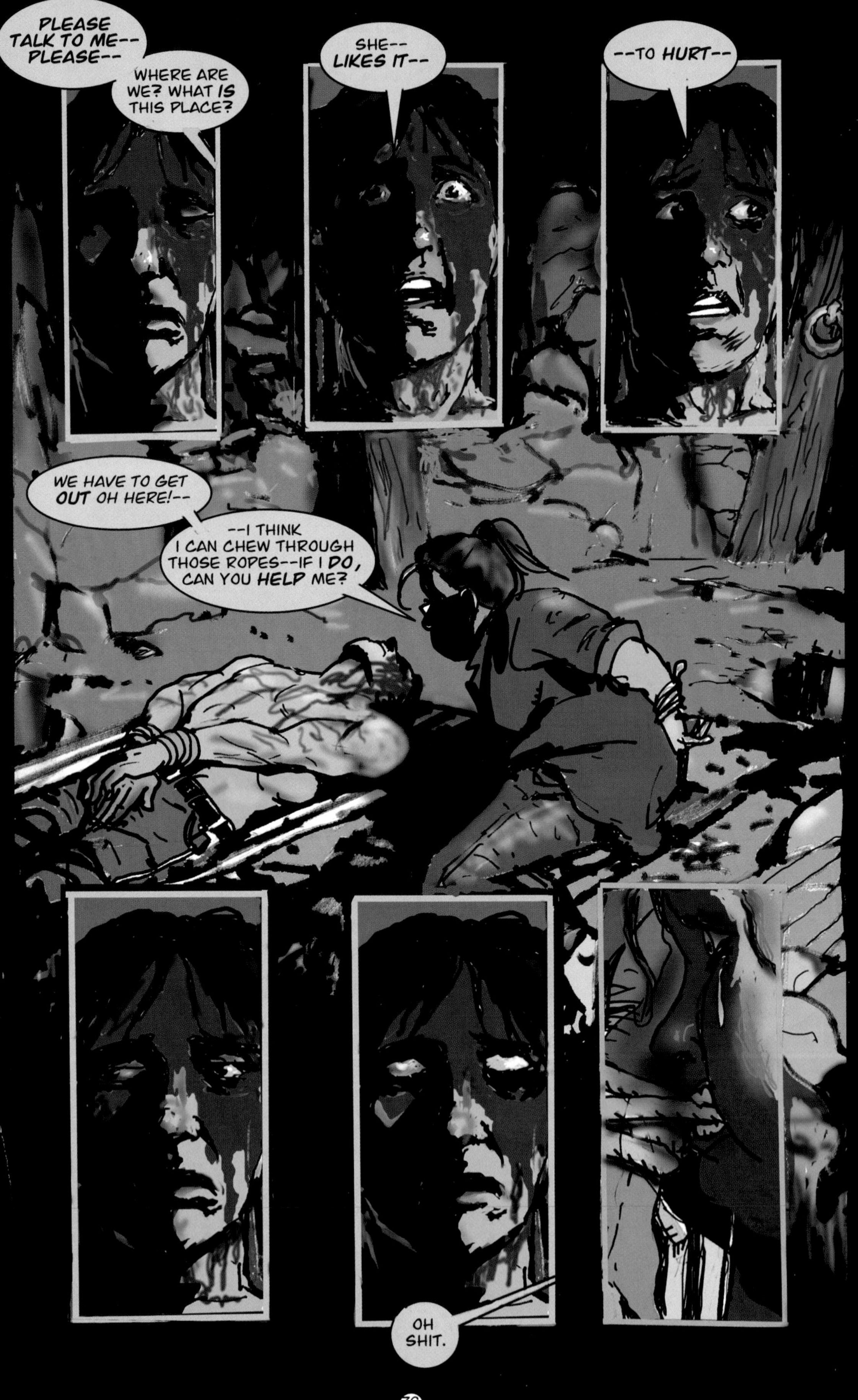
PLEASE TALK TO ME-- PLEASE--
WHERE ARE WE? WHAT IS THIS PLACE?
SHE-- LIKES IT--
--TO HURT--
WE HAVE TO GET OUT OH HERE!--
--I THINK I CAN CHEW THROUGH THOSE ROPES--IF I DO, CAN YOU HELP ME?
OH SHIT.

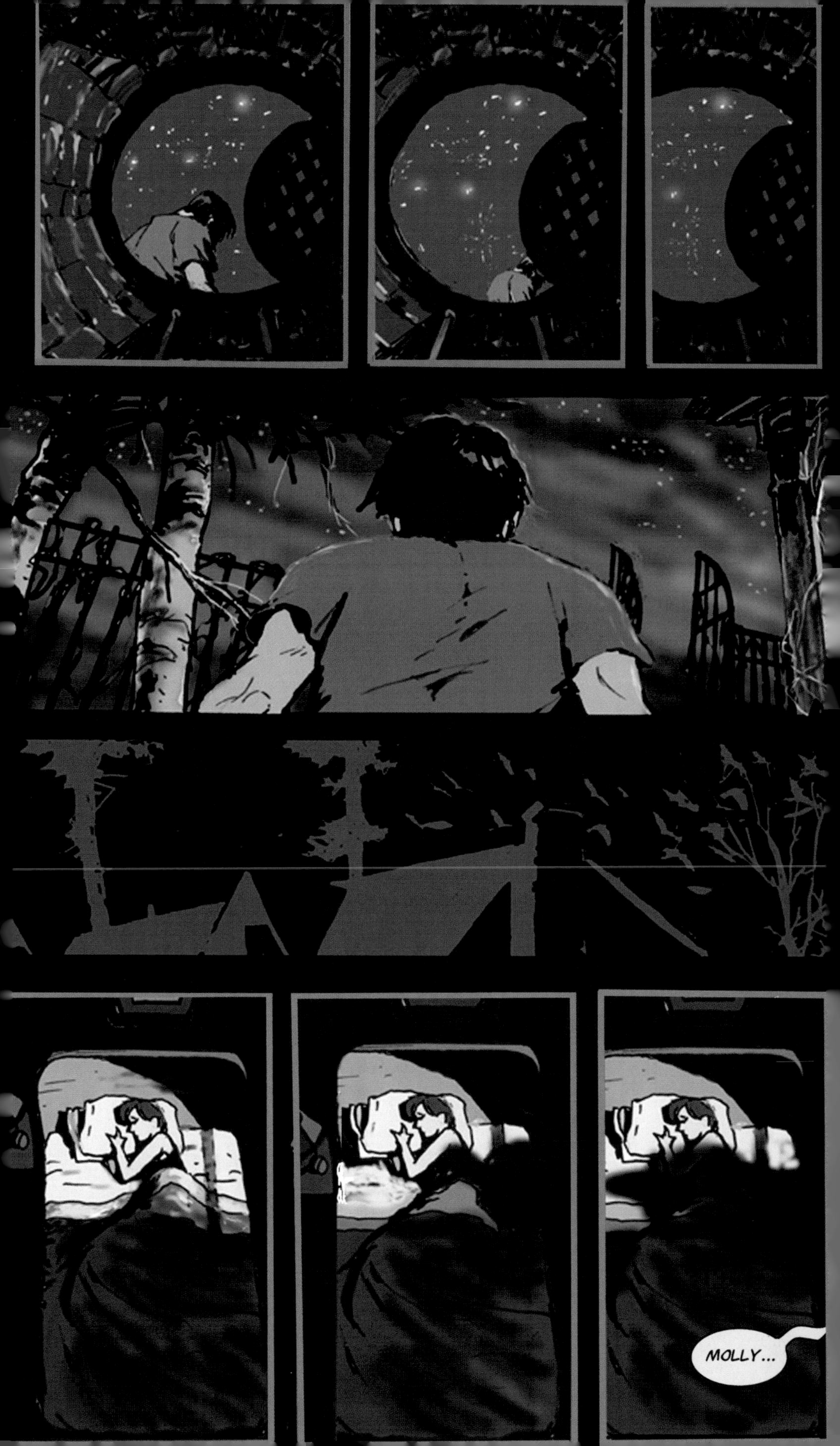
MOLLY...

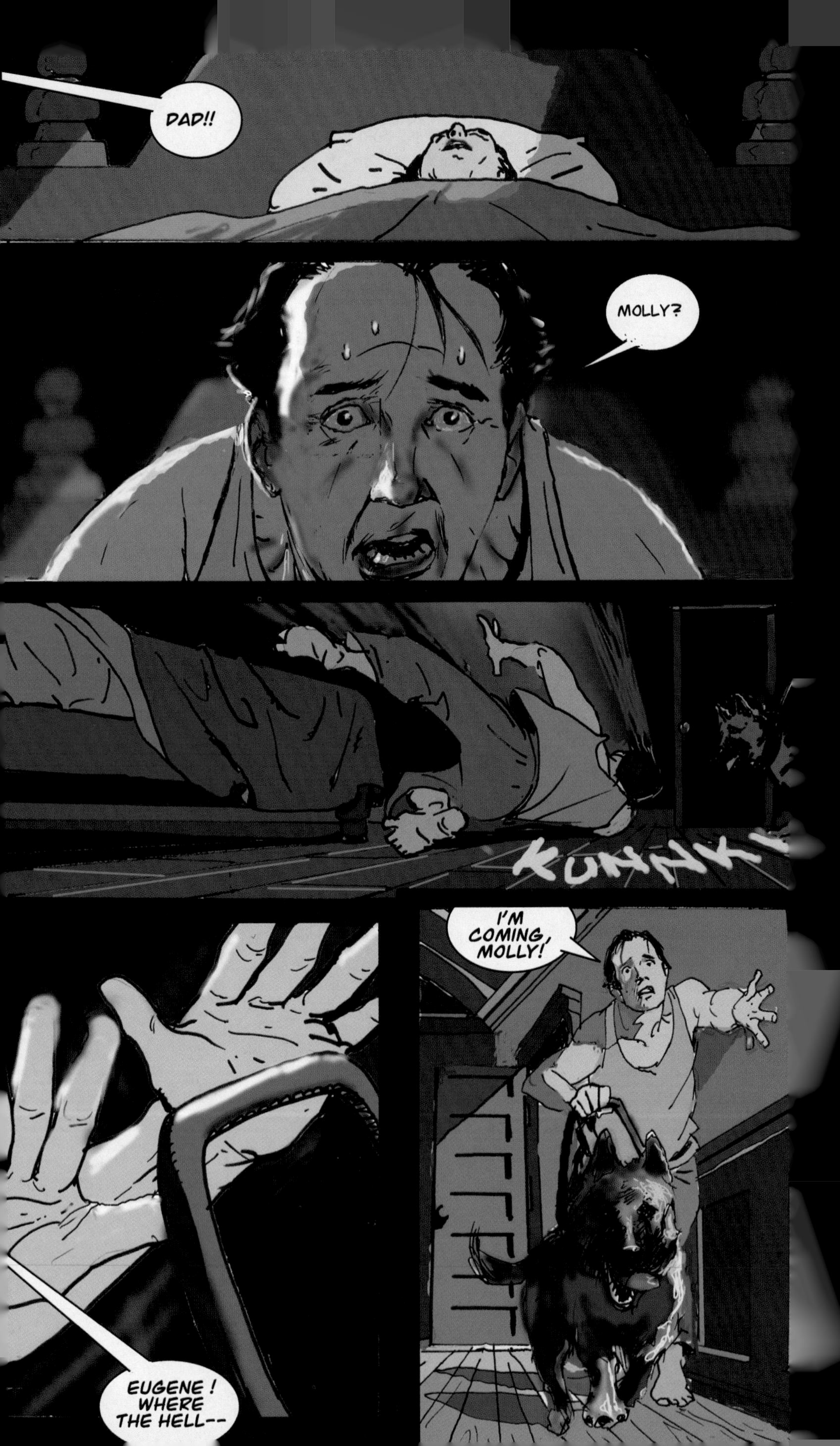

DAD!!
MOLLY?
KUNNK!
I'M COMING, MOLLY!
EUGENE ! WHERE THE HELL--

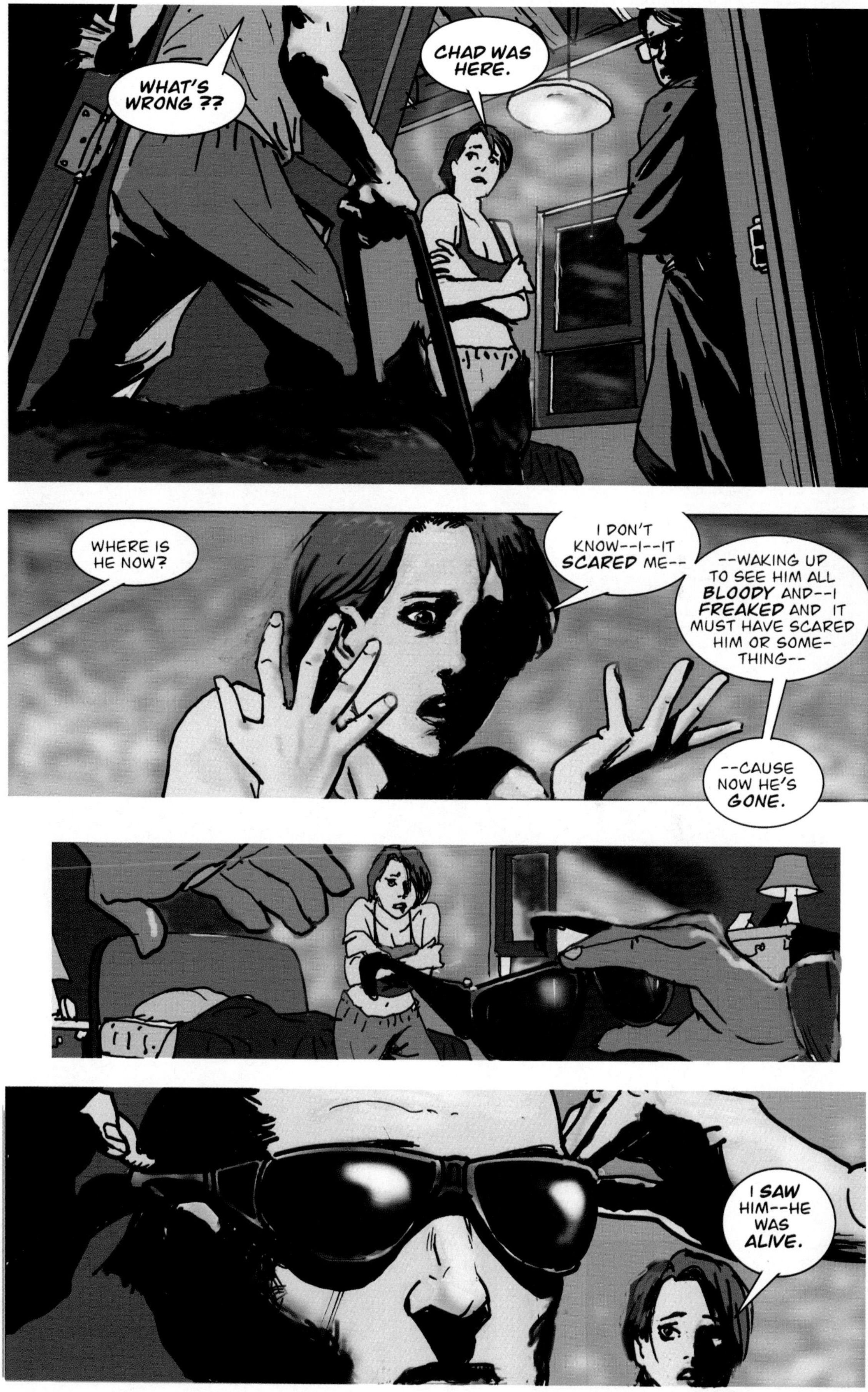
WHAT'S WRONG ??
CHAD WAS HERE.
WHERE IS HE NOW?
I DON'T KNOW--I--IT SCARED ME--
--WAKING UP TO SEE HIM ALL BLOODY AND--I FREAKED AND IT MUST HAVE SCARED HIM OR SOME-THING--
--CAUSE NOW HE'S GONE.
I SAW HIM--HE WAS ALIVE.

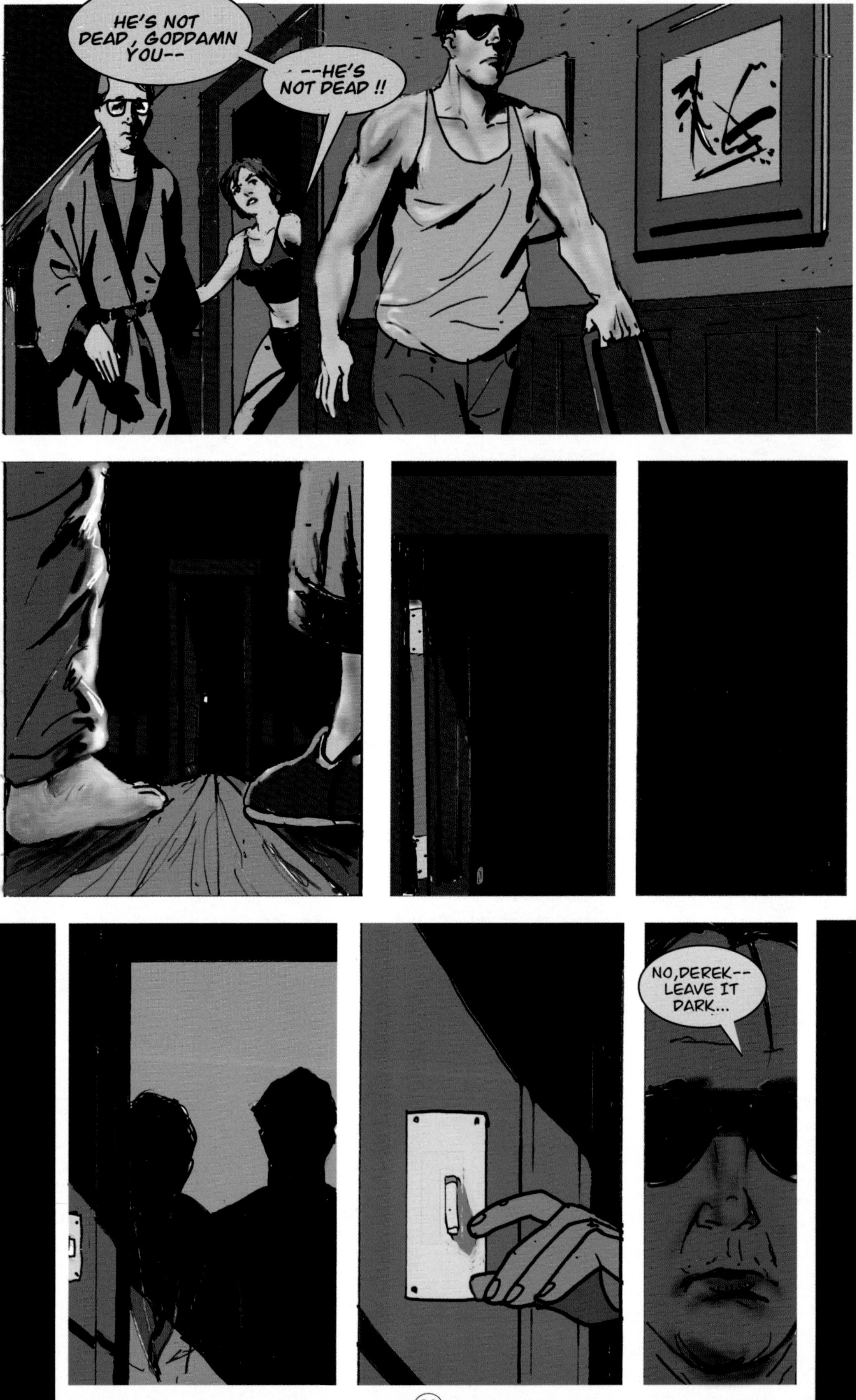
HE'S NOT DEAD, GODDAMN YOU--
--HE'S NOT DEAD !!
NO, DEREK-- LEAVE IT DARK...

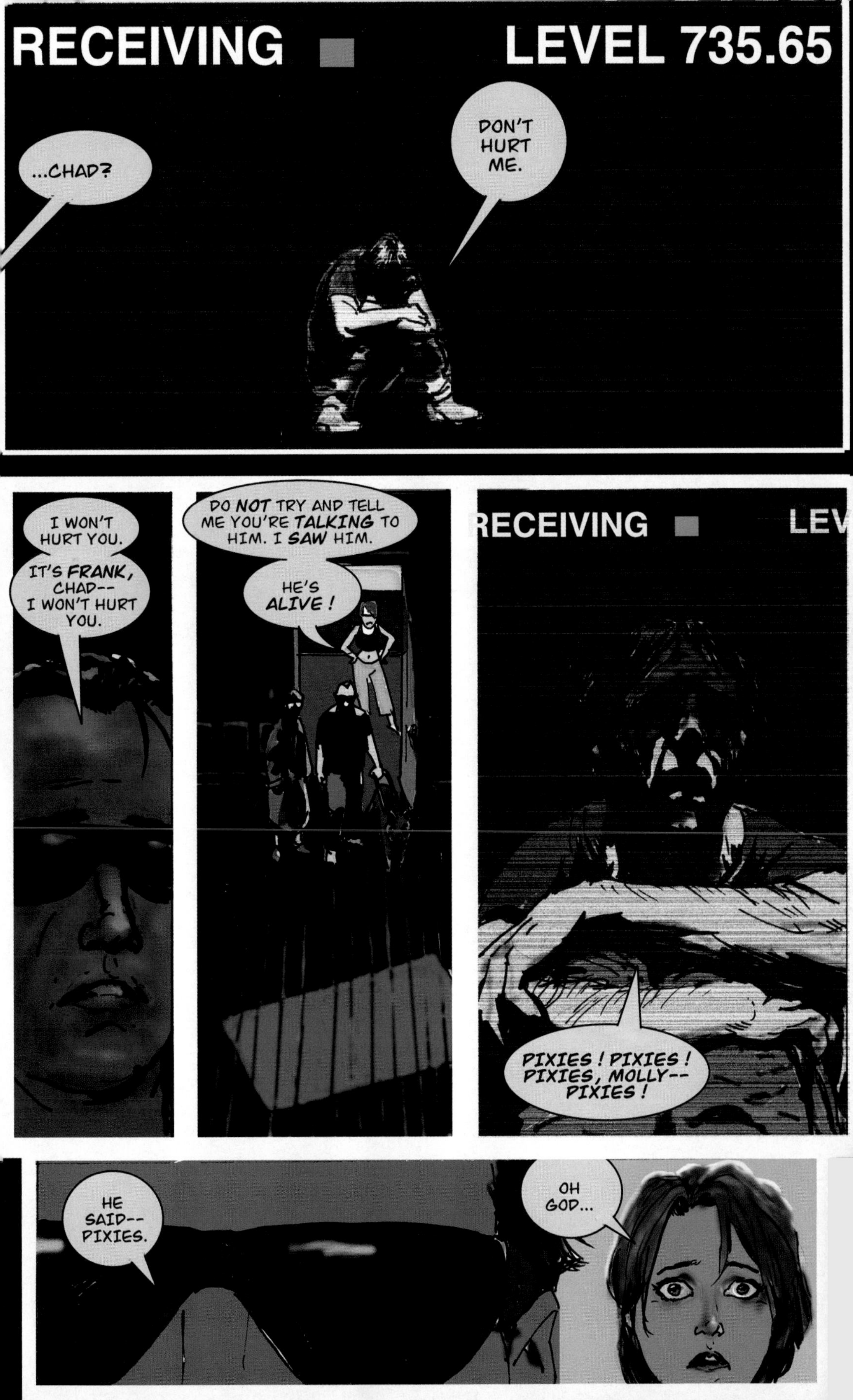
RECEIVING LEVEL 735.65
...CHAD?
DON'T HURT ME.
I WON'T HURT YOU.
IT'S FRANK, CHAD-- I WON'T HURT YOU.
DO NOT TRY AND TELL ME YOU'RE TALKING TO HIM. I SAW HIM.
HE'S ALIVE!
RECEIVING LEV
PIXIES! PIXIES! PIXIES, MOLLY-- PIXIES!
HE SAID-- PIXIES.
OH GOD...

OH CHAD...
...WHERE IS HE?
EVEL 44566

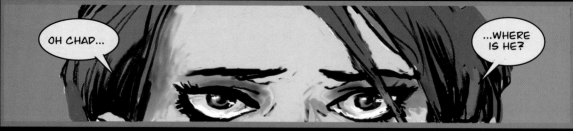

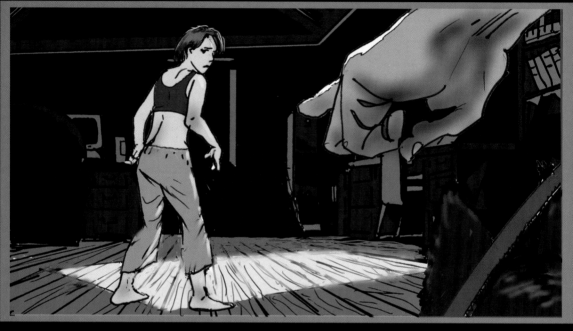

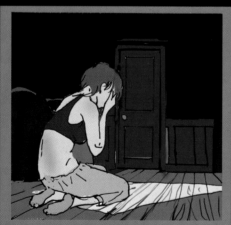

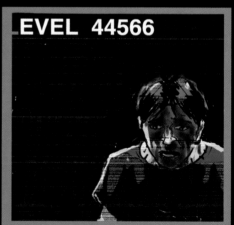

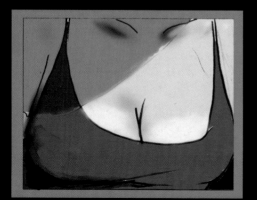

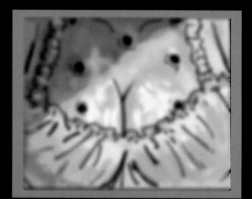

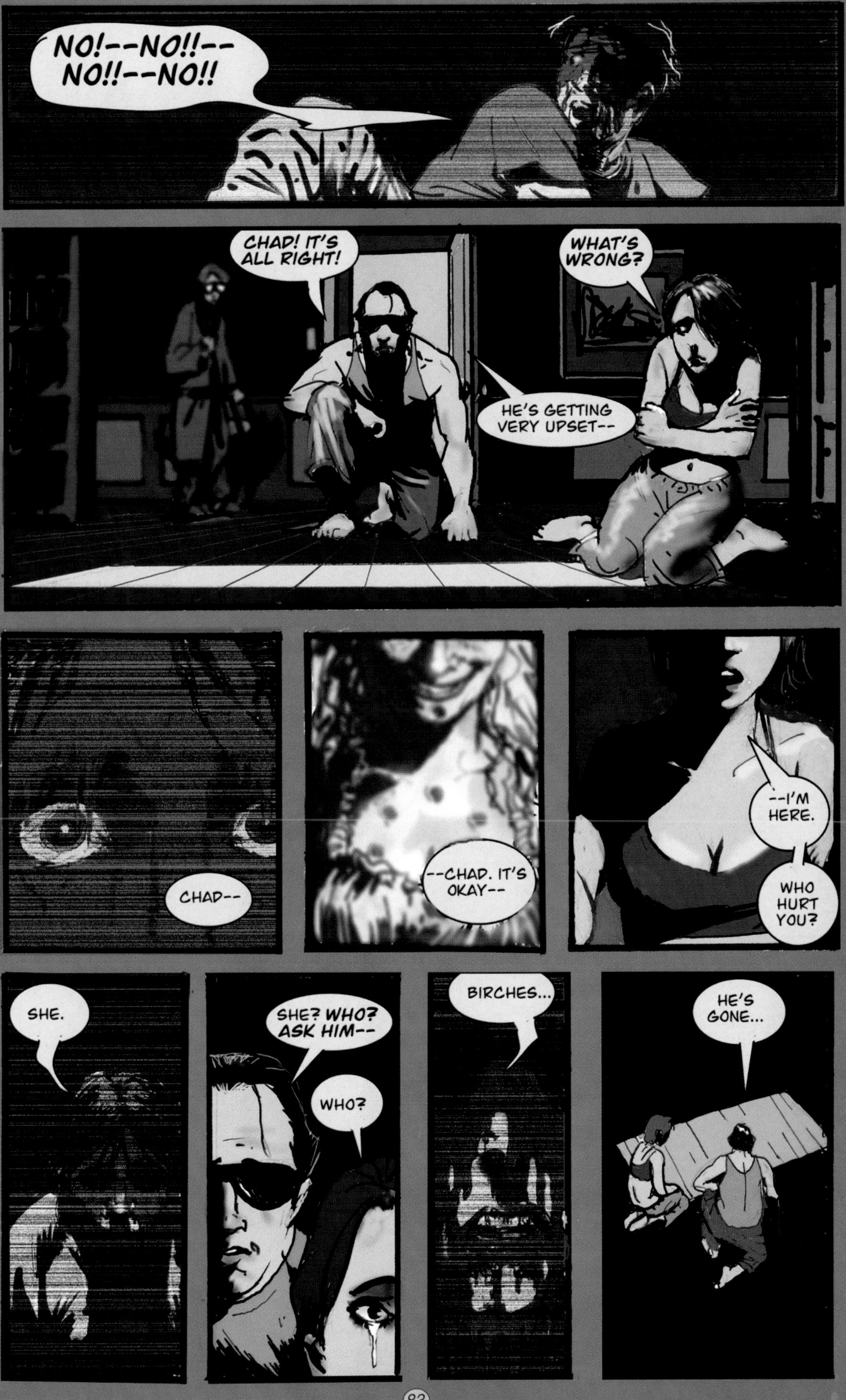
NO!--NO!!--
NO!!--NO!!
CHAD! IT'S ALL RIGHT!
WHAT'S WRONG?
HE'S GETTING VERY UPSET--
CHAD--
--CHAD. IT'S OKAY--
--I'M HERE.
WHO HURT YOU?
SHE.
SHE? WHO? ASK HIM--
WHO?
BIRCHES...
HE'S GONE...

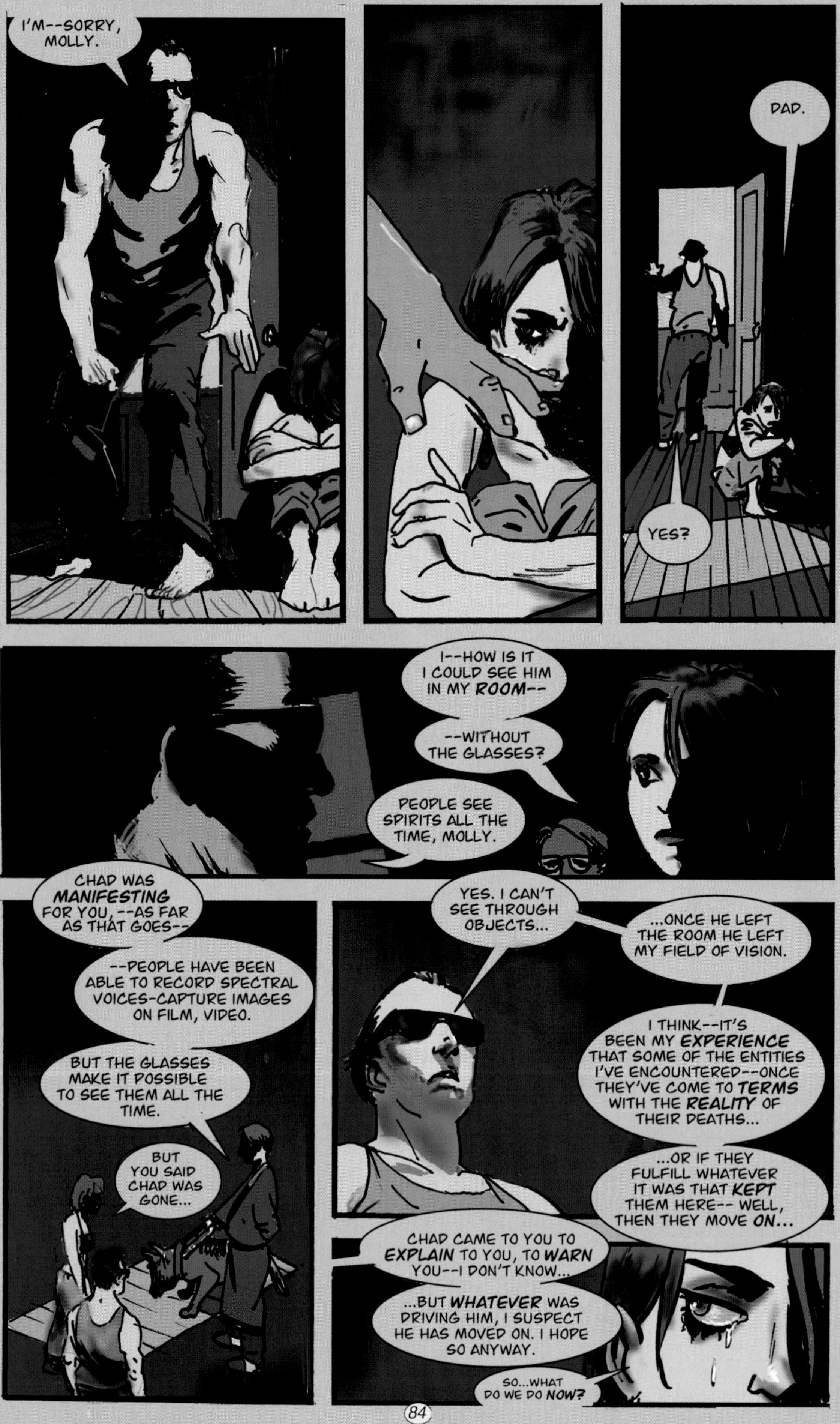

I'M--SORRY, MOLLY.
DAD.
YES?
I--HOW IS IT I COULD SEE HIM IN MY ROOM--
--WITHOUT THE GLASSES?
PEOPLE SEE SPIRITS ALL THE TIME, MOLLY.
CHAD WAS MANIFESTING FOR YOU, --AS FAR AS THAT GOES--
--PEOPLE HAVE BEEN ABLE TO RECORD SPECTRAL VOICES-CAPTURE IMAGES ON FILM, VIDEO.
BUT THE GLASSES MAKE IT POSSIBLE TO SEE THEM ALL THE TIME.
BUT YOU SAID CHAD WAS GONE...
YES. I CAN'T SEE THROUGH OBJECTS...
...ONCE HE LEFT THE ROOM HE LEFT MY FIELD OF VISION.
I THINK--IT'S BEEN MY EXPERIENCE THAT SOME OF THE ENTITIES I'VE ENCOUNTERED--ONCE THEY'VE COME TO TERMS WITH THE REALITY OF THEIR DEATHS...
...OR IF THEY FULFILL WHATEVER IT WAS THAT KEPT THEM HERE-- WELL, THEN THEY MOVE ON...
CHAD CAME TO YOU TO EXPLAIN TO YOU, TO WARN YOU--I DON'T KNOW...
...BUT WHATEVER WAS DRIVING HIM, I SUSPECT HE HAS MOVED ON. I HOPE SO ANYWAY.
SO...WHAT DO WE DO NOW?

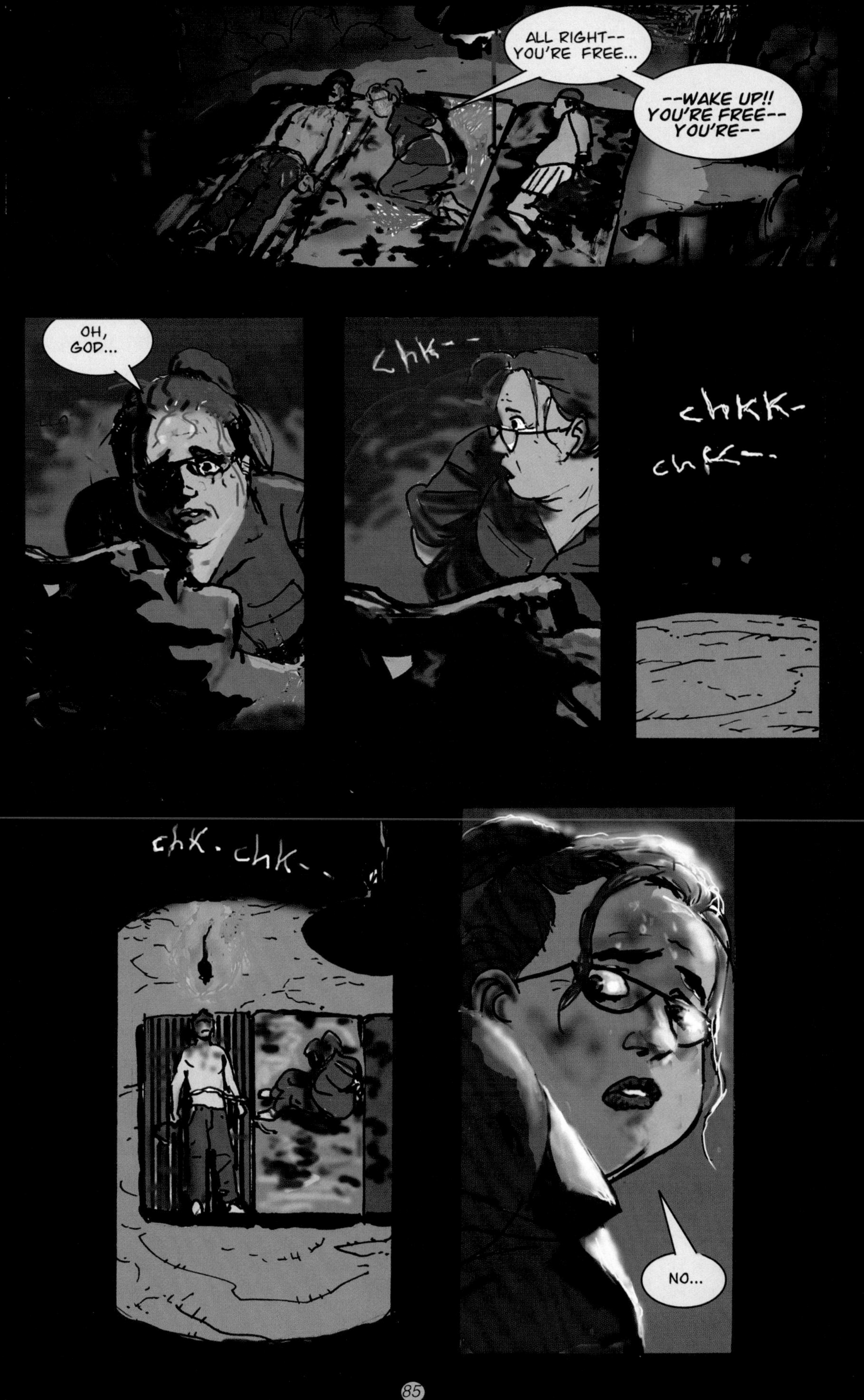
ALL RIGHT--
YOU'RE FREE...
--WAKE UP!!
YOU'RE FREE--
YOU'RE--
OH,
GOD...
chk--
chkk-
chk--
chk. chk--
NO...

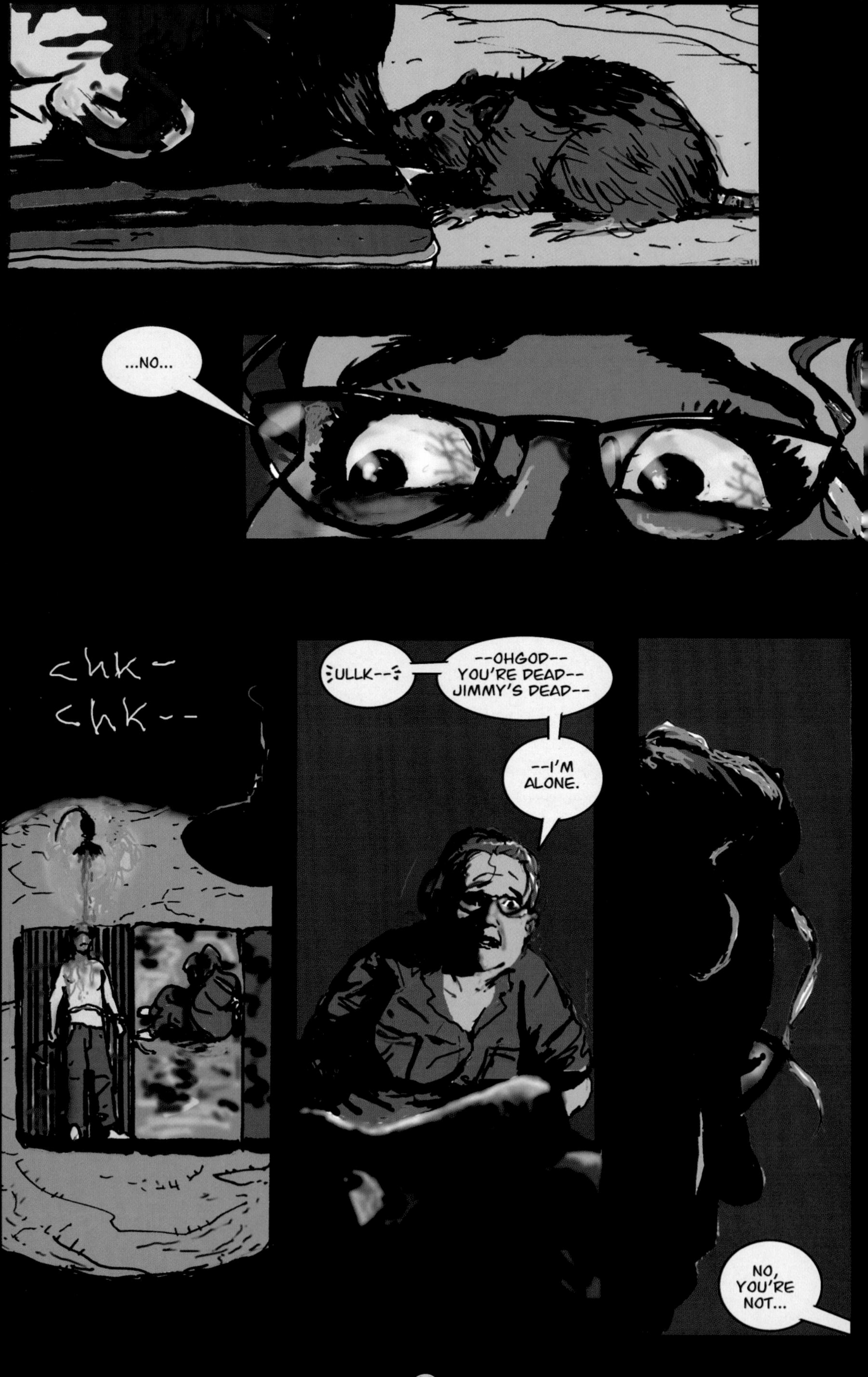
...NO...
chk-
chk--
ULLK--
--OHGOD--
YOU'RE DEAD--
JIMMY'S DEAD--
--I'M
ALONE.
NO,
YOU'RE
NOT...

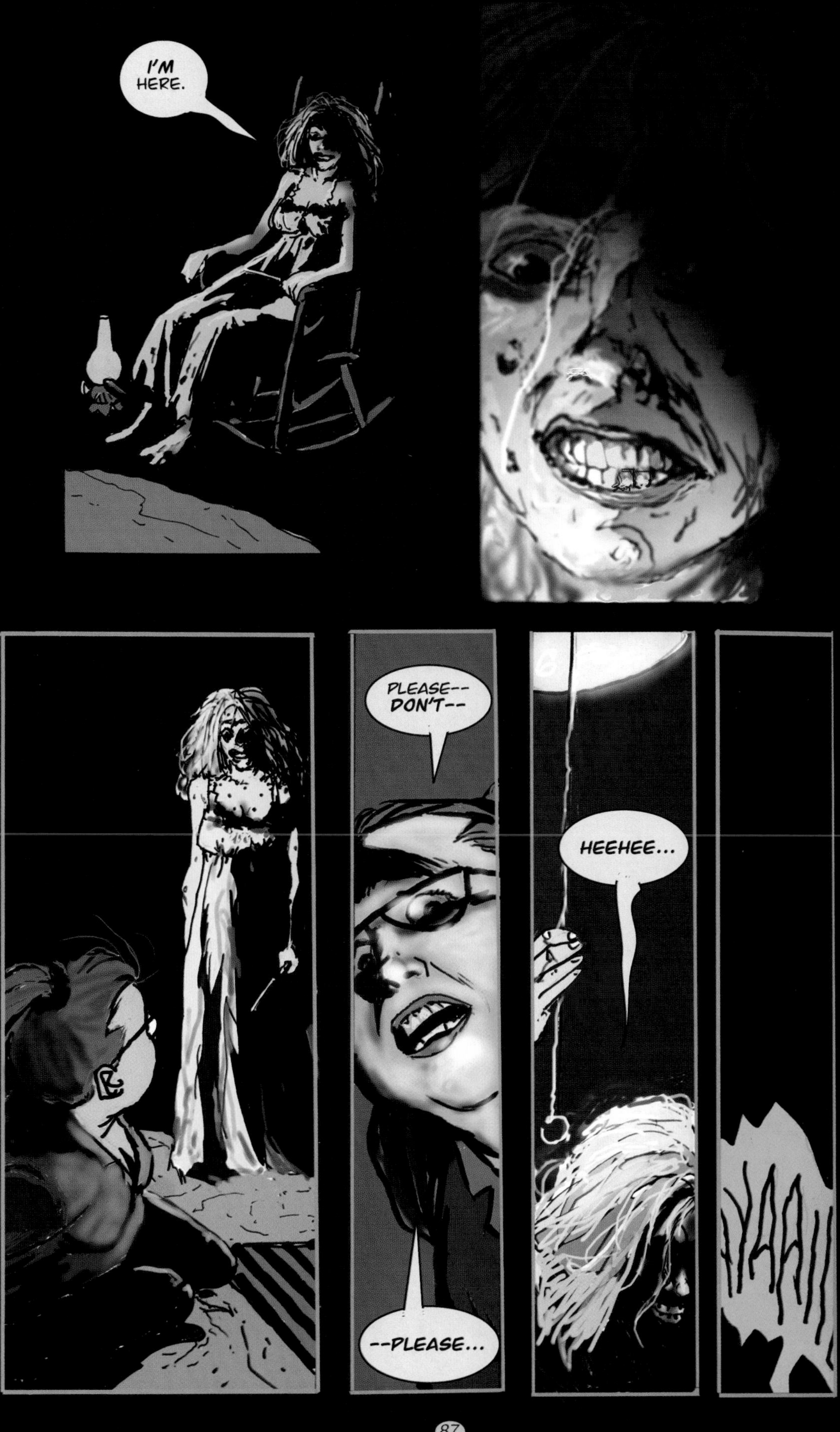
I'M HERE.
PLEASE-- DON'T--
--PLEASE...
HEEHEE...
YAAH

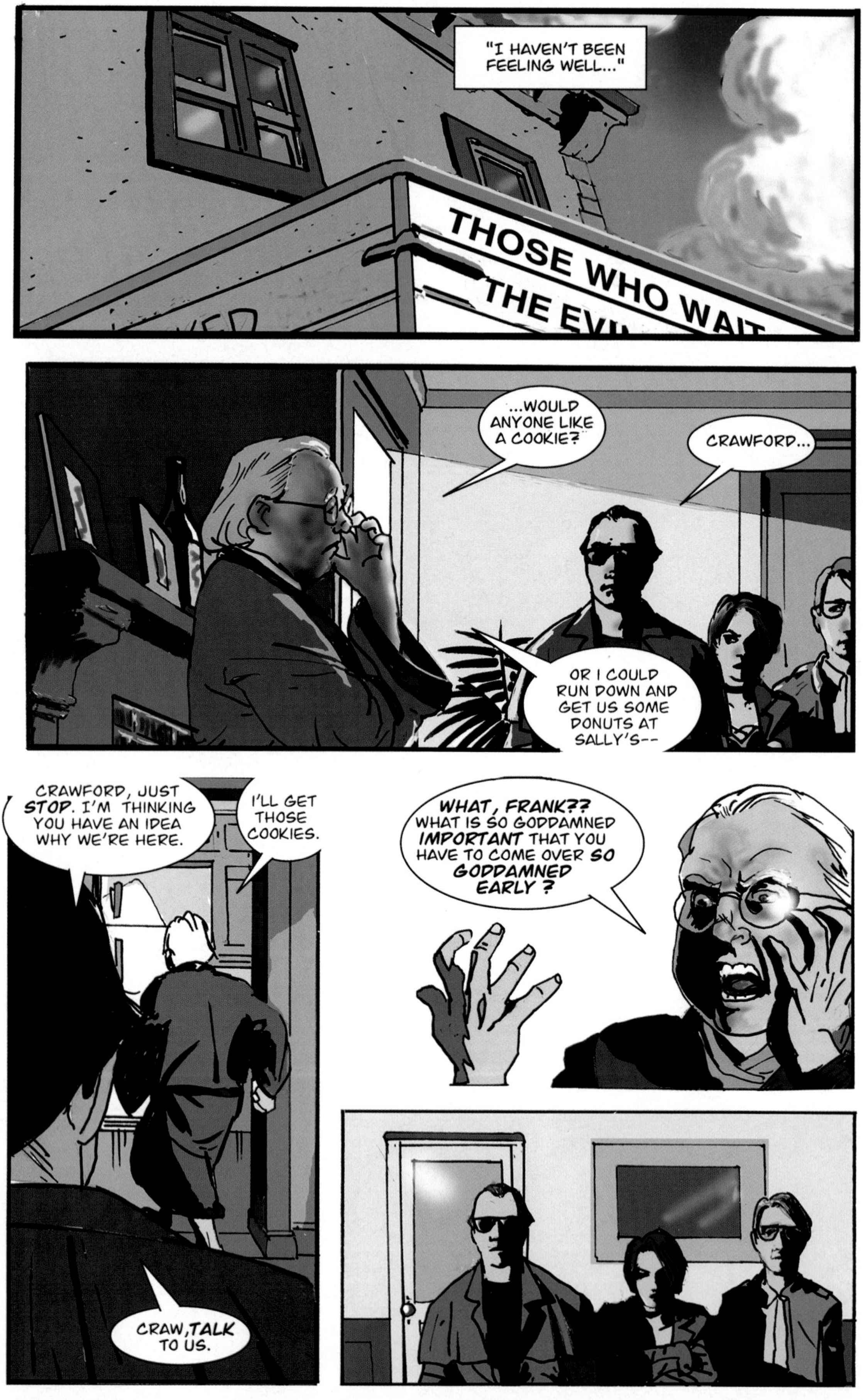
"I HAVEN'T BEEN FEELING WELL..."
THOSE WHO WAIT
...WOULD ANYONE LIKE A COOKIE?
CRAWFORD...
OR I COULD RUN DOWN AND GET US SOME DONUTS AT SALLY'S--
CRAWFORD, JUST STOP. I'M THINKING YOU HAVE AN IDEA WHY WE'RE HERE.
I'LL GET THOSE COOKIES.
CRAW, TALK TO US.
WHAT, FRANK?? WHAT IS SO GODDAMNED IMPORTANT THAT YOU HAVE TO COME OVER SO GODDAMNED EARLY ?

I THINK YOU *KNOW.*

I THINK THAT'S WHY YOU'RE SO PISSY.

I'M--*"PISSY"*--THANK YOU FOR THE STEREOTYPICAL DIG, FRANK,--

--BECAUSE MY MEDS HAVE BEEN UPSETTING MY STOMACH.

OH, FOR CRYIN' OUT *LOUD*--DON'T *PLAY* ME.

IT'S ABOUT *CHAD*-- HE'S *DEAD.*

I'M SORRY.

YOU DON'T SEEM SURPRISED.

WHY WOULD I BE?

I SAW HIM. *WE--SAW HIM--HIS SPIRIT--*

--THIS MORNING--

WHY WOULD HE TELL US ABOUT A *WOMAN*...AND THE *BIRCHES,* CRAW?

SHE'S A REAL CHIP OFF THE OLD *BLOCK,* ISN'T SHE, FRANK? PLAYING WITH YOUR LITTLE OUIJA GLASSES, SEEING *SPOOKS*--

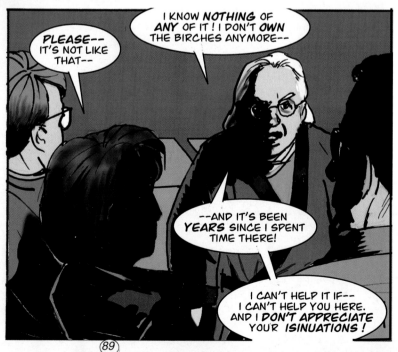

PLEASE-- IT'S NOT LIKE THAT--

I KNOW *NOTHING* OF *ANY* OF IT ! I DON'T *OWN* THE BIRCHES ANYMORE--

--AND IT'S BEEN *YEARS* SINCE I SPENT TIME THERE!

I CAN'T HELP IT IF-- I CAN'T HELP YOU HERE. AND I *DON'T* APPRECIATE YOUR *ISINUATIONS* !

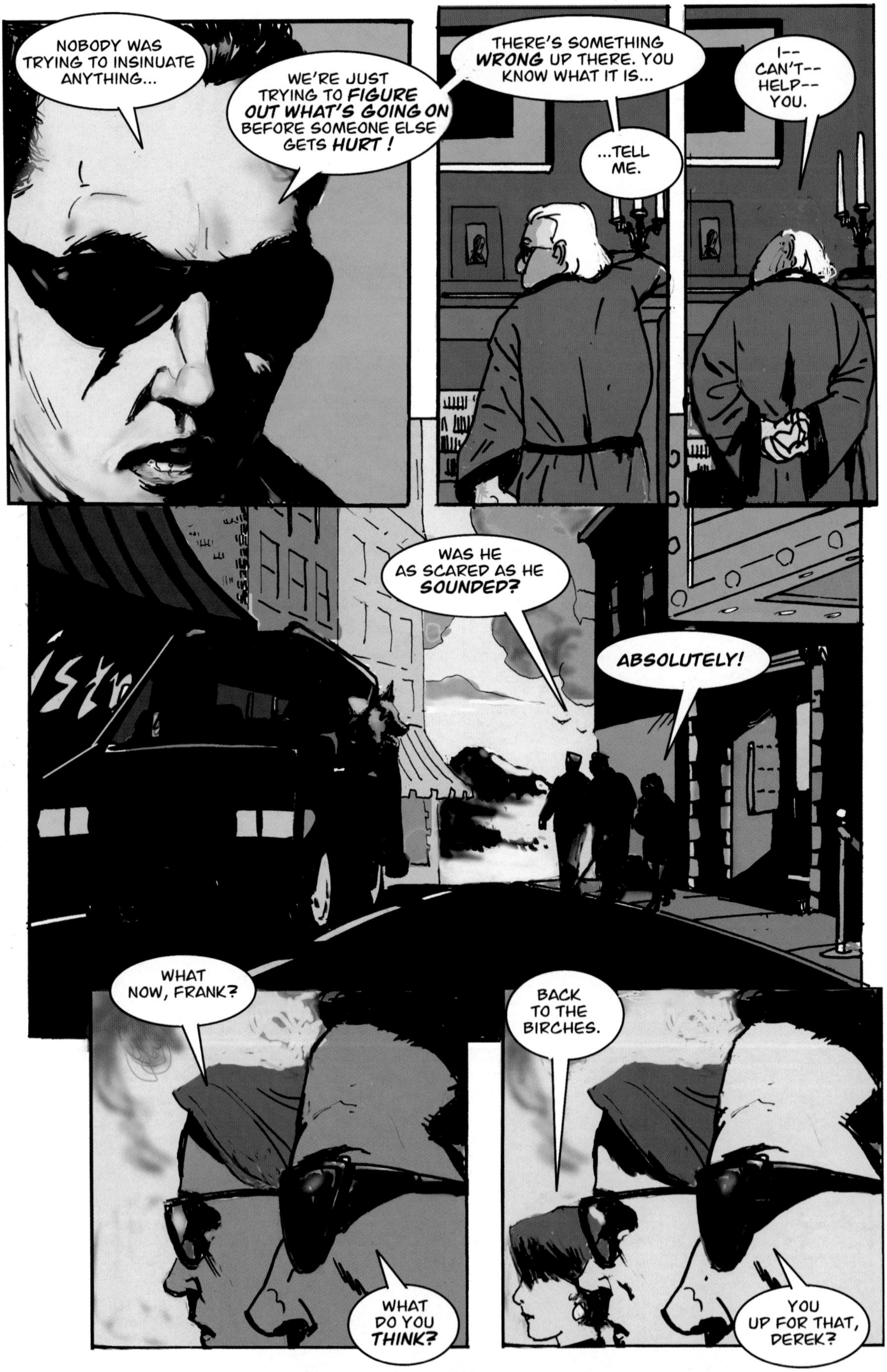
NOBODY WAS TRYING TO INSINUATE ANYTHING...
WE'RE JUST TRYING TO FIGURE OUT WHAT'S GOING ON BEFORE SOMEONE ELSE GETS HURT !
THERE'S SOMETHING WRONG UP THERE. YOU KNOW WHAT IT IS...
...TELL ME.
I-- CAN'T-- HELP-- YOU.
WAS HE AS SCARED AS HE SOUNDED?
ABSOLUTELY!
WHAT NOW, FRANK?
WHAT DO YOU THINK?
BACK TO THE BIRCHES.
YOU UP FOR THAT, DEREK?

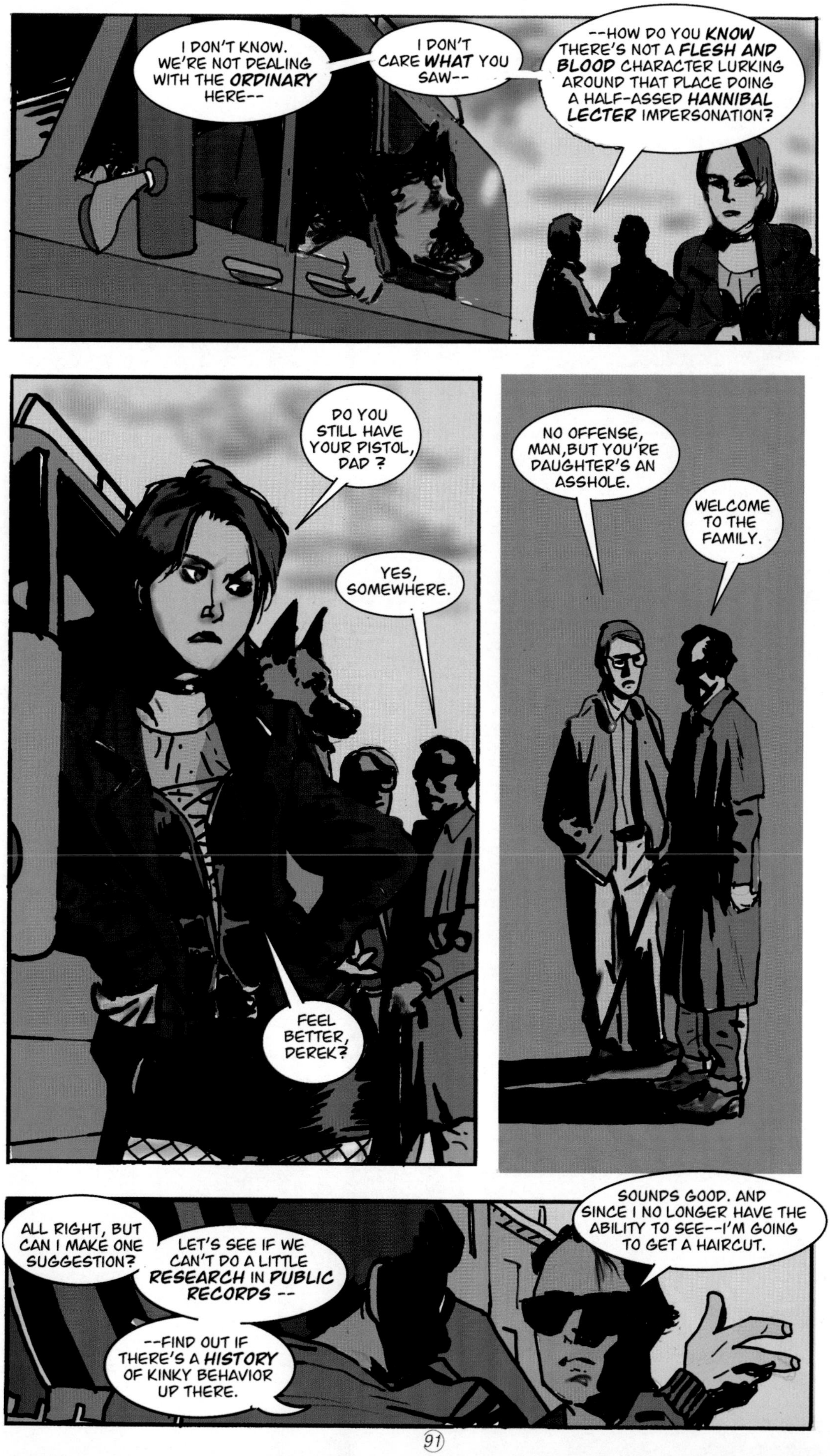
I DON'T KNOW. WE'RE NOT DEALING WITH THE ORDINARY HERE--
I DON'T CARE WHAT YOU SAW--
--HOW DO YOU KNOW THERE'S NOT A FLESH AND BLOOD CHARACTER LURKING AROUND THAT PLACE DOING A HALF-ASSED HANNIBAL LECTER IMPERSONATION?
DO YOU STILL HAVE YOUR PISTOL, DAD ?
YES, SOMEWHERE.
FEEL BETTER, DEREK?
NO OFFENSE, MAN,BUT YOU'RE DAUGHTER'S AN ASSHOLE.
WELCOME TO THE FAMILY.
ALL RIGHT, BUT CAN I MAKE ONE SUGGESTION?
LET'S SEE IF WE CAN'T DO A LITTLE RESEARCH IN PUBLIC RECORDS --
--FIND OUT IF THERE'S A HISTORY OF KINKY BEHAVIOR UP THERE.
SOUNDS GOOD. AND SINCE I NO LONGER HAVE THE ABILITY TO SEE--I'M GOING TO GET A HAIRCUT.

"I TAKE IT BACK. YOU'RE *BOTH* ASSHOLES".

PUBLIC LIBRARY

LOCAL BUSINESSMAN DIES

Fontaine Halliday, of the Birches, dies. Was descendant of area's first settlers.

MUST HAVE BEEN CRAWFORD'S GREAT-GRAND-FATHER, HUH?

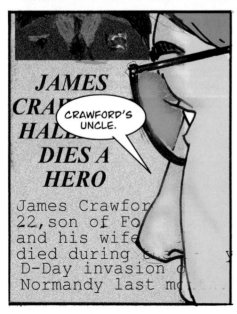

JAMES CRAWFORD HALLIDAY DIES A HERO

CRAWFORD'S UNCLE.

James Crawfor
22, son of Fo
and his wife
died during
D-Day invasion o
Normandy last m

HALLIDAY-BRODERICK NUPTIALS

THEY LOOK LIKE THEY WERE A LOT OF FUN.

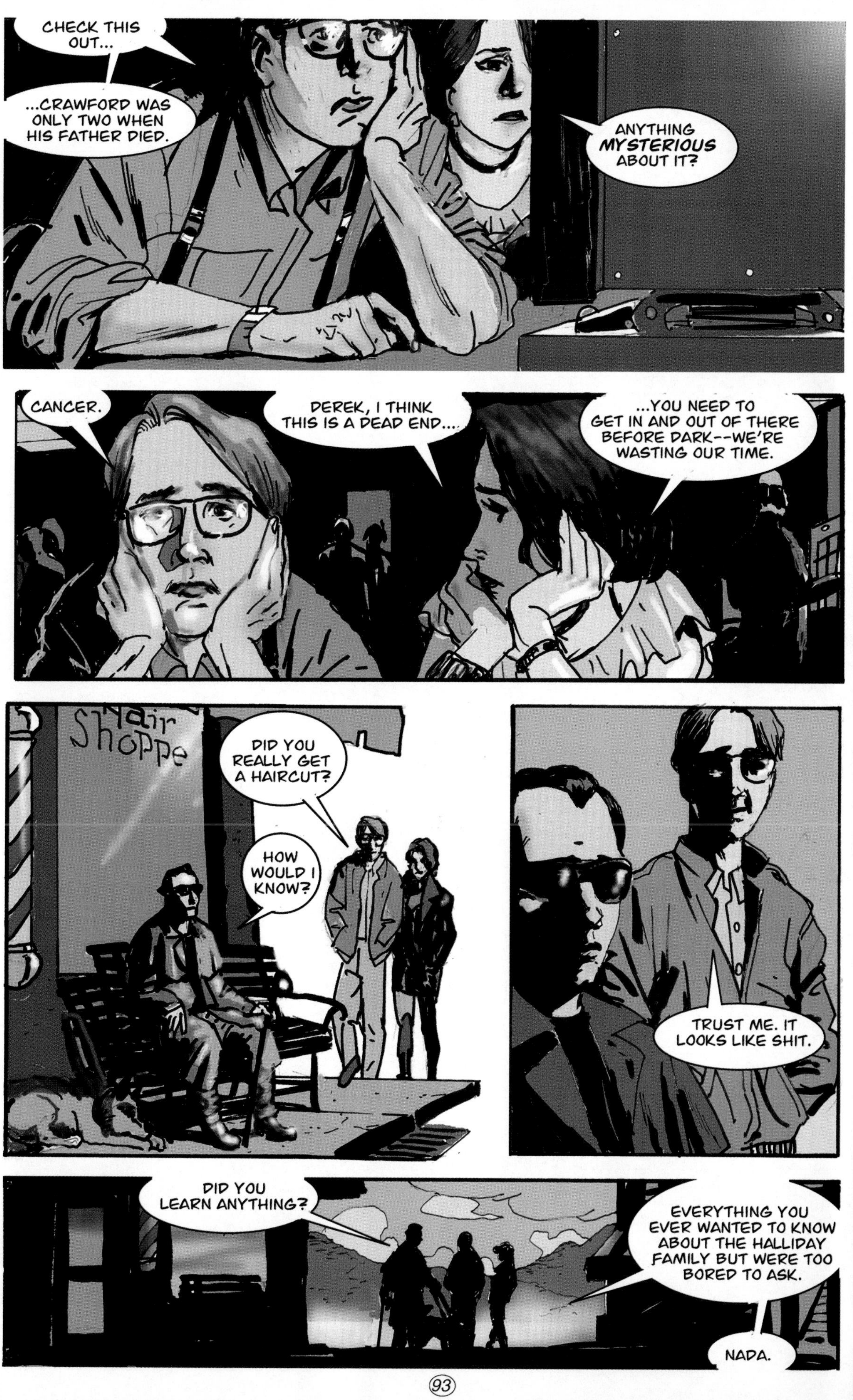
CHECK THIS OUT...
...CRAWFORD WAS ONLY TWO WHEN HIS FATHER DIED.
ANYTHING *MYSTERIOUS* ABOUT IT?
CANCER.
DEREK, I THINK THIS IS A DEAD END....
...YOU NEED TO GET IN AND OUT OF THERE BEFORE DARK--WE'RE WASTING OUR TIME.
Hair Shoppe
DID YOU REALLY GET A HAIRCUT?
HOW WOULD I KNOW?
TRUST ME. IT LOOKS LIKE SHIT.
DID YOU LEARN ANYTHING?
EVERYTHING YOU EVER WANTED TO KNOW ABOUT THE HALLIDAY FAMILY BUT WERE TOO BORED TO ASK.
NADA.

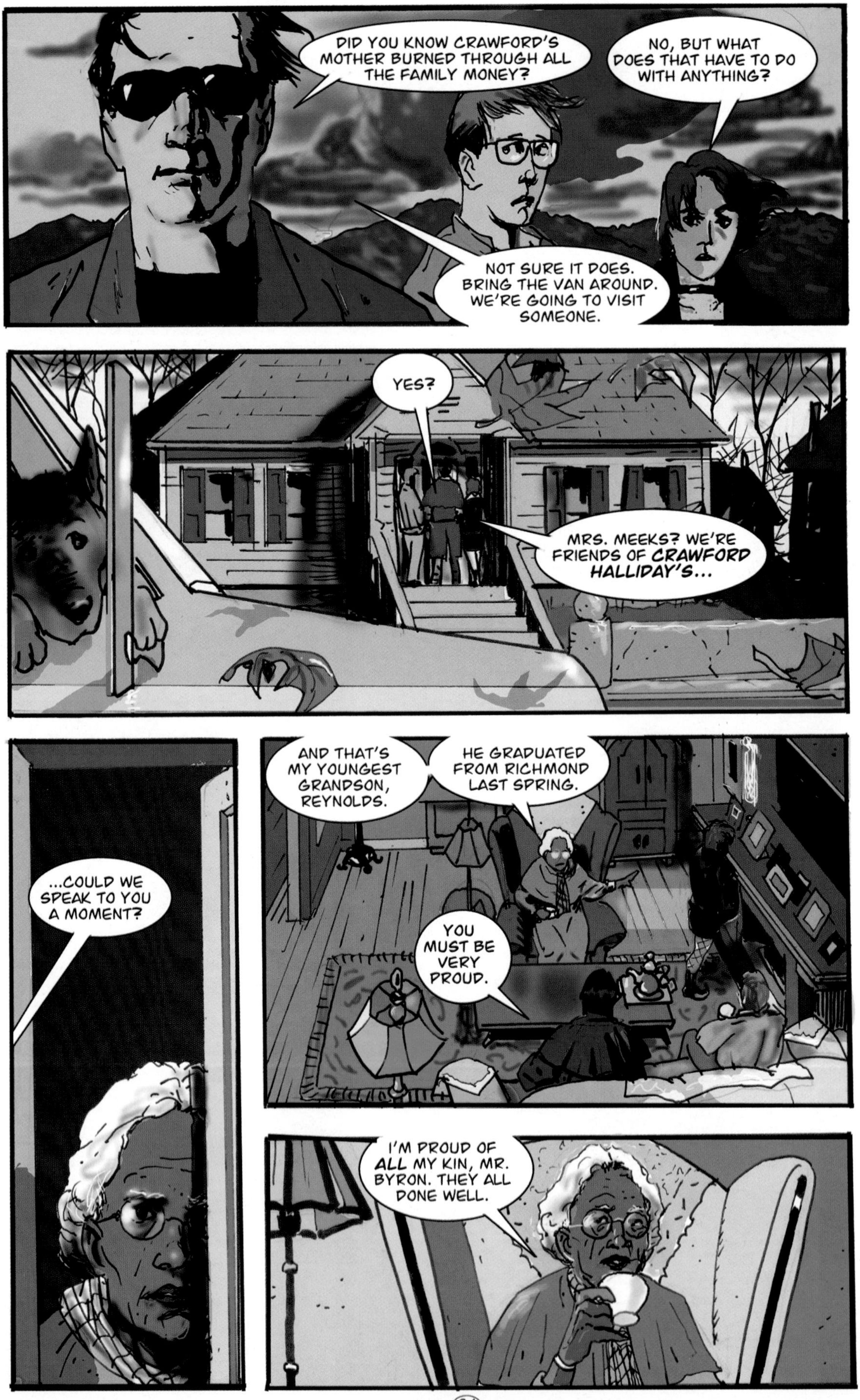
DID YOU KNOW CRAWFORD'S MOTHER BURNED THROUGH ALL THE FAMILY MONEY?
NO, BUT WHAT DOES THAT HAVE TO DO WITH ANYTHING?
NOT SURE IT DOES. BRING THE VAN AROUND. WE'RE GOING TO VISIT SOMEONE.
YES?
MRS. MEEKS? WE'RE FRIENDS OF CRAWFORD HALLIDAY'S...
...COULD WE SPEAK TO YOU A MOMENT?
AND THAT'S MY YOUNGEST GRANDSON, REYNOLDS.
HE GRADUATED FROM RICHMOND LAST SPRING.
YOU MUST BE VERY PROUD.
I'M PROUD OF ALL MY KIN, MR. BYRON. THEY ALL DONE WELL.

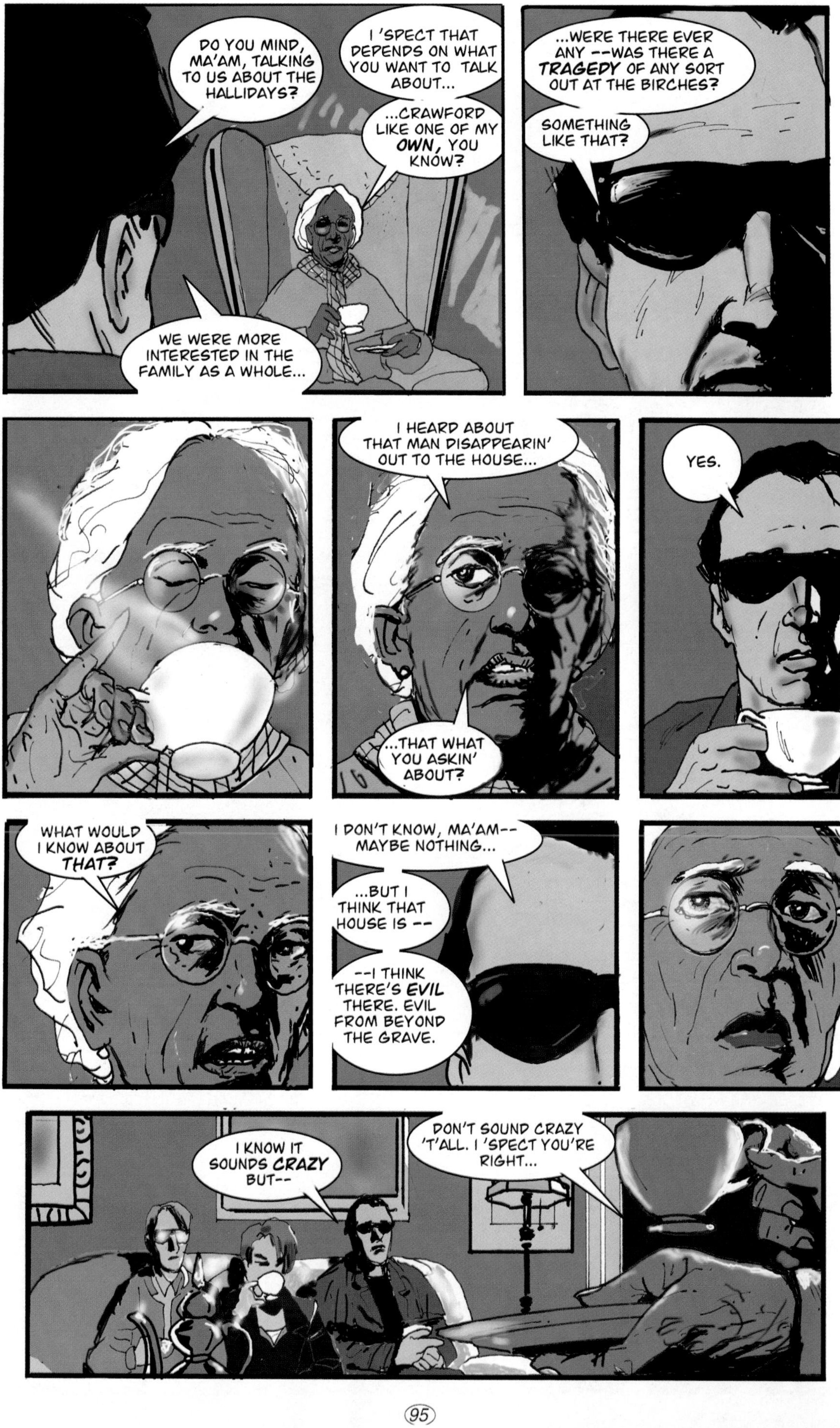
DO YOU MIND, MA'AM, TALKING TO US ABOUT THE HALLIDAYS?
I 'SPECT THAT DEPENDS ON WHAT YOU WANT TO TALK ABOUT...
WE WERE MORE INTERESTED IN THE FAMILY AS A WHOLE...
...CRAWFORD LIKE ONE OF MY OWN, YOU KNOW?
...WERE THERE EVER ANY --WAS THERE A TRAGEDY OF ANY SORT OUT AT THE BIRCHES?
SOMETHING LIKE THAT?
I HEARD ABOUT THAT MAN DISAPPEARIN' OUT TO THE HOUSE...
...THAT WHAT YOU ASKIN' ABOUT?
YES.
WHAT WOULD I KNOW ABOUT THAT?
I DON'T KNOW, MA'AM-- MAYBE NOTHING...
...BUT I THINK THAT HOUSE IS --
--I THINK THERE'S EVIL THERE. EVIL FROM BEYOND THE GRAVE.
I KNOW IT SOUNDS CRAZY BUT--
DON'T SOUND CRAZY 'T'ALL. I 'SPECT YOU'RE RIGHT...

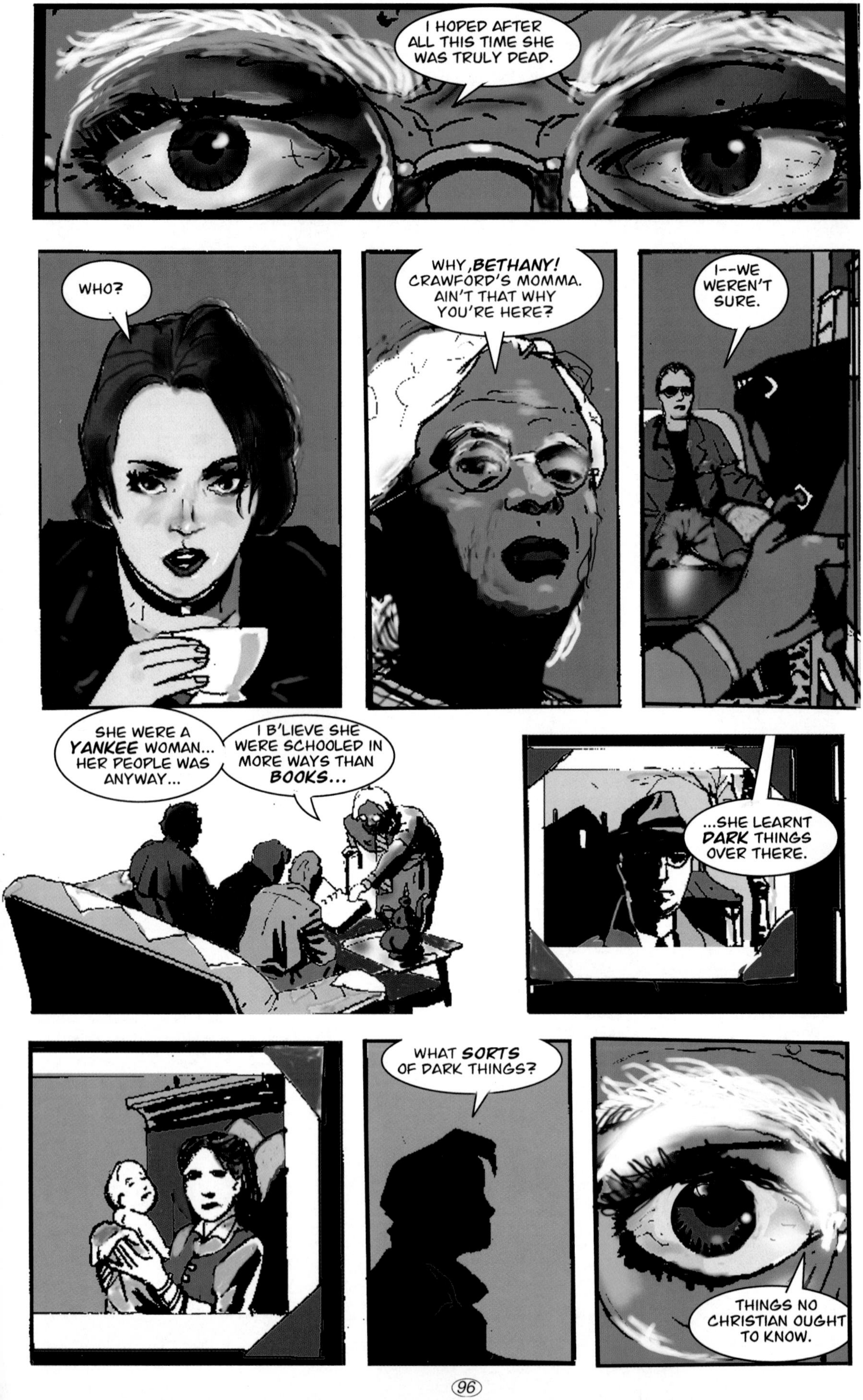
I HOPED AFTER ALL THIS TIME SHE WAS TRULY DEAD.
WHO?
WHY, BETHANY! CRAWFORD'S MOMMA. AIN'T THAT WHY YOU'RE HERE?
I--WE WEREN'T SURE.
SHE WERE A YANKEE WOMAN... HER PEOPLE WAS ANYWAY...
I B'LIEVE SHE WERE SCHOOLED IN MORE WAYS THAN BOOKS...
...SHE LEARNT DARK THINGS OVER THERE.
WHAT SORTS OF DARK THINGS?
THINGS NO CHRISTIAN OUGHT TO KNOW.

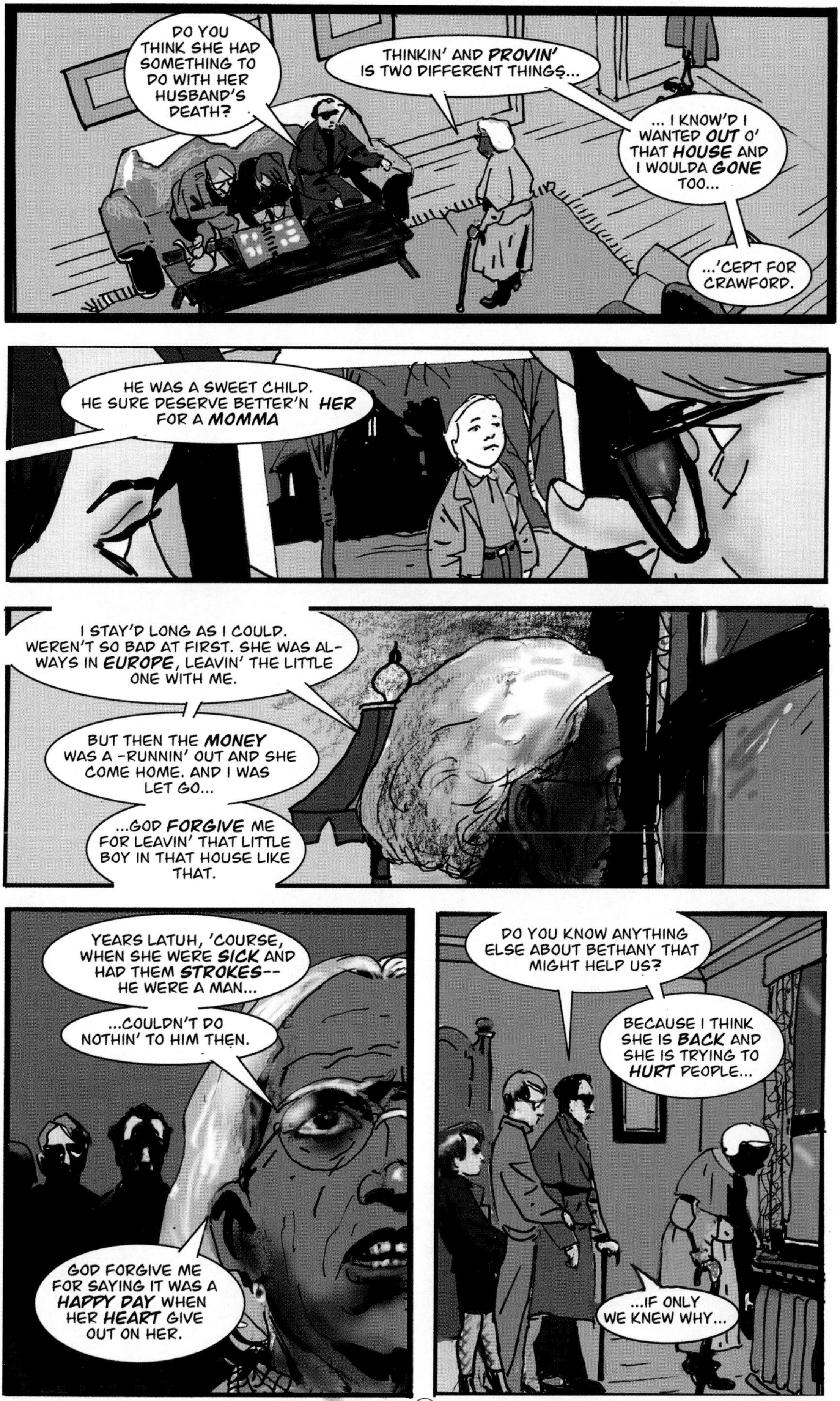
DO YOU THINK SHE HAD SOMETHING TO DO WITH HER HUSBAND'S DEATH?
THINKIN' AND PROVIN' IS TWO DIFFERENT THINGS...
... I KNOW'D I WANTED OUT O' THAT HOUSE AND I WOULDA GONE TOO...
...'CEPT FOR CRAWFORD.
HE WAS A SWEET CHILD. HE SURE DESERVE BETTER'N HER FOR A MOMMA
I STAY'D LONG AS I COULD. WEREN'T SO BAD AT FIRST. SHE WAS ALWAYS IN EUROPE, LEAVIN' THE LITTLE ONE WITH ME.
BUT THEN THE MONEY WAS A -RUNNIN' OUT AND SHE COME HOME. AND I WAS LET GO...
...GOD FORGIVE ME FOR LEAVIN' THAT LITTLE BOY IN THAT HOUSE LIKE THAT.
YEARS LATUH, 'COURSE, WHEN SHE WERE SICK AND HAD THEM STROKES-- HE WERE A MAN...
...COULDN'T DO NOTHIN' TO HIM THEN.
GOD FORGIVE ME FOR SAYING IT WAS A HAPPY DAY WHEN HER HEART GIVE OUT ON HER.
DO YOU KNOW ANYTHING ELSE ABOUT BETHANY THAT MIGHT HELP US?
BECAUSE I THINK SHE IS BACK AND SHE IS TRYING TO HURT PEOPLE...
...IF ONLY WE KNEW WHY...

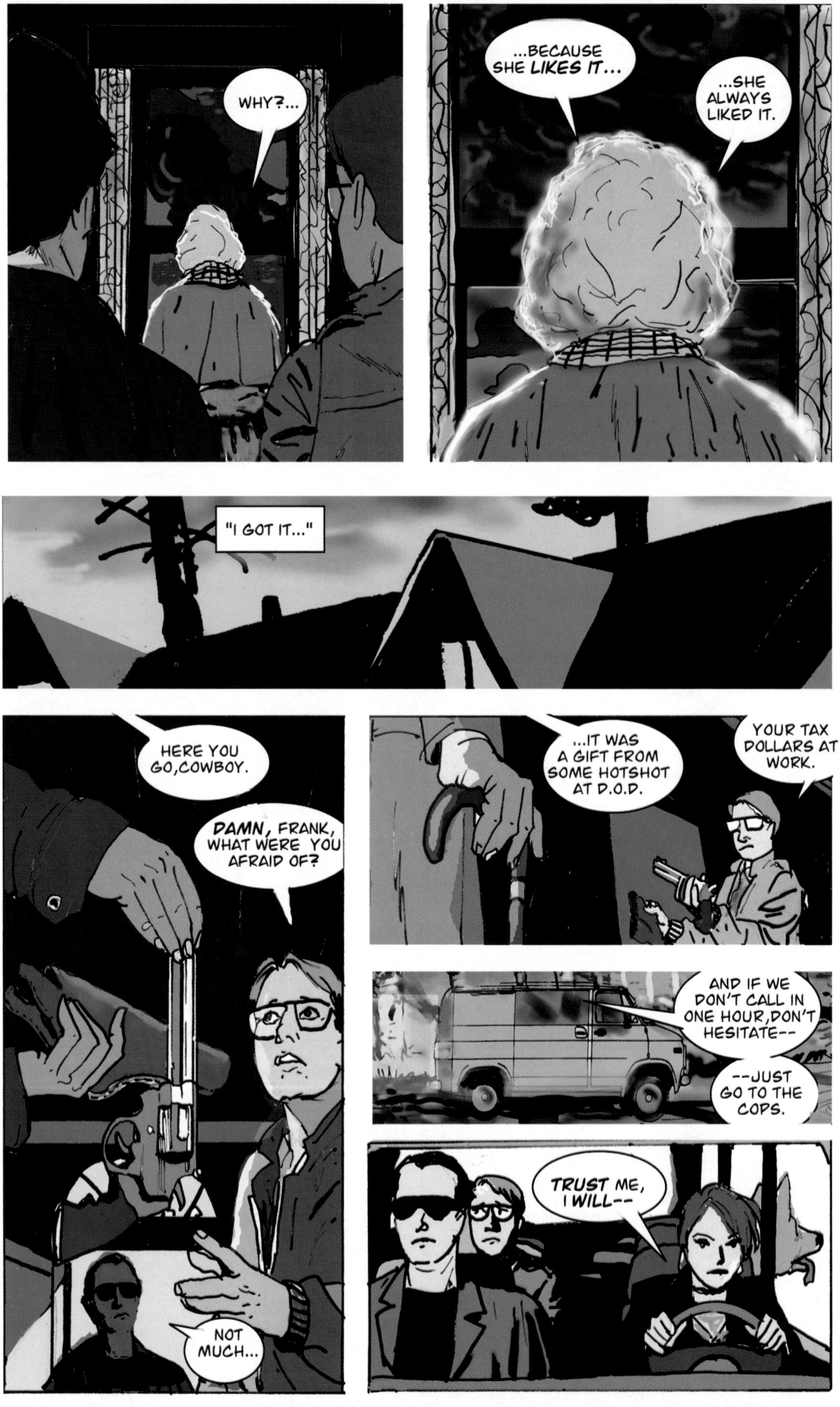
WHY?...
...BECAUSE SHE LIKES IT...
...SHE ALWAYS LIKED IT.
"I GOT IT..."
HERE YOU GO,COWBOY.
DAMN, FRANK, WHAT WERE YOU AFRAID OF?
NOT MUCH...
...IT WAS A GIFT FROM SOME HOTSHOT AT D.O.D.
YOUR TAX DOLLARS AT WORK.
AND IF WE DON'T CALL IN ONE HOUR,DON'T HESITATE--
--JUST GO TO THE COPS.
TRUST ME, I WILL--

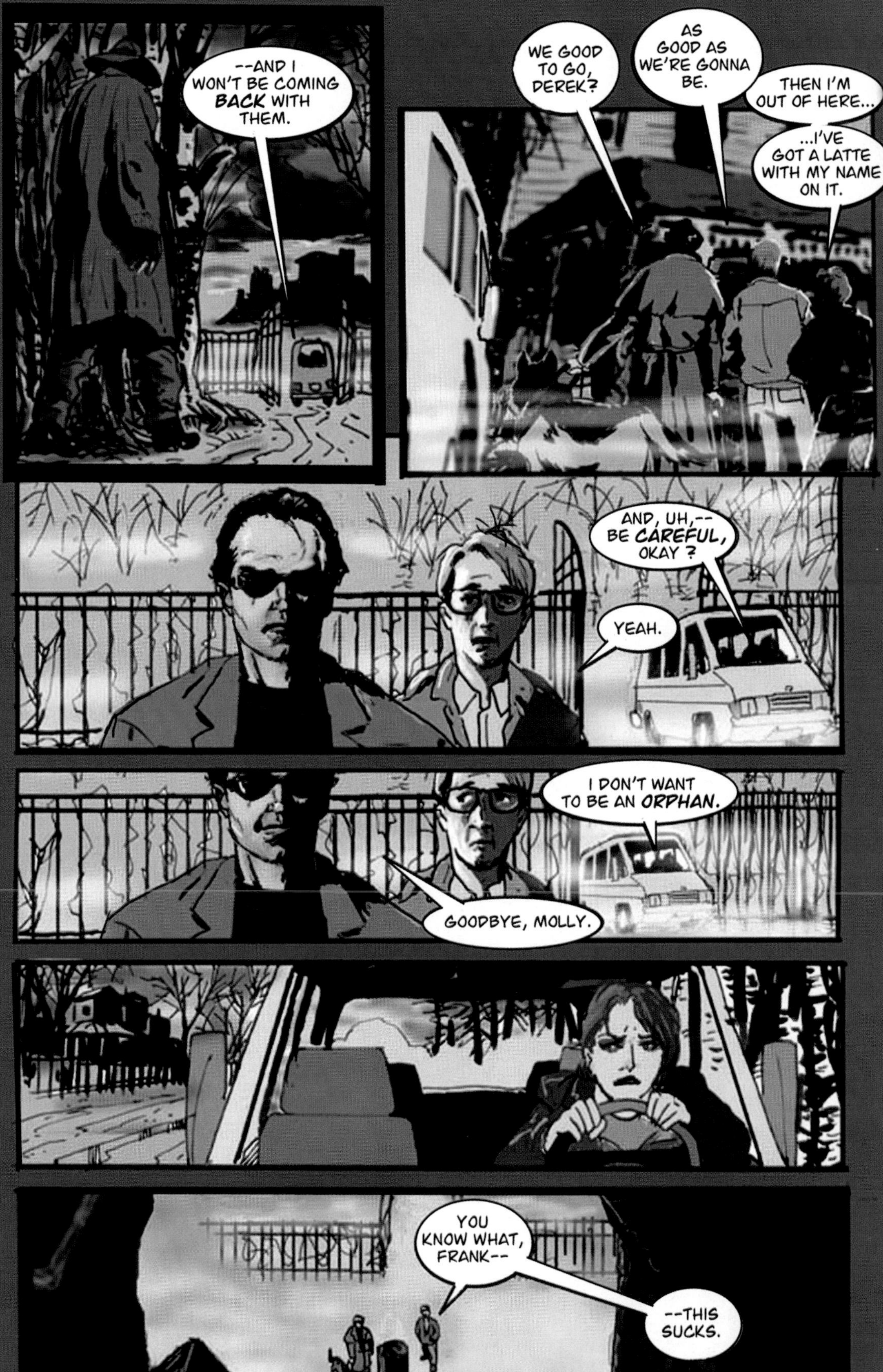
--AND I WON'T BE COMING BACK WITH THEM.
WE GOOD TO GO, DEREK?
AS GOOD AS WE'RE GONNA BE.
THEN I'M OUT OF HERE...
...I'VE GOT A LATTE WITH MY NAME ON IT.
AND, UH,-- BE CAREFUL, OKAY ?
YEAH.
I DON'T WANT TO BE AN ORPHAN.
GOODBYE, MOLLY.
YOU KNOW WHAT, FRANK--
--THIS SUCKS.

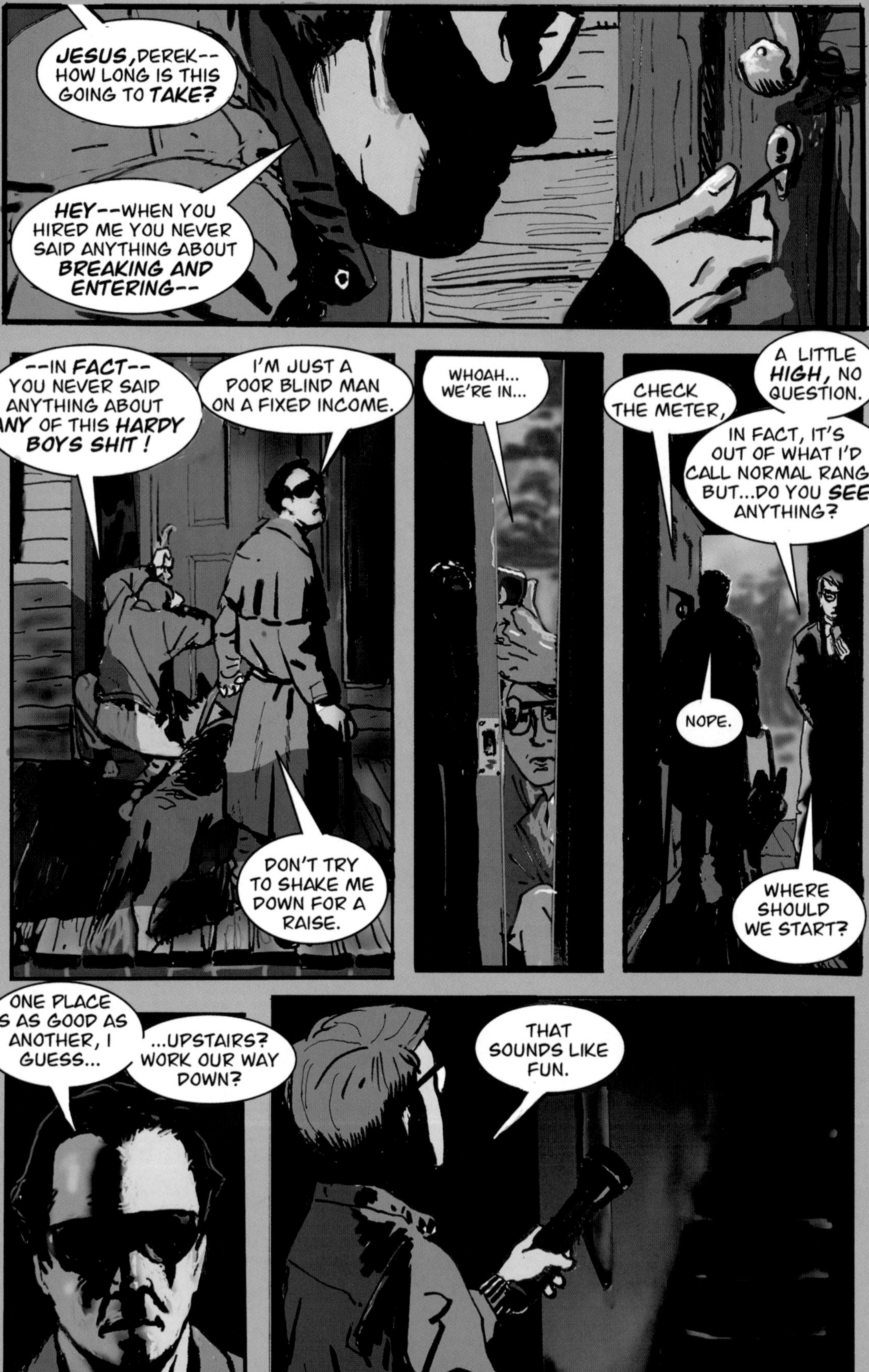
JESUS, DEREK-- HOW LONG IS THIS GOING TO TAKE?
HEY--WHEN YOU HIRED ME YOU NEVER SAID ANYTHING ABOUT BREAKING AND ENTERING--
--IN FACT-- YOU NEVER SAID ANYTHING ABOUT ANY OF THIS HARDY BOYS SHIT!
I'M JUST A POOR BLIND MAN ON A FIXED INCOME.
DON'T TRY TO SHAKE ME DOWN FOR A RAISE.
WHOAH... WE'RE IN...
CHECK THE METER,
A LITTLE HIGH, NO QUESTION.
IN FACT, IT'S OUT OF WHAT I'D CALL NORMAL RANGE. BUT...DO YOU SEE ANYTHING?
NOPE.
WHERE SHOULD WE START?
ONE PLACE IS AS GOOD AS ANOTHER, I GUESS...
...UPSTAIRS? WORK OUR WAY DOWN?
THAT SOUNDS LIKE FUN.

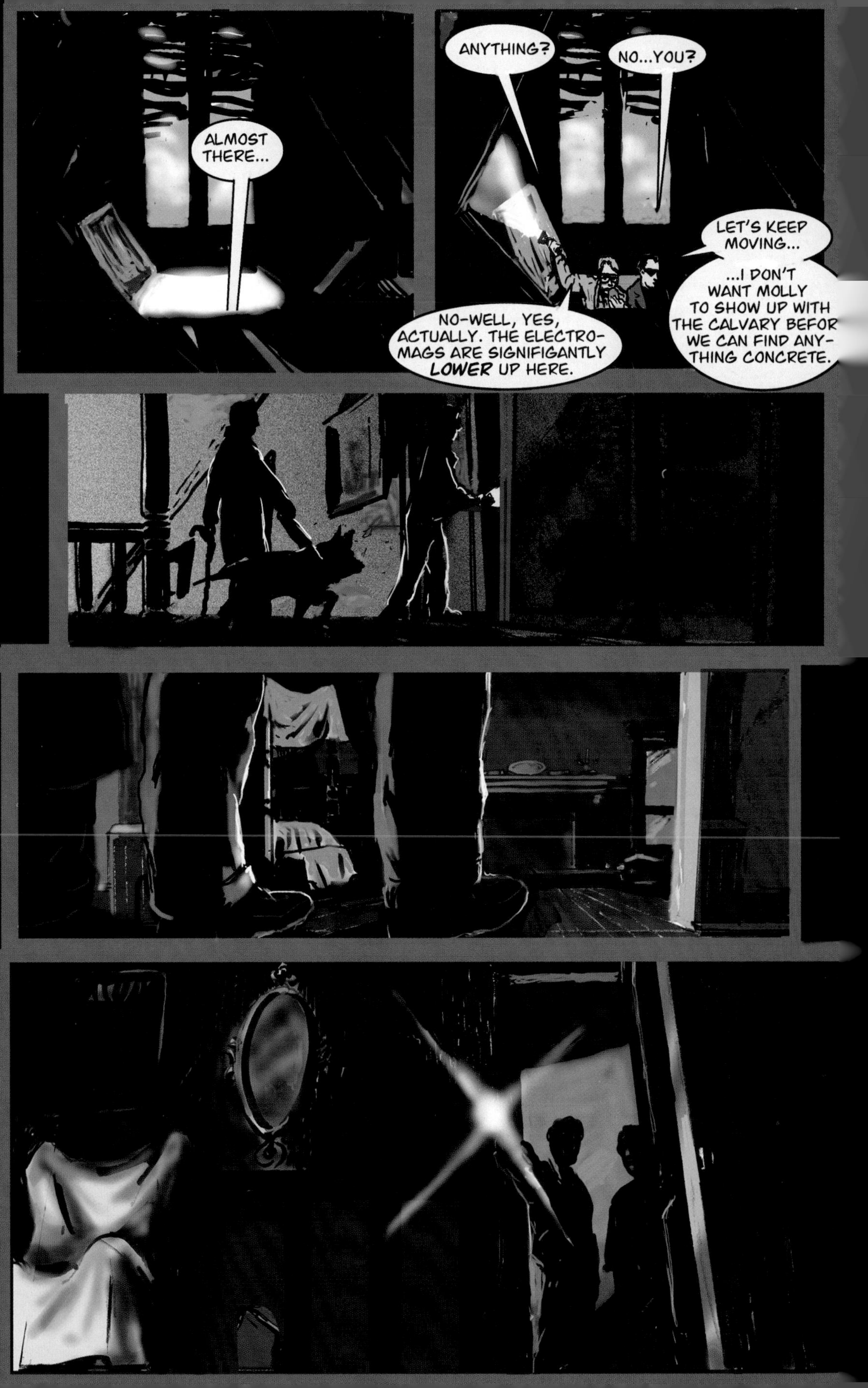
ALMOST THERE...
ANYTHING?
NO...YOU?
NO-WELL, YES, ACTUALLY. THE ELECTRO-MAGS ARE SIGNIFIGANTLY LOWER UP HERE.
LET'S KEEP MOVING...
...I DON'T WANT MOLLY TO SHOW UP WITH THE CALVARY BEFOR WE CAN FIND ANY-THING CONCRETE.

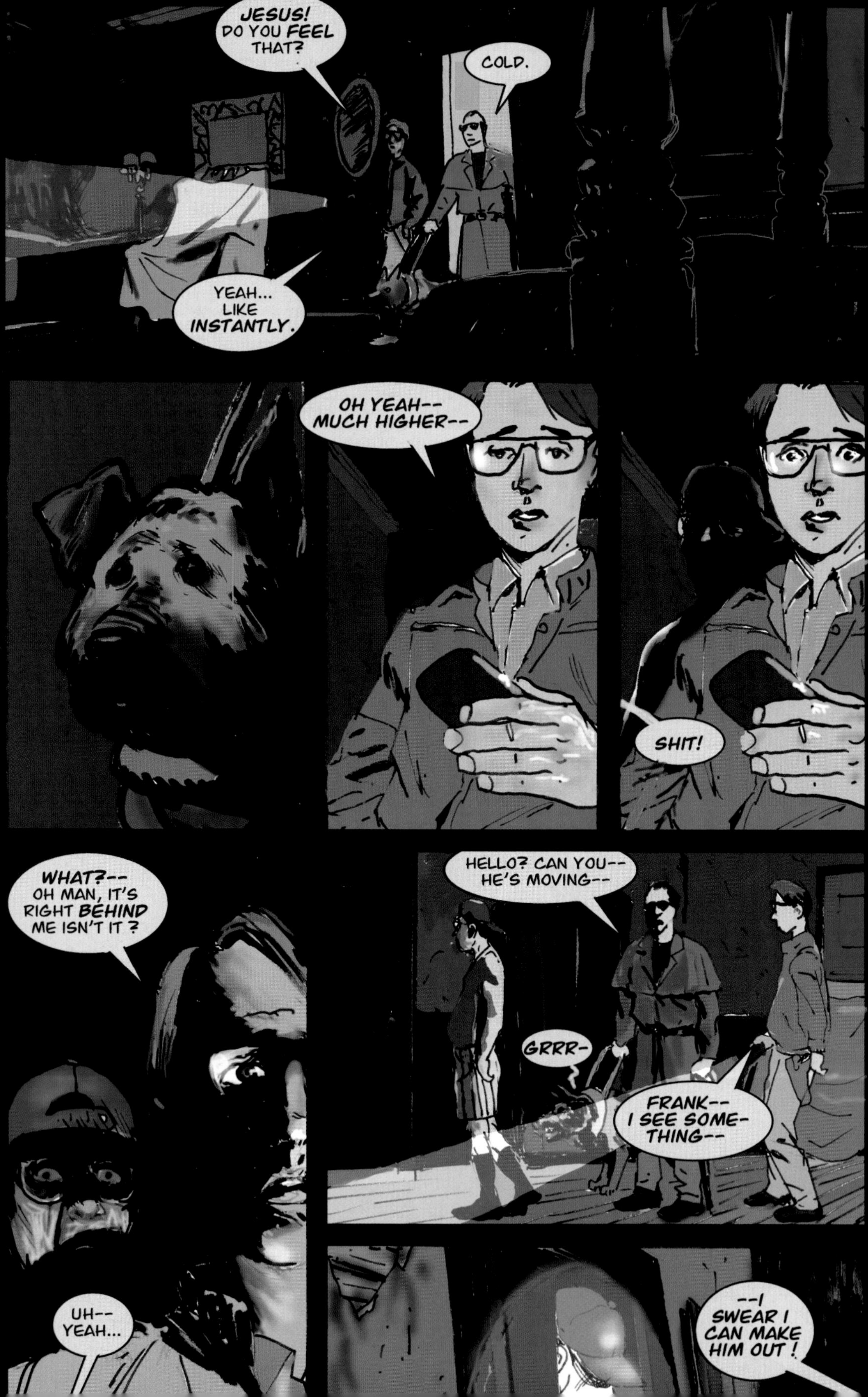
JESUS! DO YOU FEEL THAT?
COLD.
YEAH... LIKE INSTANTLY.
OH YEAH-- MUCH HIGHER--
SHIT!
WHAT?-- OH MAN, IT'S RIGHT BEHIND ME ISN'T IT ?
UH-- YEAH...
HELLO? CAN YOU-- HE'S MOVING--
GRRR-
FRANK-- I SEE SOME-THING--
--I SWEAR I CAN MAKE HIM OUT !

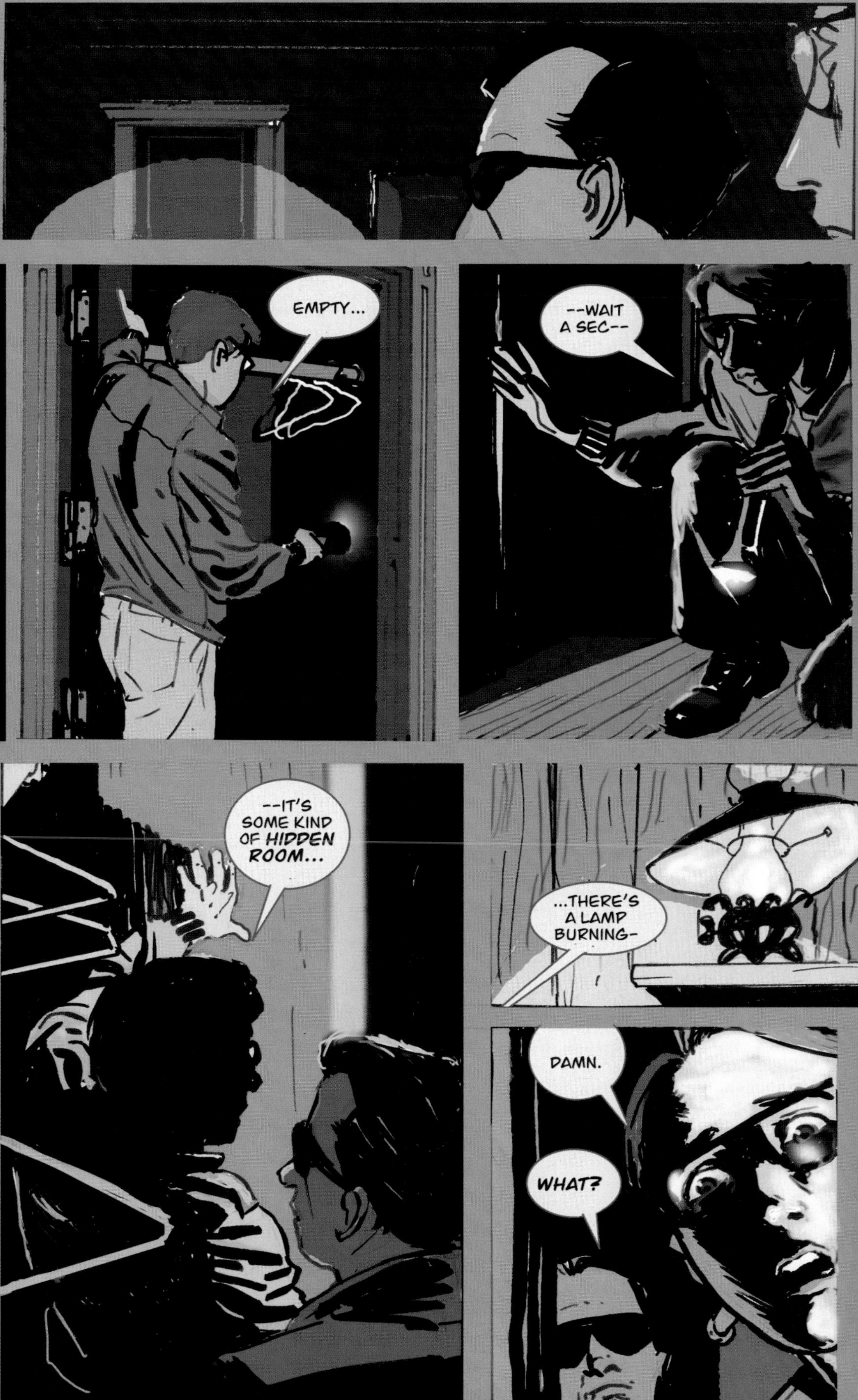
EMPTY...
--WAIT A SEC--
--IT'S SOME KIND OF *HIDDEN ROOM...*
...THERE'S A LAMP BURNING-
DAMN.
WHAT?

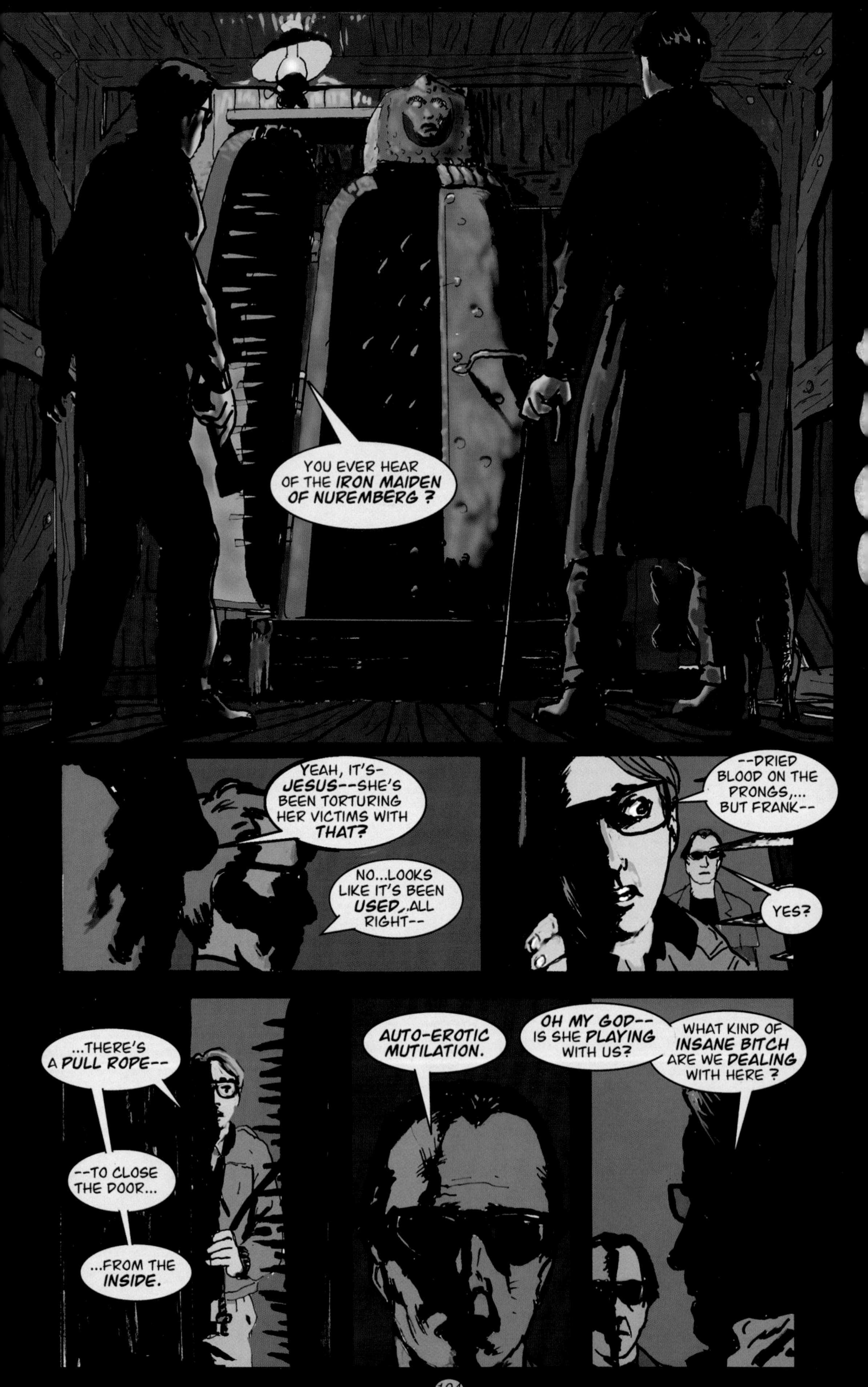
YOU EVER HEAR OF THE IRON MAIDEN OF NUREMBERG ?
YEAH, IT'S- JESUS--SHE'S BEEN TORTURING HER VICTIMS WITH THAT?
NO...LOOKS LIKE IT'S BEEN USED, ALL RIGHT--
--DRIED BLOOD ON THE PRONGS,... BUT FRANK--
YES?
...THERE'S A PULL ROPE--
--TO CLOSE THE DOOR...
...FROM THE INSIDE.
AUTO-EROTIC MUTILATION.
OH MY GOD-- IS SHE PLAYING WITH US?
WHAT KIND OF INSANE BITCH ARE WE DEALING WITH HERE ?

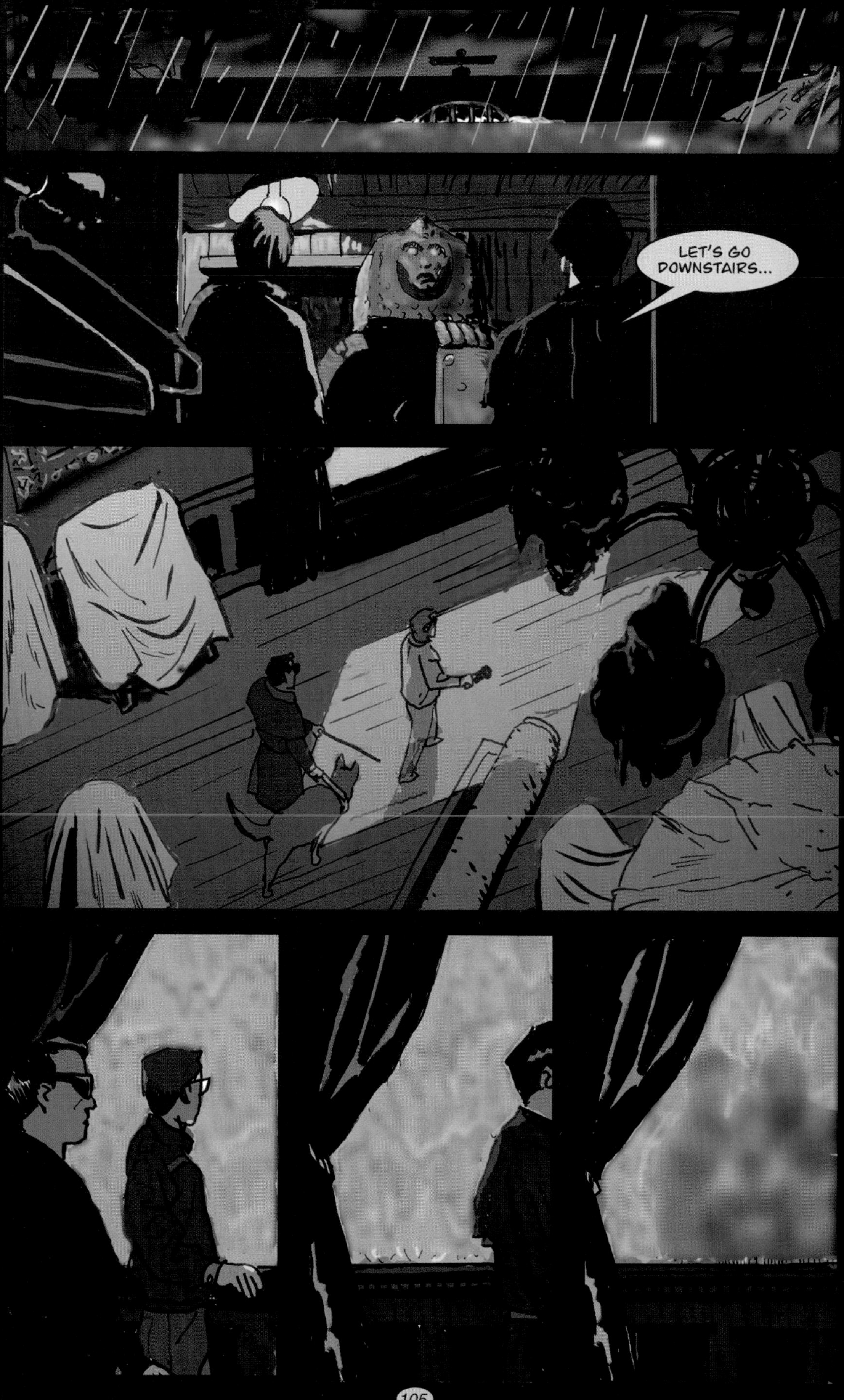
LET'S GO DOWNSTAIRS...

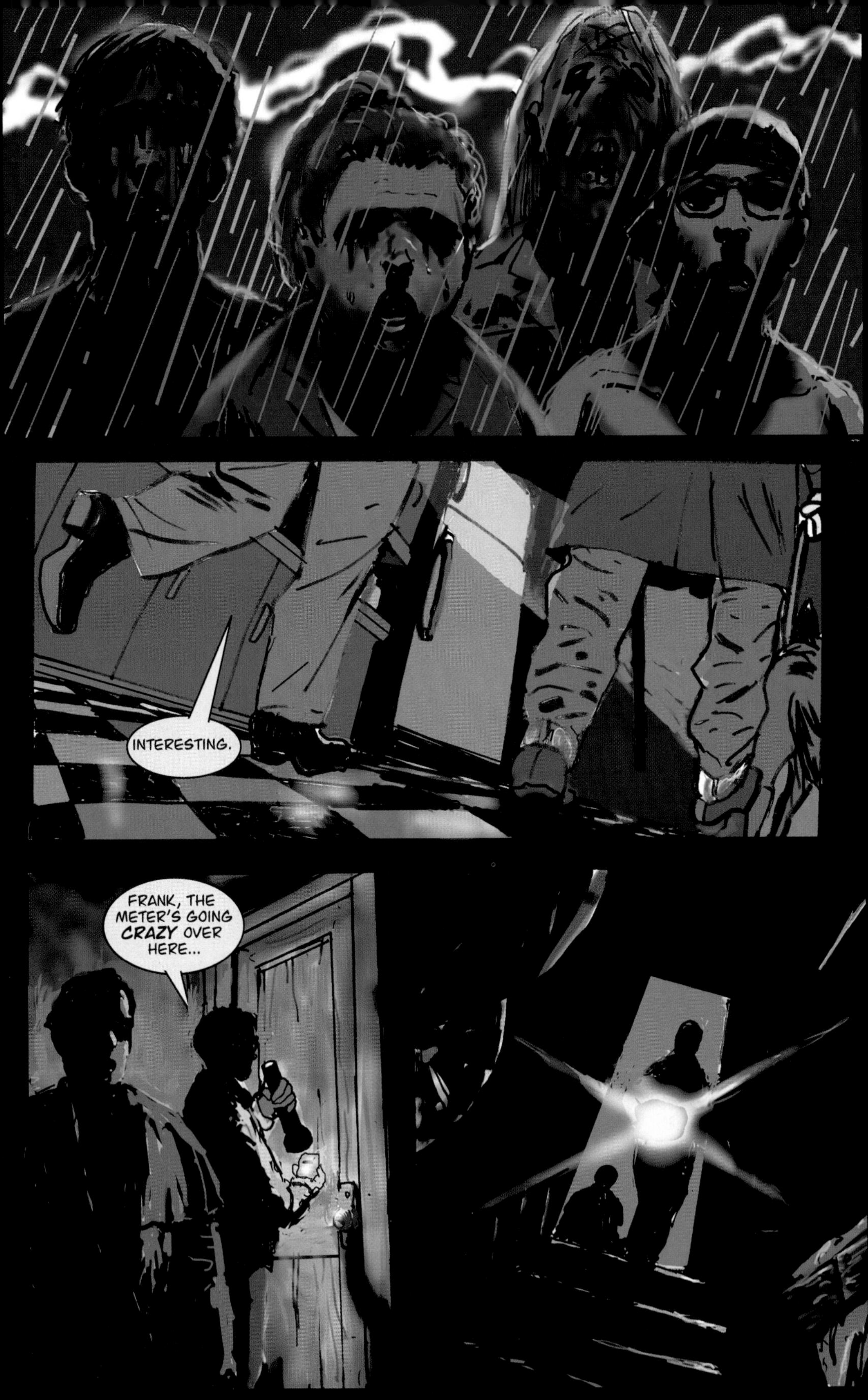
INTERESTING.
FRANK, THE METER'S GOING CRAZY OVER HERE...

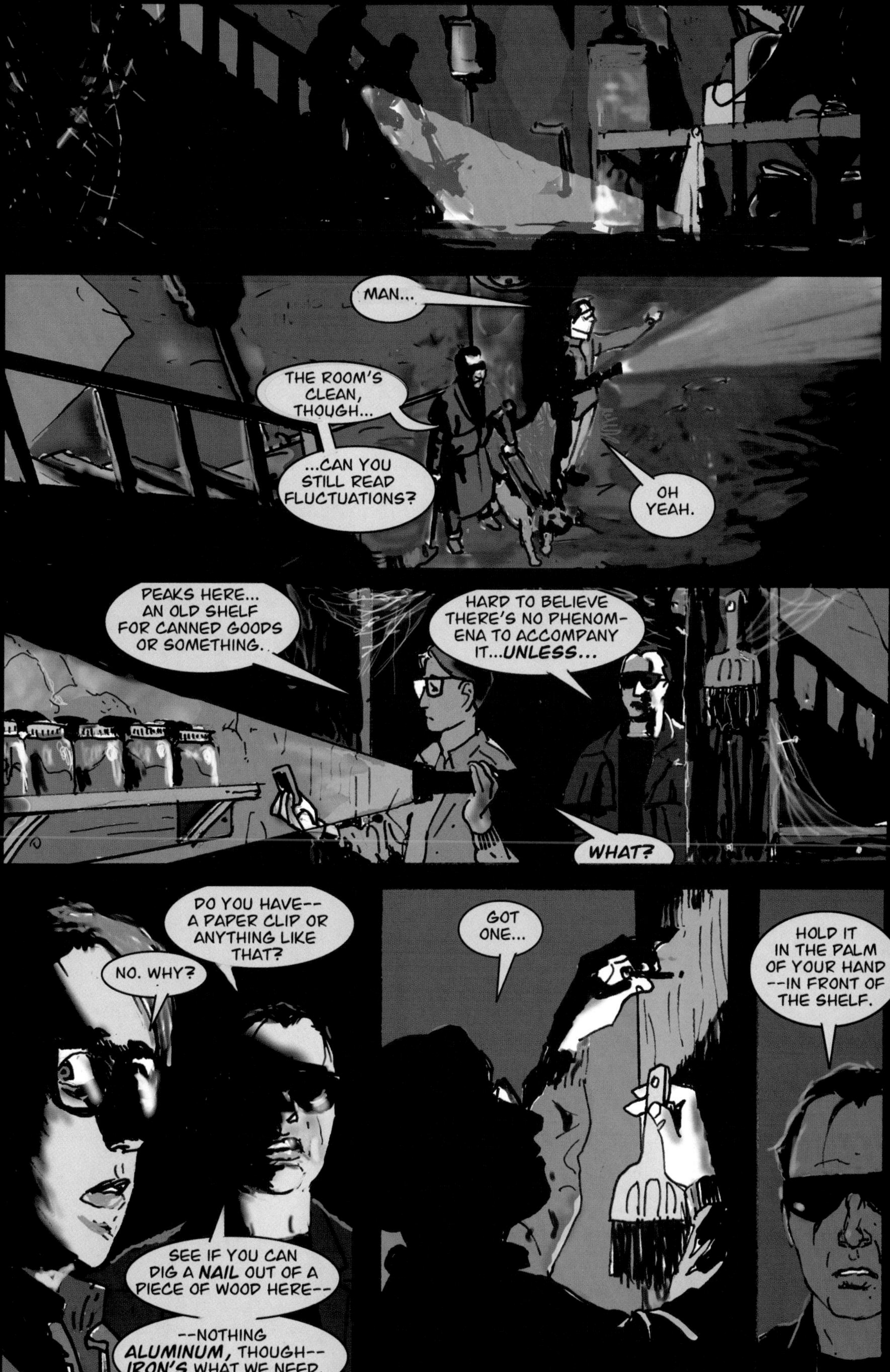
MAN...
THE ROOM'S CLEAN, THOUGH...
...CAN YOU STILL READ FLUCTUATIONS?
OH YEAH.
PEAKS HERE... AN OLD SHELF FOR CANNED GOODS OR SOMETHING.
HARD TO BELIEVE THERE'S NO PHENOMENA TO ACCOMPANY IT...UNLESS...
WHAT?
DO YOU HAVE-- A PAPER CLIP OR ANYTHING LIKE THAT?
NO. WHY?
SEE IF YOU CAN DIG A NAIL OUT OF A PIECE OF WOOD HERE--
--NOTHING ALUMINUM, THOUGH-- IRON'S WHAT WE NEED.
GOT ONE...
HOLD IT IN THE PALM OF YOUR HAND --IN FRONT OF THE SHELF.

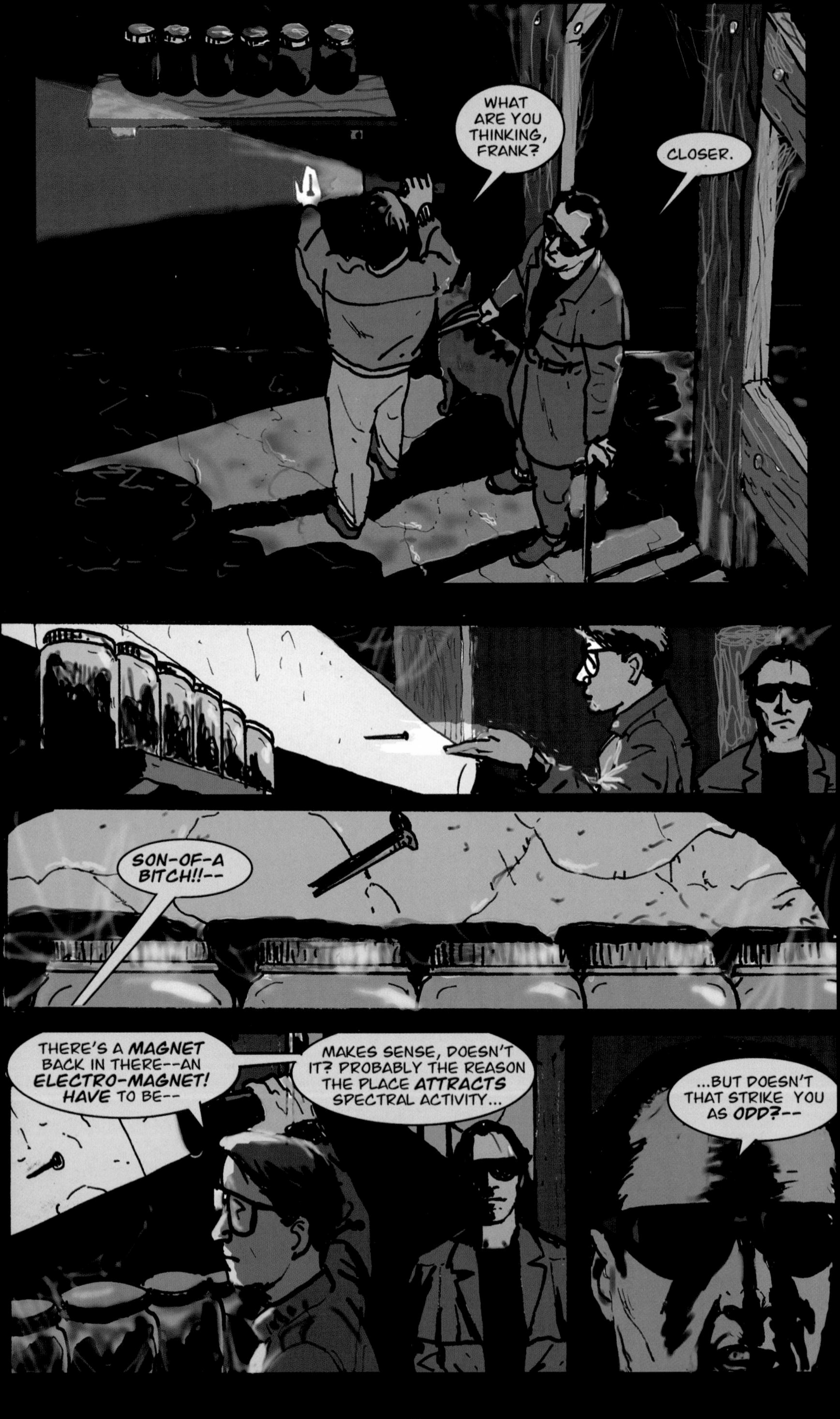

WHAT ARE YOU THINKING, FRANK?
CLOSER.
SON-OF-A BITCH!!--
THERE'S A MAGNET BACK IN THERE--AN ELECTRO-MAGNET! HAVE TO BE--
MAKES SENSE, DOESN'T IT? PROBABLY THE REASON THE PLACE ATTRACTS SPECTRAL ACTIVITY...
...BUT DOESN'T THAT STRIKE YOU AS ODD?--

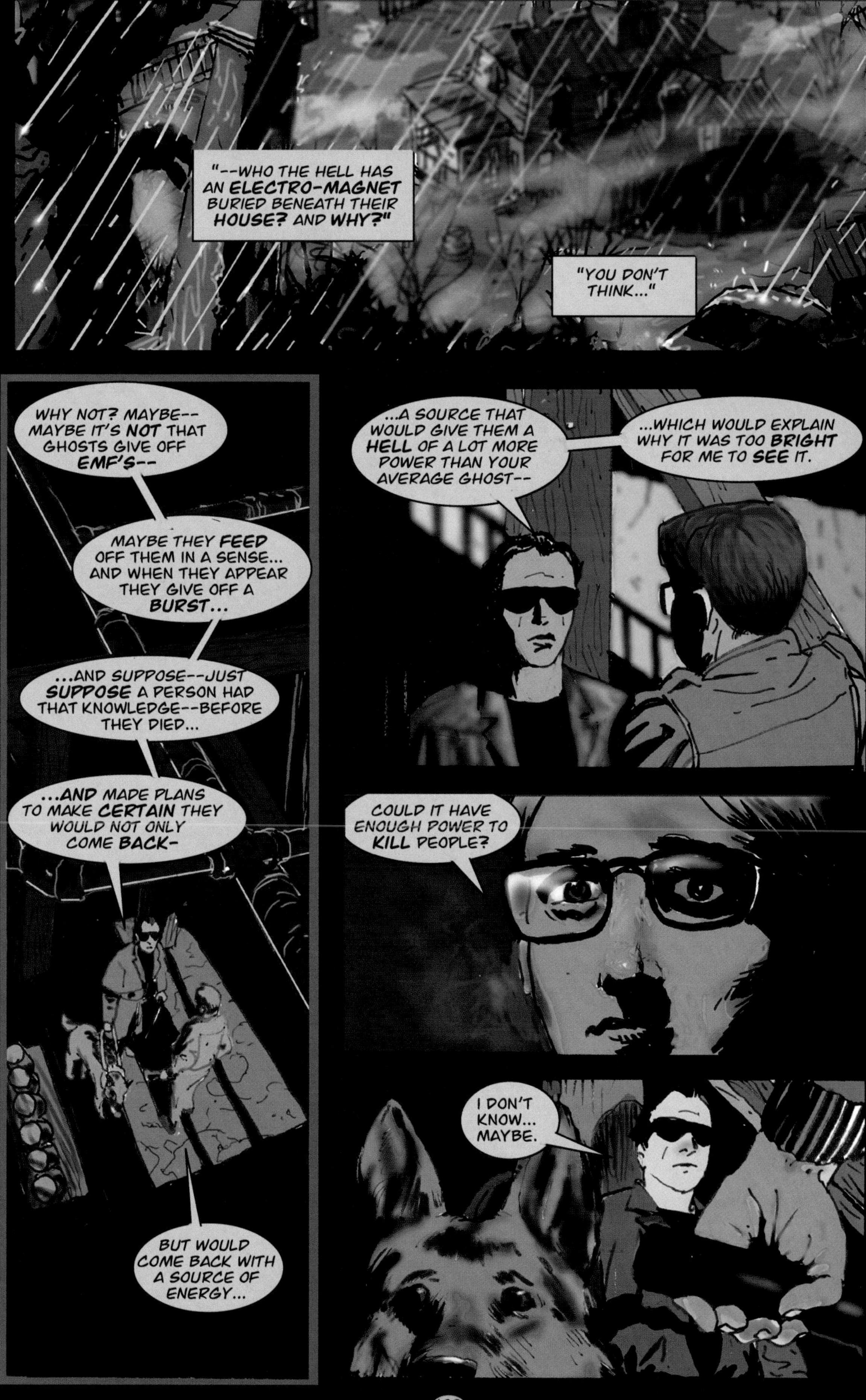
"--WHO THE HELL HAS AN ELECTRO-MAGNET BURIED BENEATH THEIR HOUSE? AND WHY?"
"YOU DON'T THINK..."
WHY NOT? MAYBE--MAYBE IT'S NOT THAT GHOSTS GIVE OFF EMF'S--
MAYBE THEY FEED OFF THEM IN A SENSE... AND WHEN THEY APPEAR THEY GIVE OFF A BURST...
...AND SUPPOSE--JUST SUPPOSE A PERSON HAD THAT KNOWLEDGE--BEFORE THEY DIED...
...AND MADE PLANS TO MAKE CERTAIN THEY WOULD NOT ONLY COME BACK-
BUT WOULD COME BACK WITH A SOURCE OF ENERGY...
...A SOURCE THAT WOULD GIVE THEM A HELL OF A LOT MORE POWER THAN YOUR AVERAGE GHOST--
...WHICH WOULD EXPLAIN WHY IT WAS TOO BRIGHT FOR ME TO SEE IT.
COULD IT HAVE ENOUGH POWER TO KILL PEOPLE?
I DON'T KNOW... MAYBE.

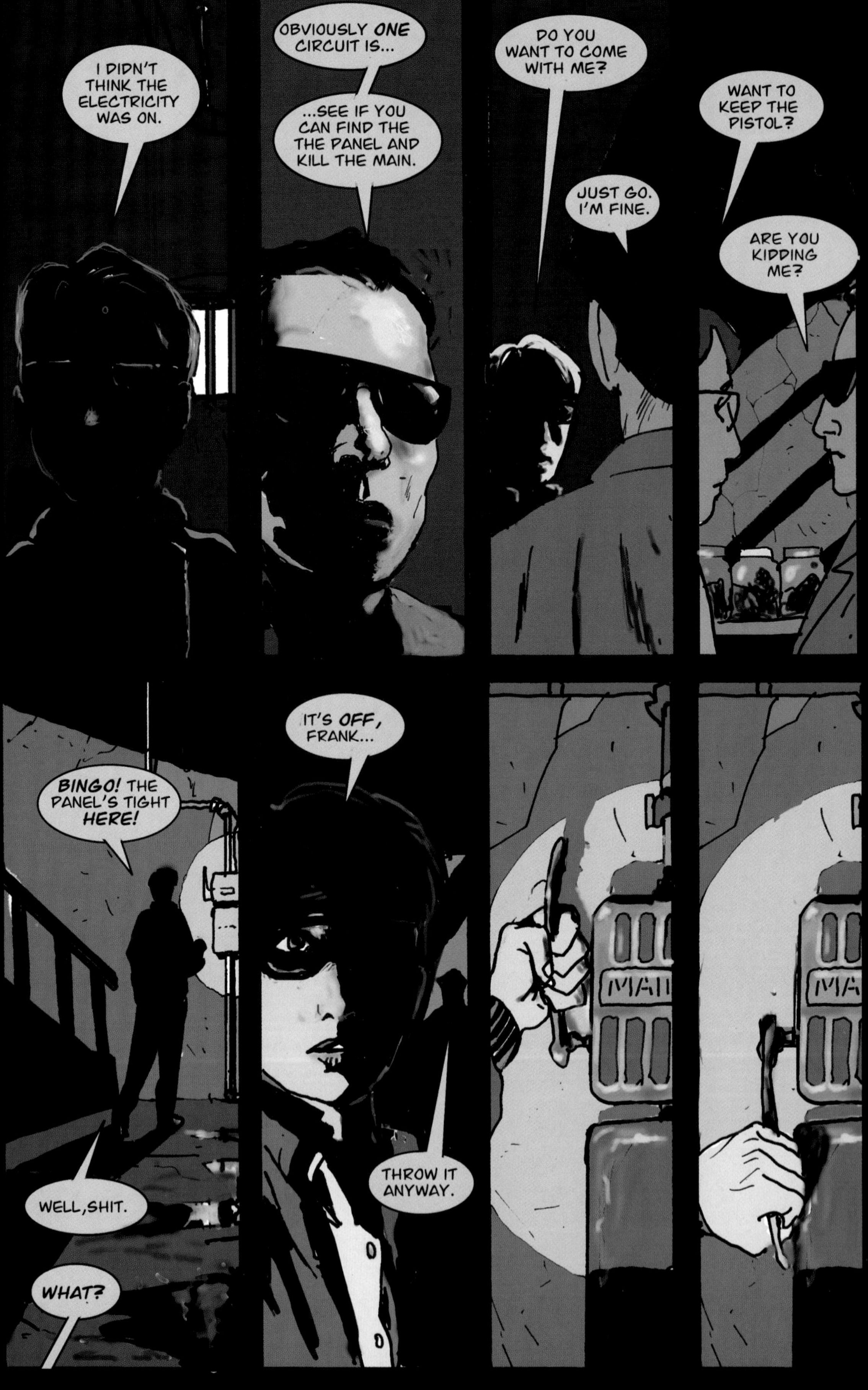
I DIDN'T THINK THE ELECTRICITY WAS ON.
OBVIOUSLY ONE CIRCUIT IS...
...SEE IF YOU CAN FIND THE THE PANEL AND KILL THE MAIN.
DO YOU WANT TO COME WITH ME?
JUST GO. I'M FINE.
WANT TO KEEP THE PISTOL?
ARE YOU KIDDING ME?
BINGO! THE PANEL'S TIGHT HERE!
WELL, SHIT.
WHAT?
IT'S OFF, FRANK...
THROW IT ANYWAY.

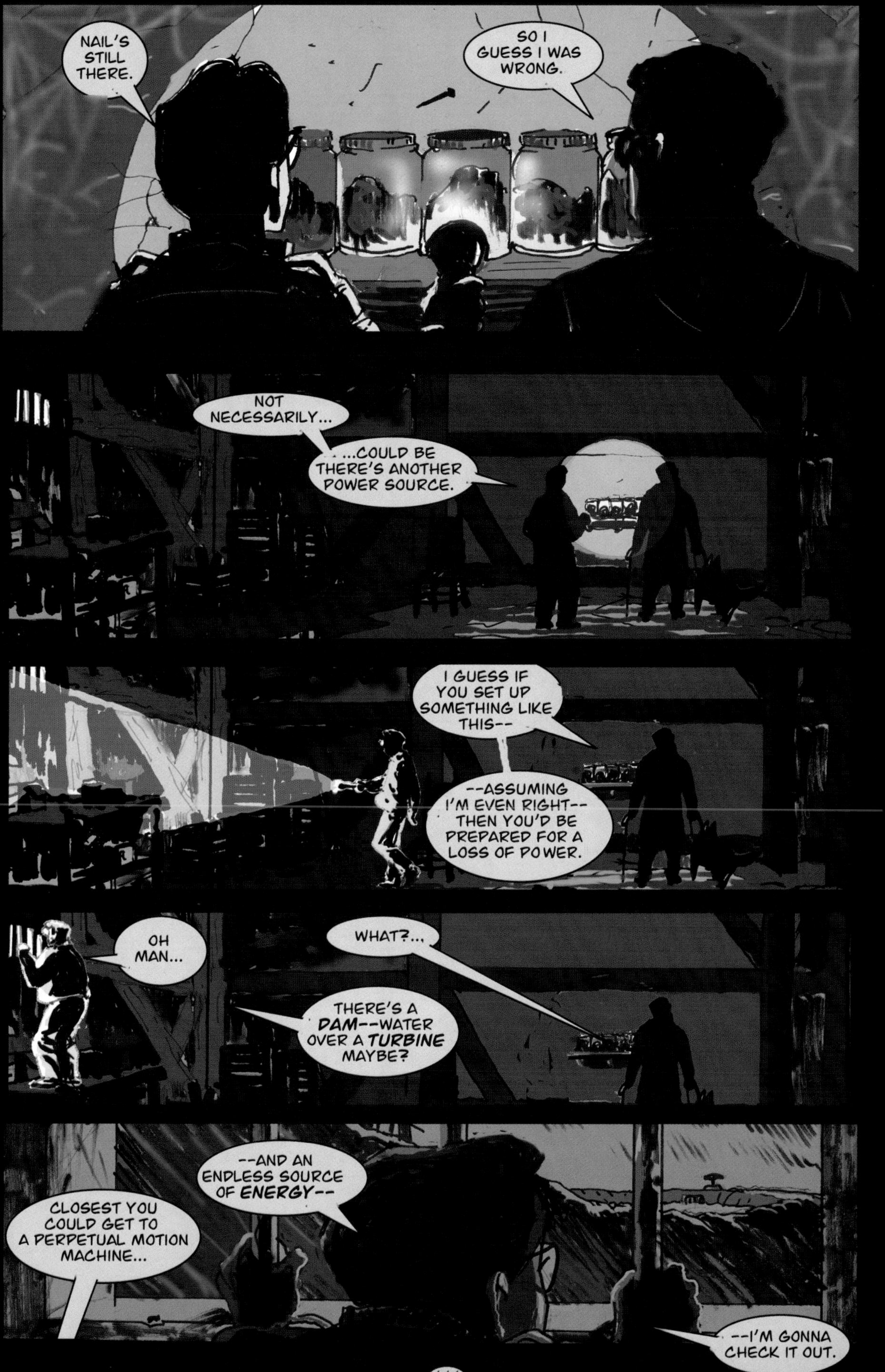
NAIL'S STILL THERE.
SO I GUESS I WAS WRONG.
NOT NECESSARILY...
...COULD BE THERE'S ANOTHER POWER SOURCE.
I GUESS IF YOU SET UP SOMETHING LIKE THIS--
--ASSUMING I'M EVEN RIGHT-- THEN YOU'D BE PREPARED FOR A LOSS OF POWER.
OH MAN...
WHAT?...
THERE'S A DAM--WATER OVER A TURBINE MAYBE?
--AND AN ENDLESS SOURCE OF ENERGY--
CLOSEST YOU COULD GET TO A PERPETUAL MOTION MACHINE...
--I'M GONNA CHECK IT OUT.

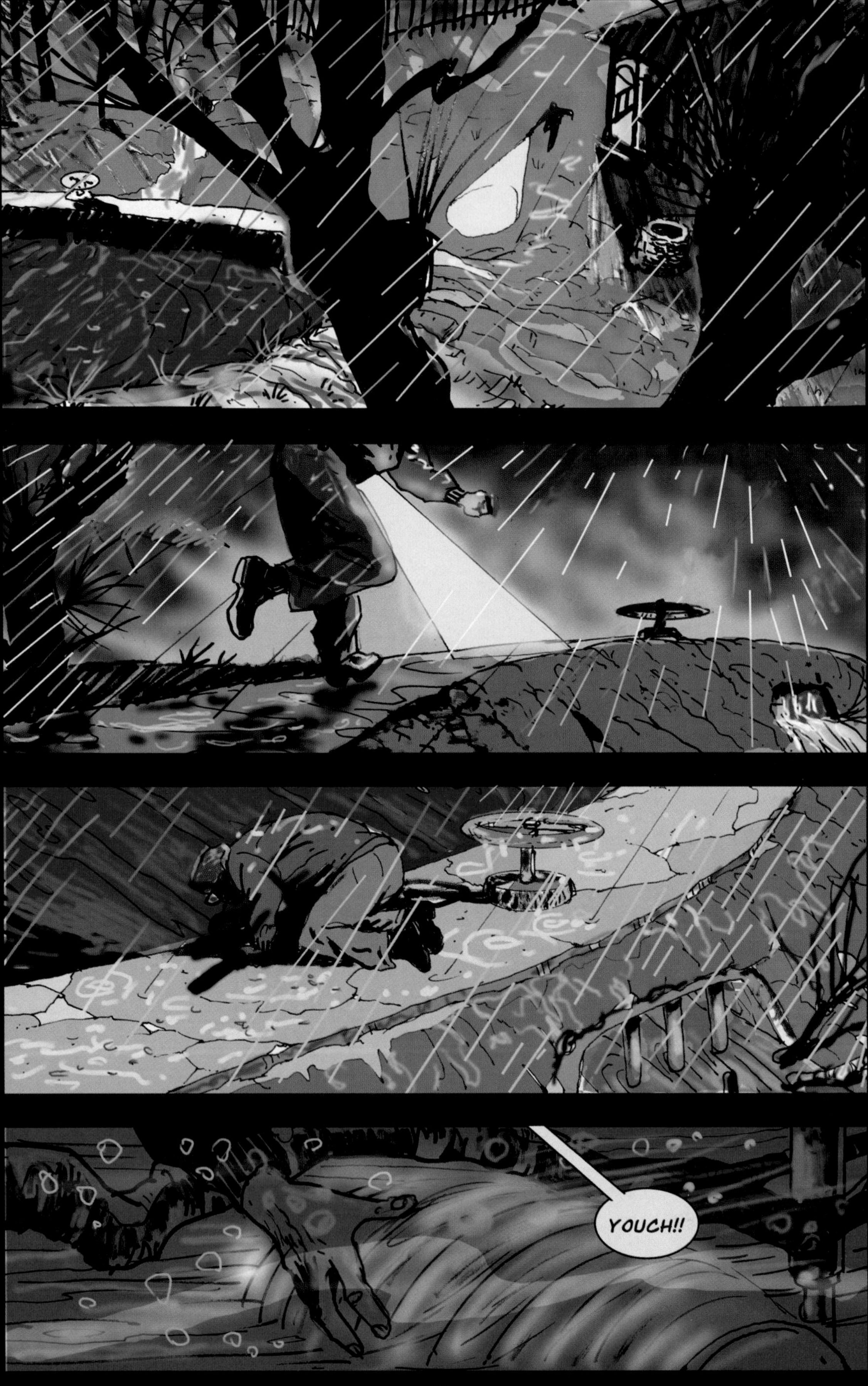
YOUCH!!

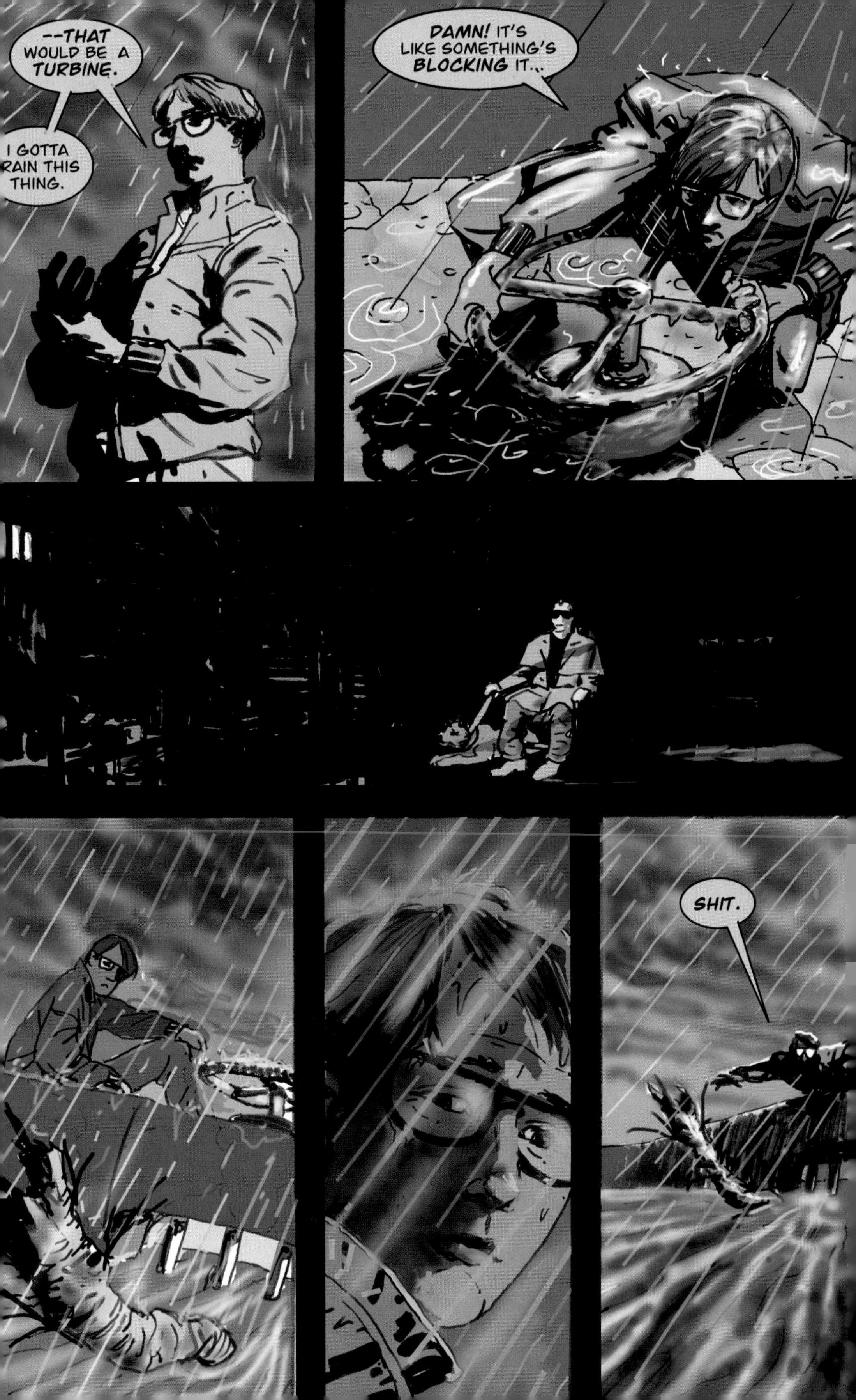
--THAT WOULD BE A TURBINE.
I GOTTA RAIN THIS THING.
DAMN! IT'S LIKE SOMETHING'S BLOCKING IT...
SHIT.

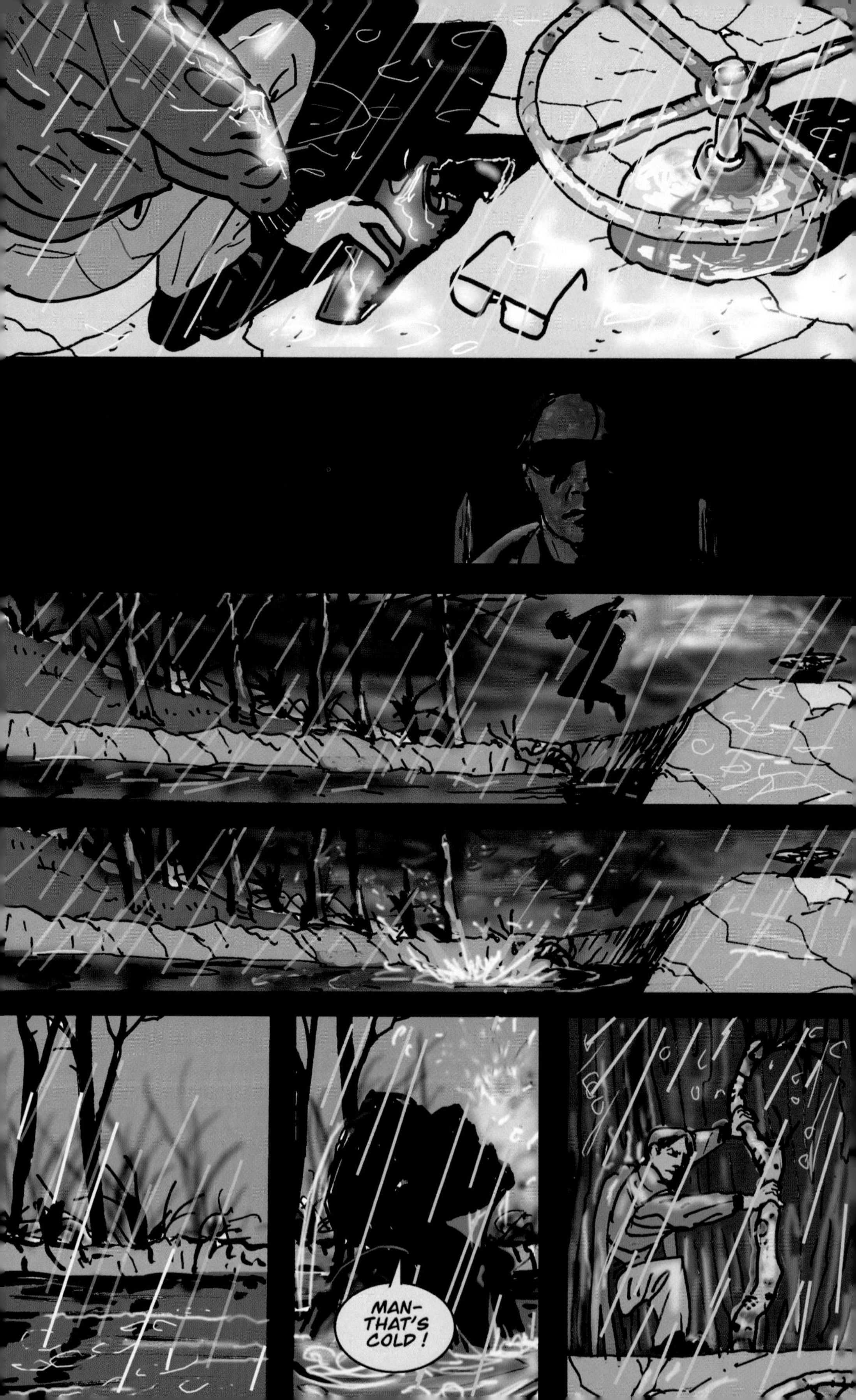
MAN-
THAT'S
COLD!

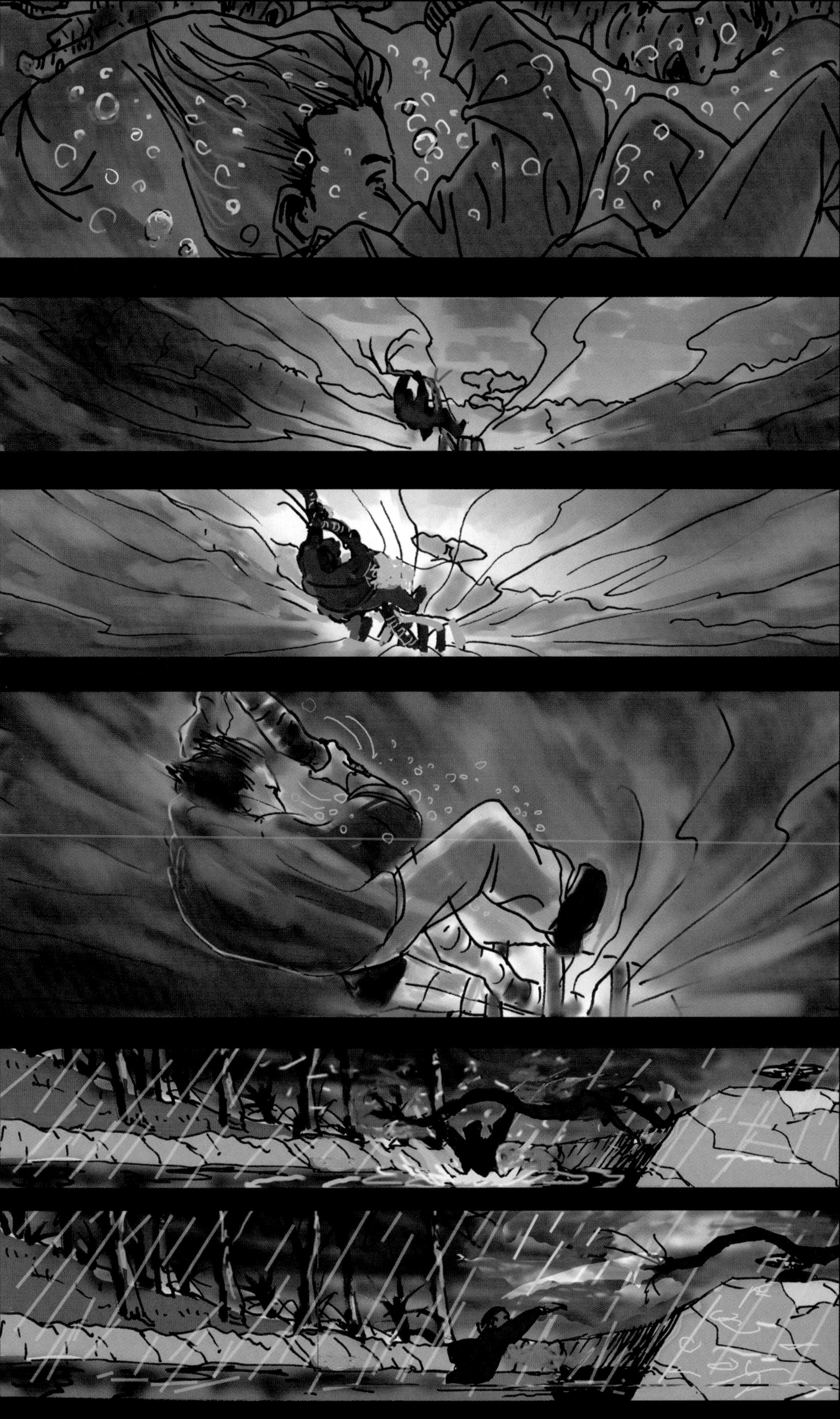

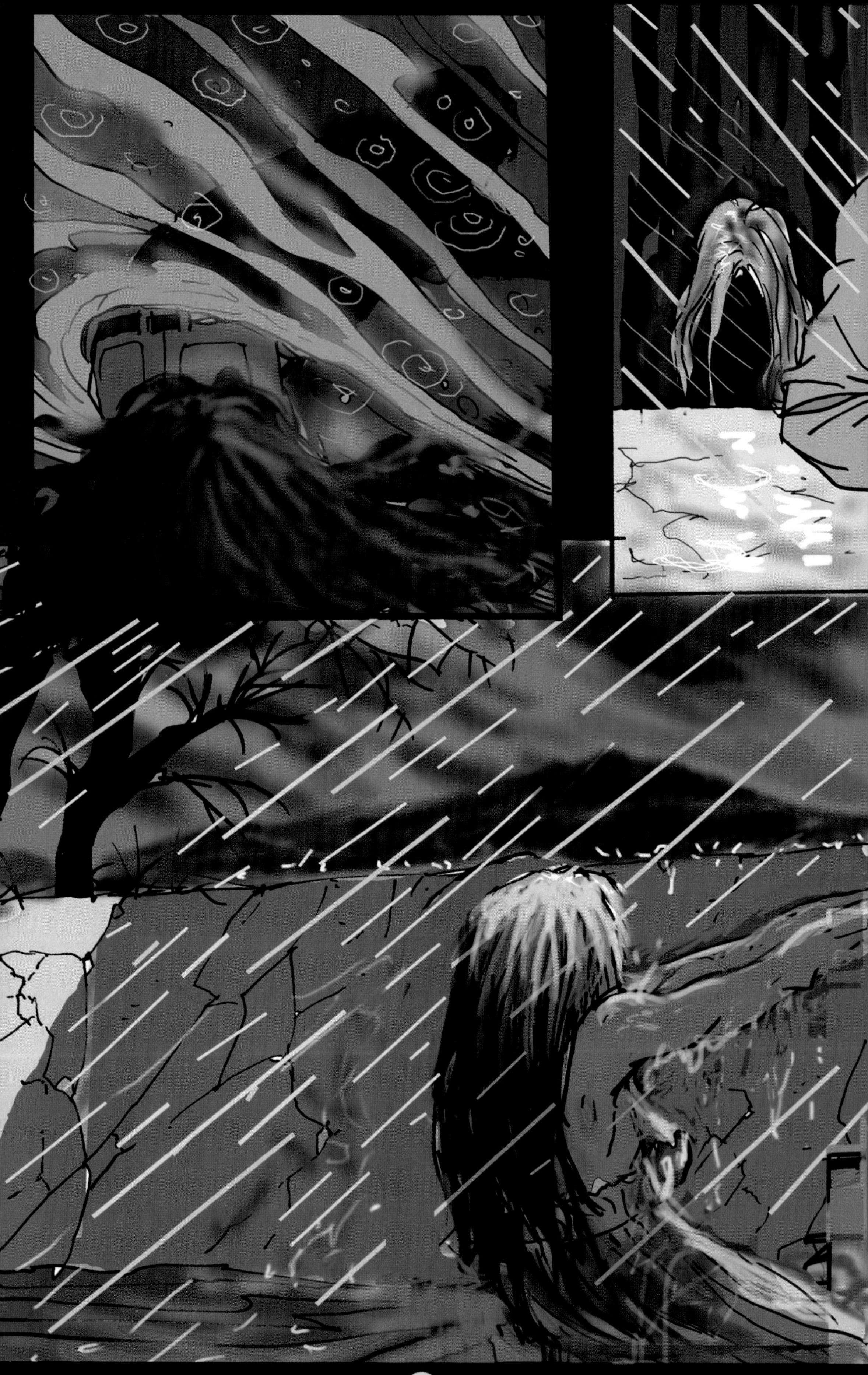

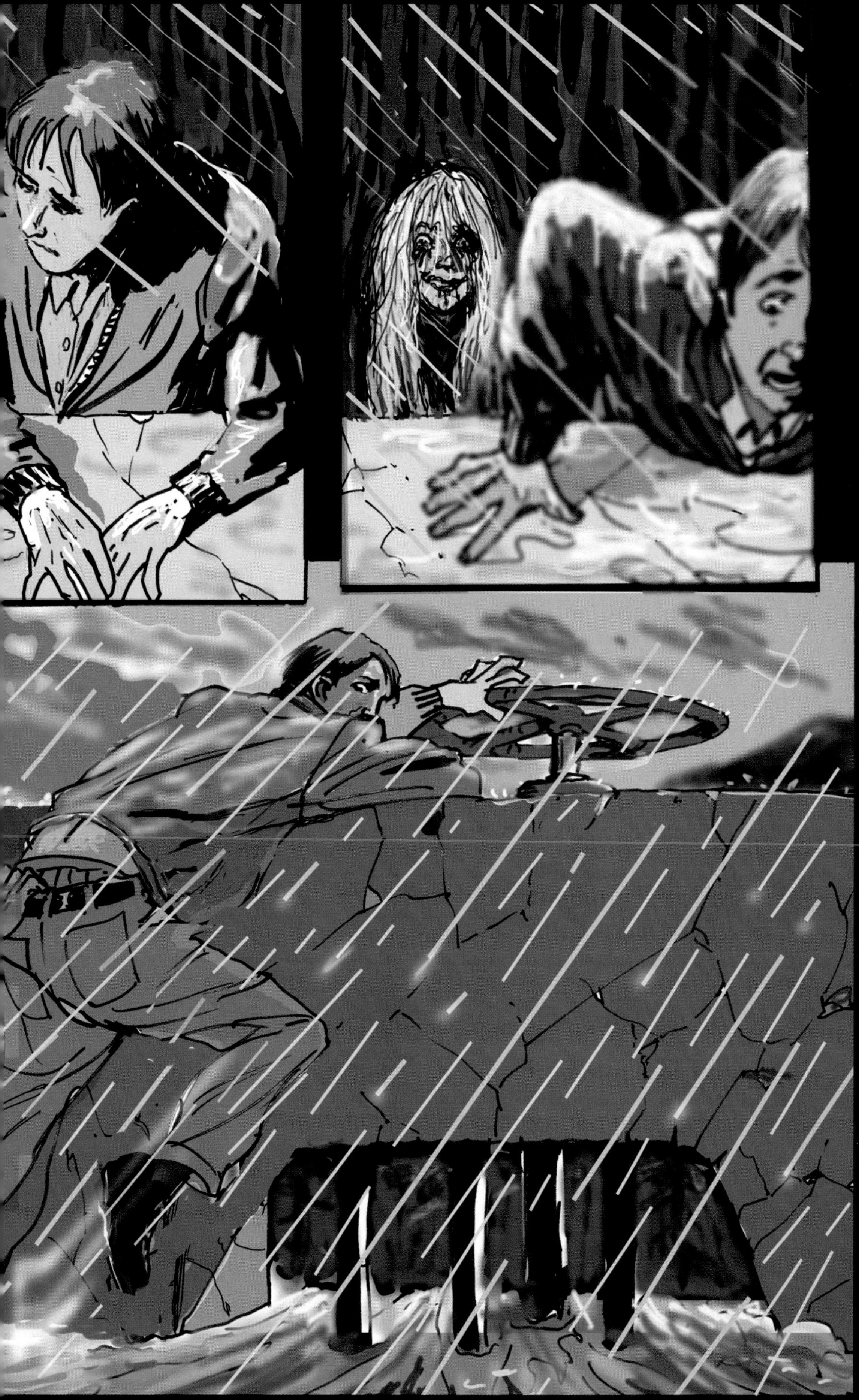

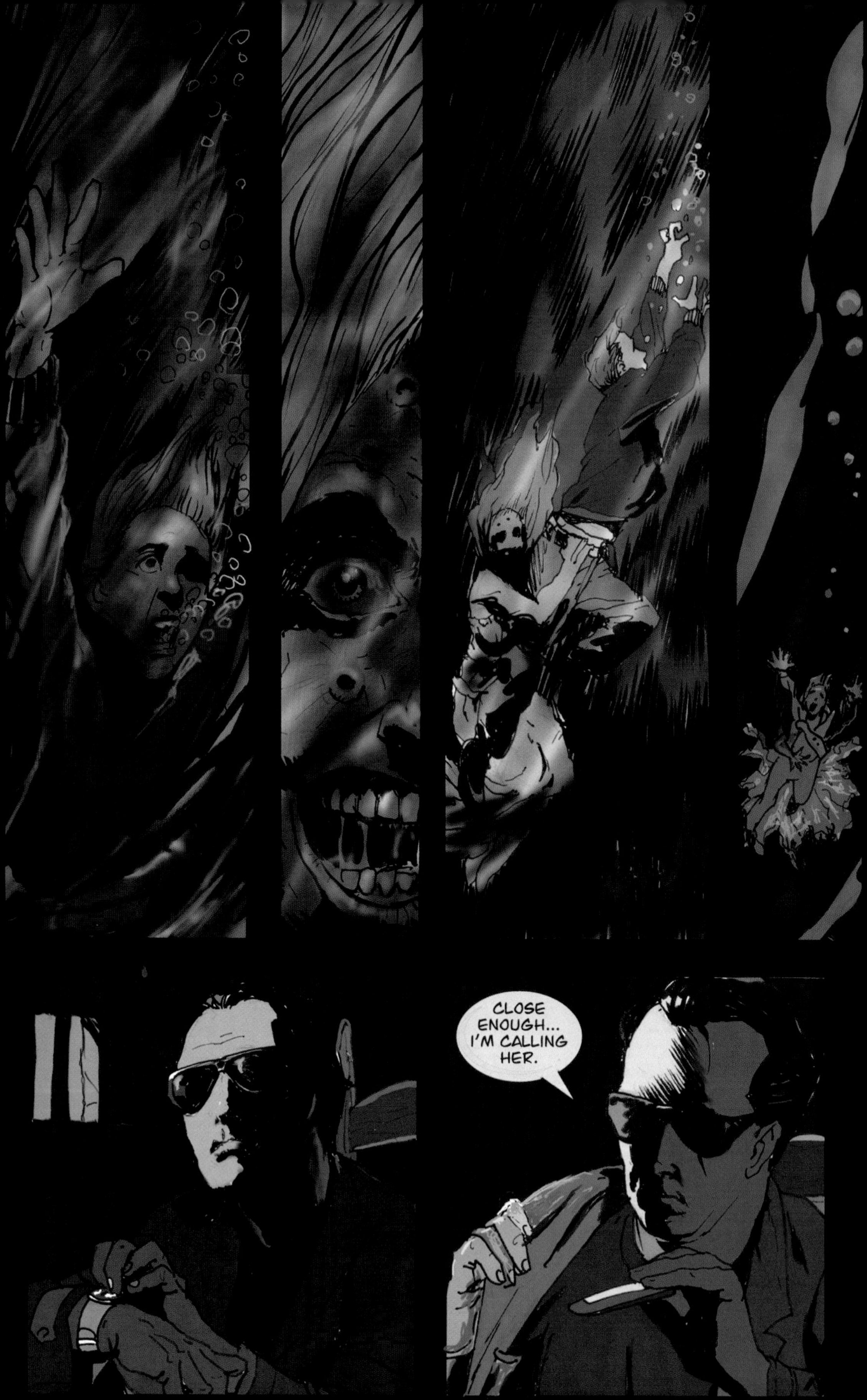
CLOSE ENOUGH... I'M CALLING HER.

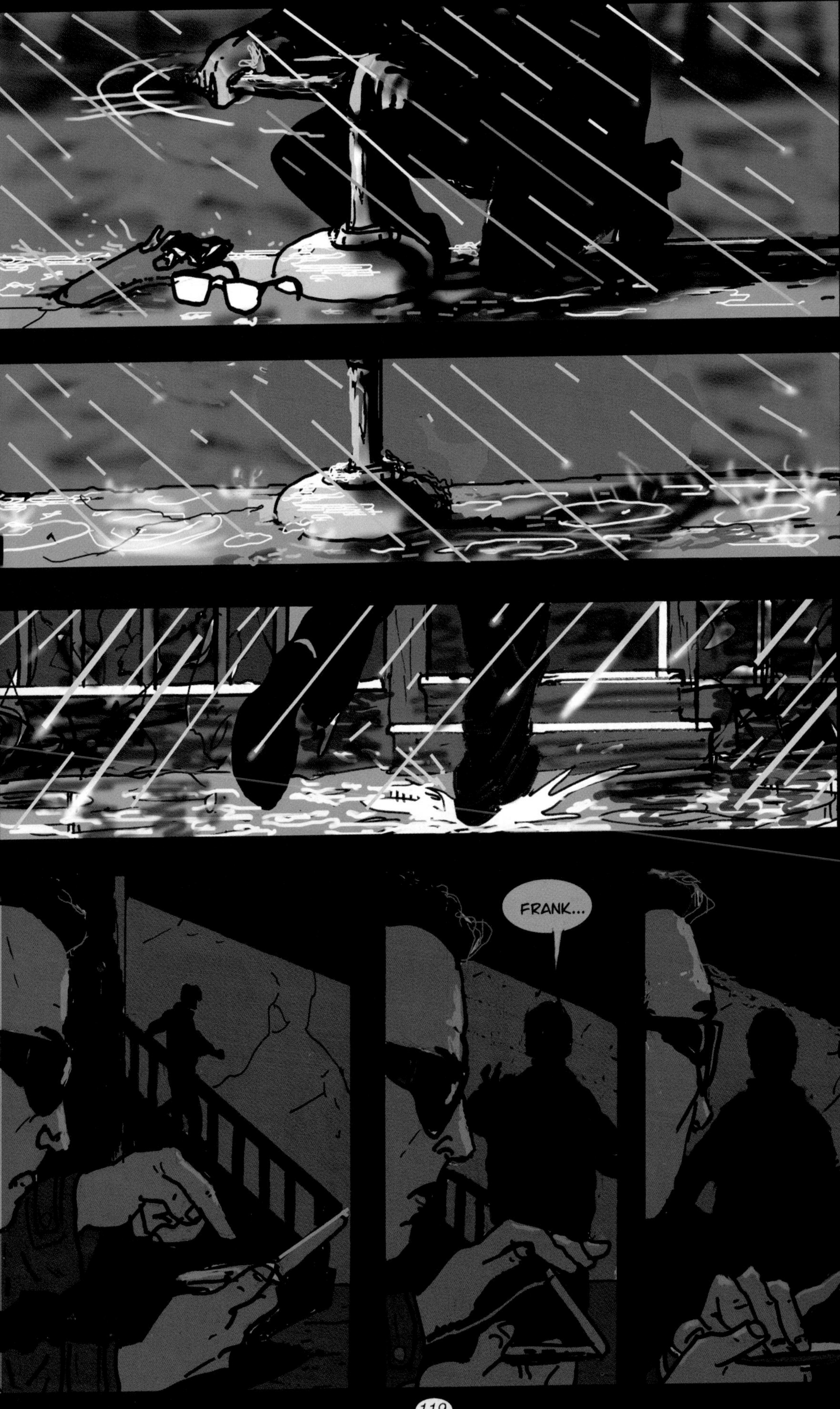
FRANK...

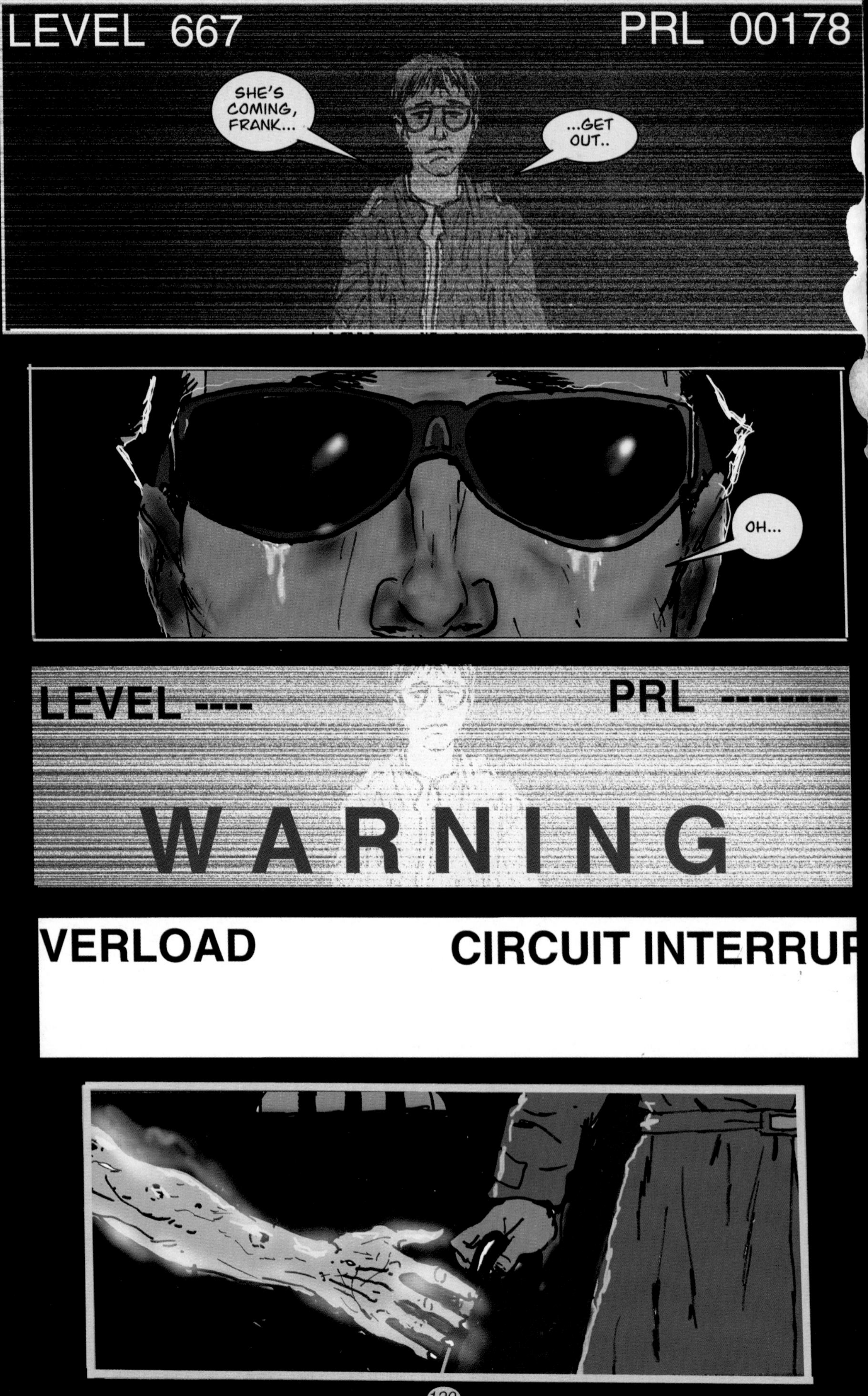
LEVEL 667
PRL 00178
SHE'S COMING, FRANK...
...GET OUT..
OH...
LEVEL ----
PRL --------
WARNING
VERLOAD
CIRCUIT INTERRUP

AR-ARRAAR-
RAHRRR--

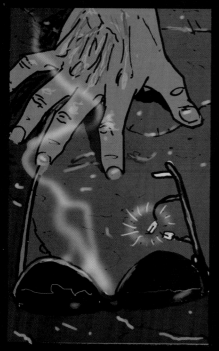

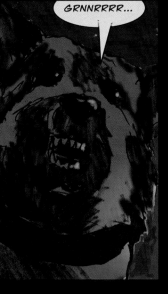

GRNNRRRR...

IF YOU HURT MY DOG, I'LL...

...I'LL...

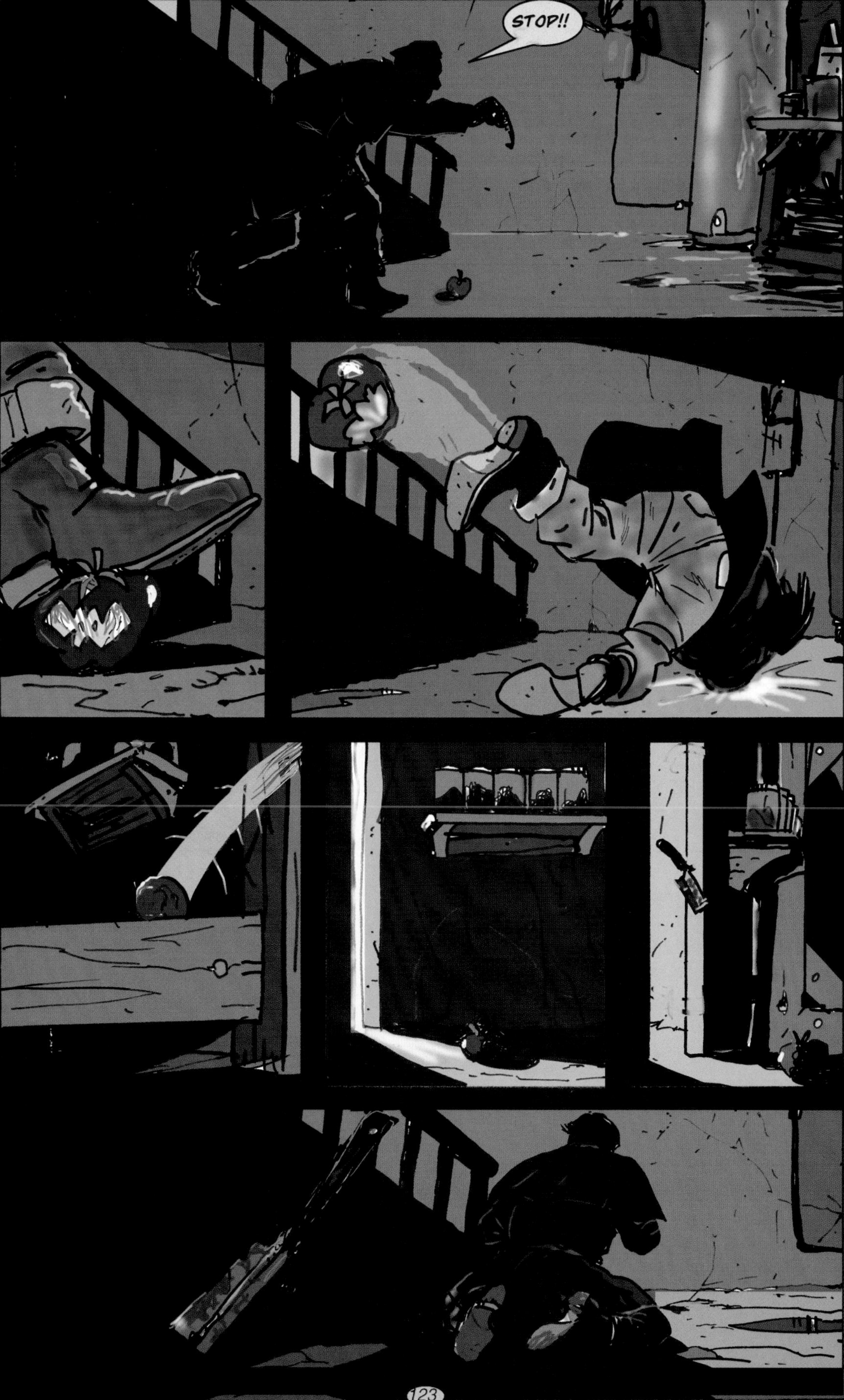
STOP!!

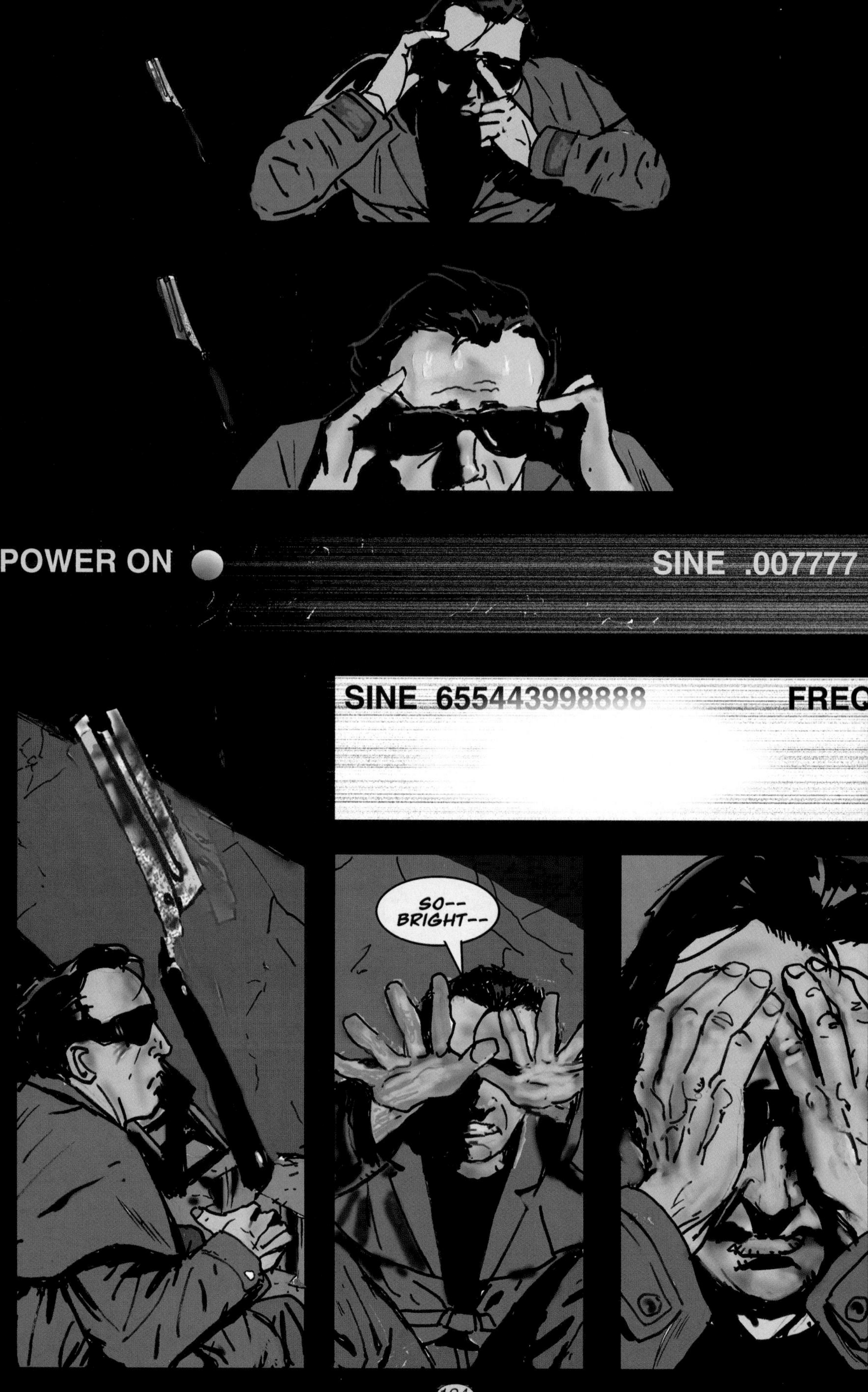
POWER ON
SINE .007777
SINE 655443998888
FREQ
SO-- BRIGHT--

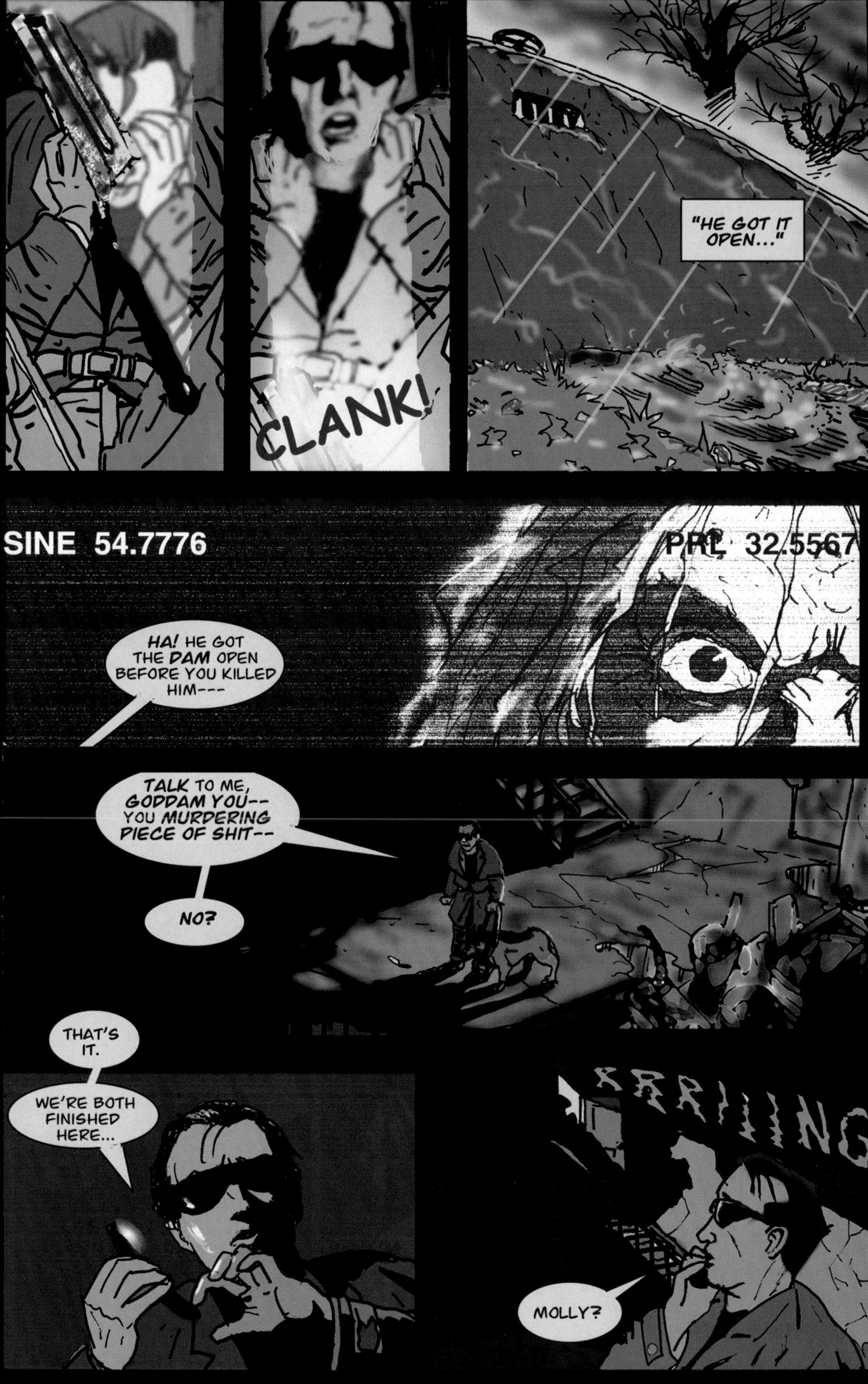
CLANK!
"HE GOT IT OPEN..."
SINE 54.7776
PRL 32.5567
HA! HE GOT THE DAM OPEN BEFORE YOU KILLED HIM---
TALK TO ME, GODDAM YOU-- YOU MURDERING PIECE OF SHIT--
NO?
THAT'S IT.
WE'RE BOTH FINISHED HERE...
KRRIING
MOLLY?

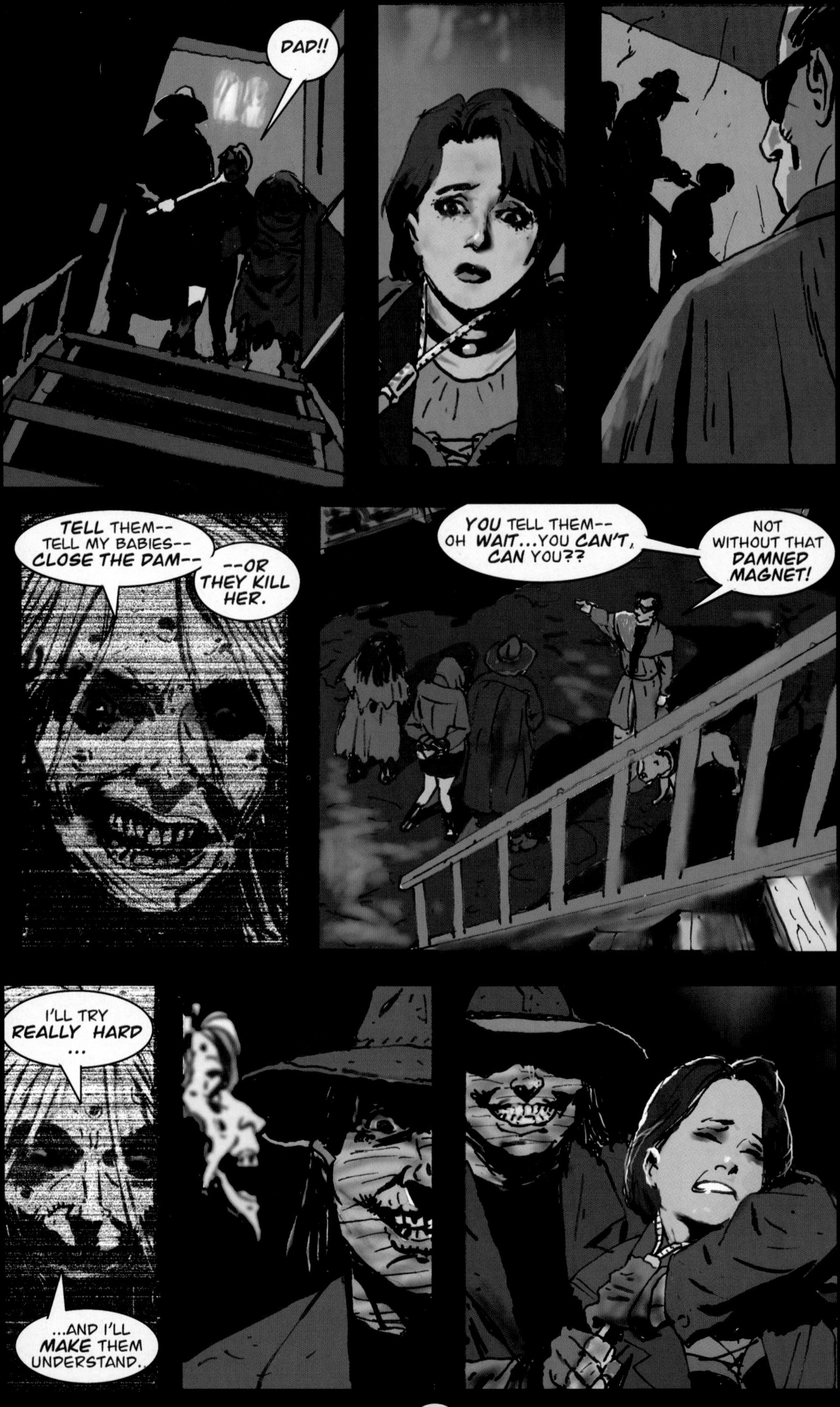
DAD!!
TELL THEM-- TELL MY BABIES-- CLOSE THE DAM--
--OR THEY KILL HER.
YOU TELL THEM-- OH WAIT...YOU CAN'T, CAN YOU??
NOT WITHOUT THAT DAMNED MAGNET!
I'LL TRY REALLY HARD ...
...AND I'LL MAKE THEM UNDERSTAND.

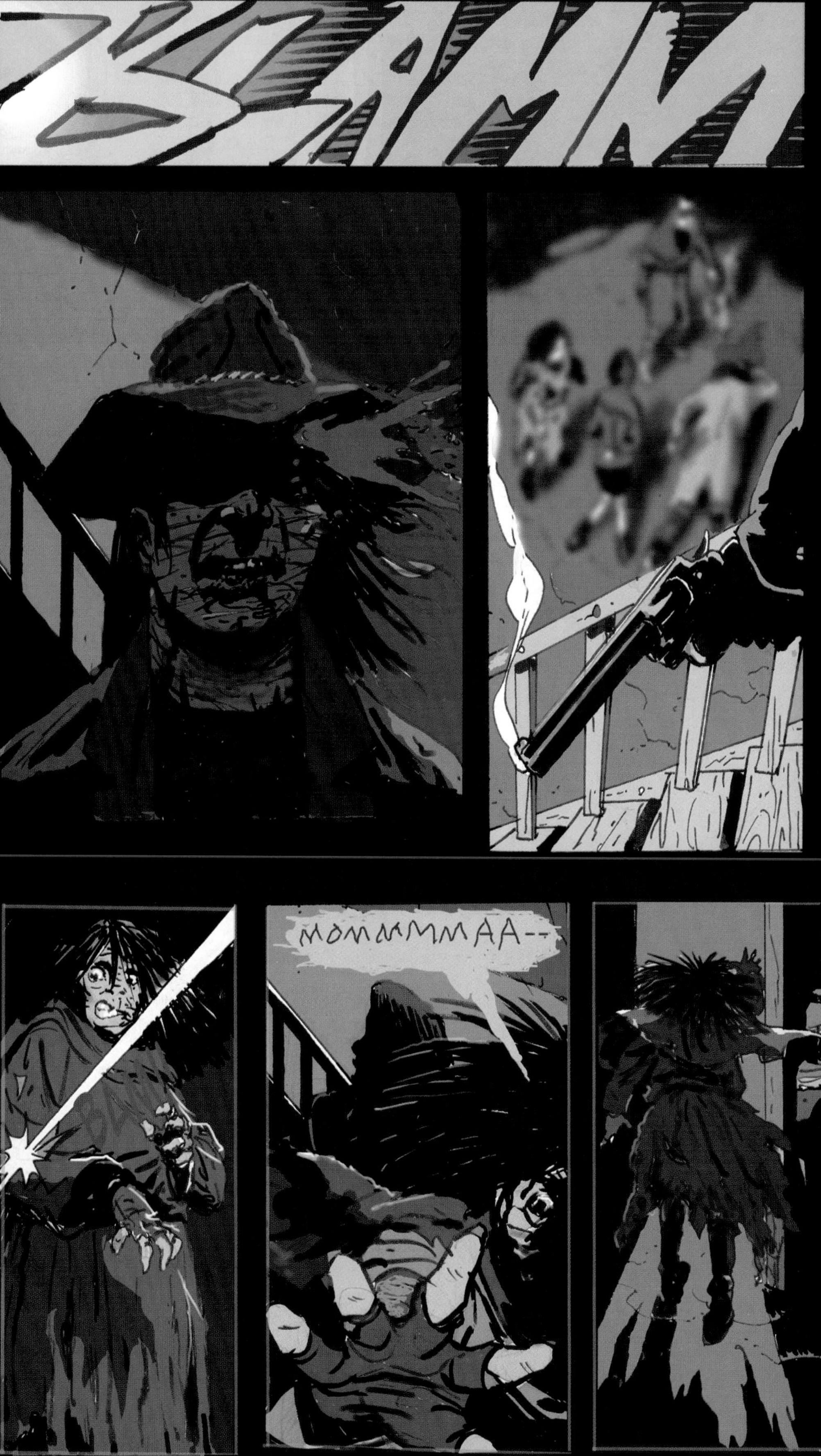
BLAMM
MOMMMMAA--

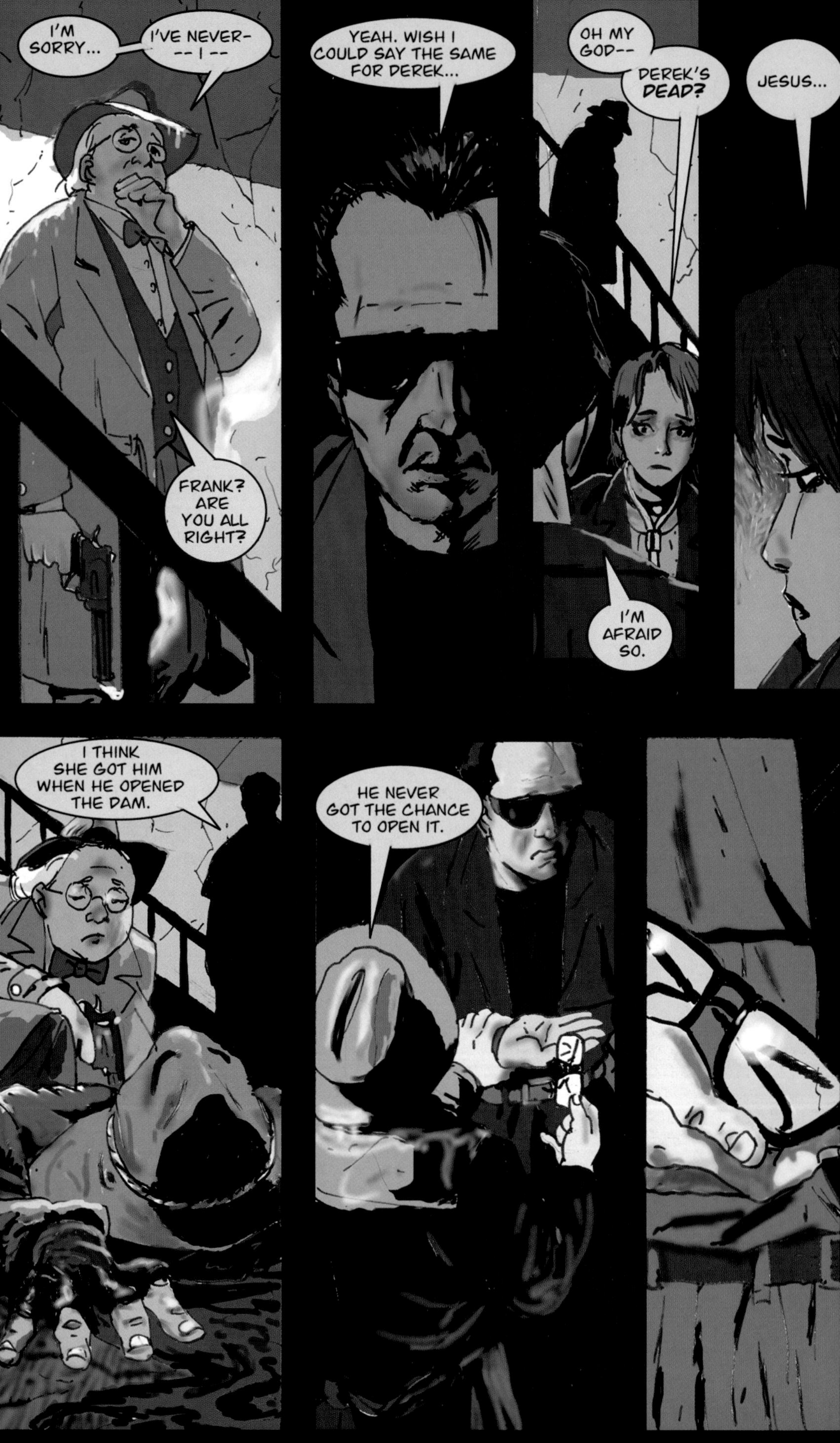
I'M SORRY...
I'VE NEVER- -- I --
FRANK? ARE YOU ALL RIGHT?
YEAH. WISH I COULD SAY THE SAME FOR DEREK...
OH MY GOD--
DEREK'S DEAD?
I'M AFRAID SO.
JESUS...
I THINK SHE GOT HIM WHEN HE OPENED THE DAM.
HE NEVER GOT THE CHANCE TO OPEN IT.

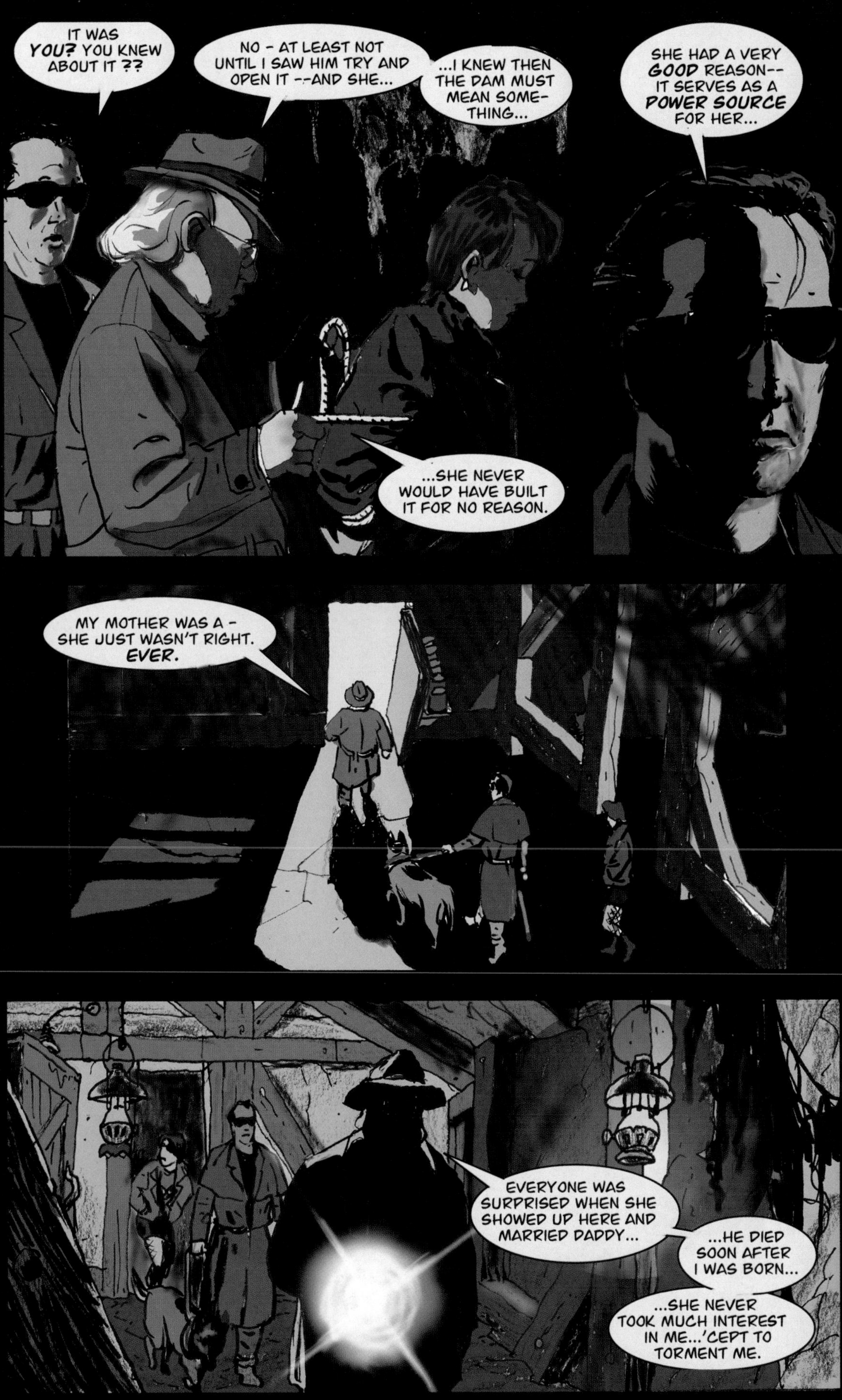
IT WAS YOU? YOU KNEW ABOUT IT ??
NO - AT LEAST NOT UNTIL I SAW HIM TRY AND OPEN IT --AND SHE...
...I KNEW THEN THE DAM MUST MEAN SOME-THING...
...SHE NEVER WOULD HAVE BUILT IT FOR NO REASON.
SHE HAD A VERY GOOD REASON-- IT SERVES AS A POWER SOURCE FOR HER...
MY MOTHER WAS A - SHE JUST WASN'T RIGHT. EVER.
EVERYONE WAS SURPRISED WHEN SHE SHOWED UP HERE AND MARRIED DADDY...
...HE DIED SOON AFTER I WAS BORN...
...SHE NEVER TOOK MUCH INTEREST IN ME...'CEPT TO TORMENT ME.

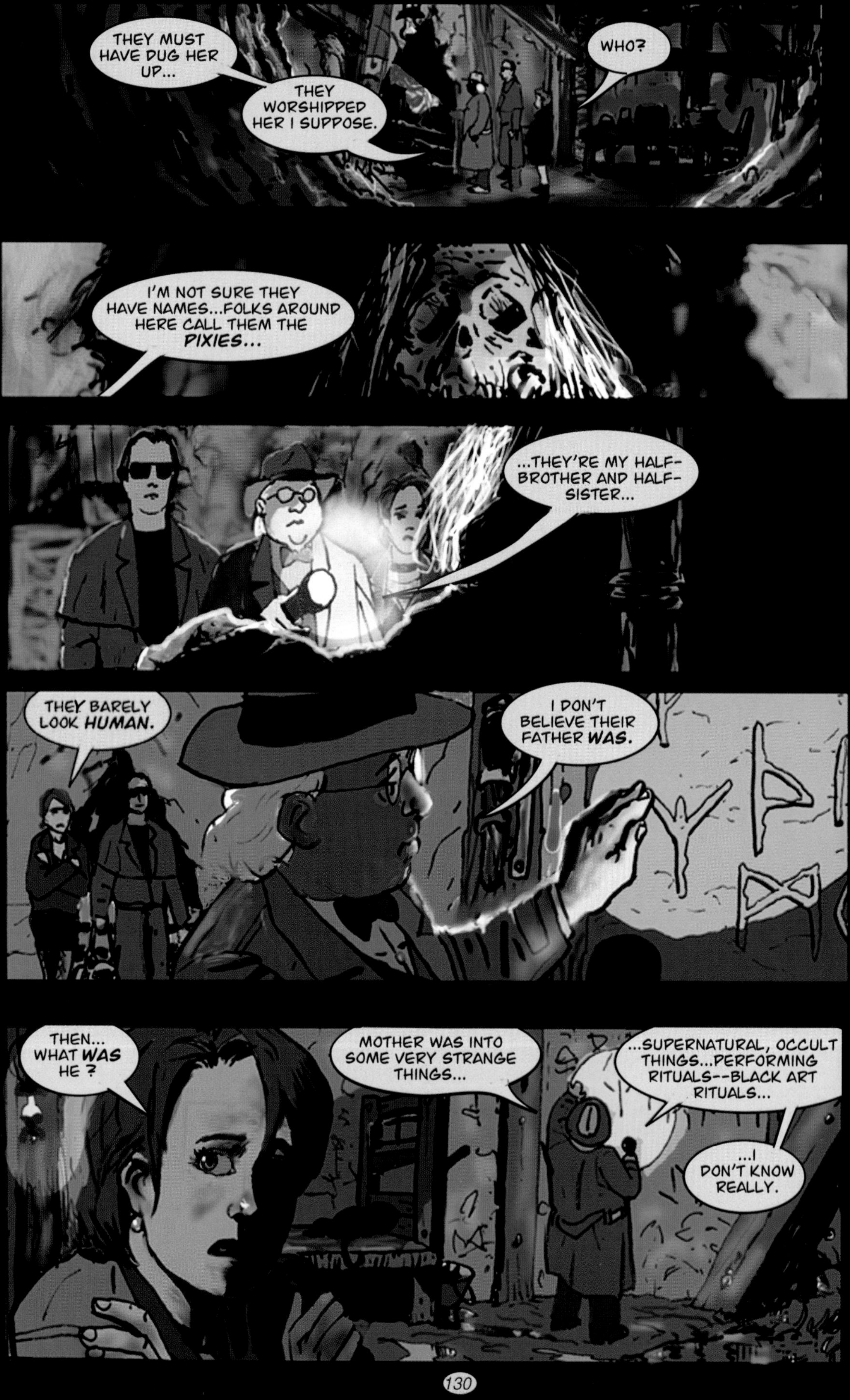
THEY MUST HAVE DUG HER UP...
THEY WORSHIPPED HER I SUPPOSE.
WHO?
I'M NOT SURE THEY HAVE NAMES...FOLKS AROUND HERE CALL THEM THE PIXIES...
...THEY'RE MY HALF-BROTHER AND HALF-SISTER...
THEY BARELY LOOK HUMAN.
I DON'T BELIEVE THEIR FATHER WAS.
THEN... WHAT WAS HE ?
MOTHER WAS INTO SOME VERY STRANGE THINGS...
...SUPERNATURAL, OCCULT THINGS...PERFORMING RITUALS--BLACK ART RITUALS...
...I DON'T KNOW REALLY.

WHEN SHE STARTED HAVING THE STROKES, I MOVED BACK TO HALLIDAY SPRINGS TO CARE FOR HER...

THE **PIXIES** WERE JUST SMALL THEN...I SAW THEM ON OCCASION-- CREEPING AROUND THE WOODS AT THE EDGE OF THE YARD...

...I SUPPOSE IT WAS THE RIGHT THING TO DO.

I CAN REMEMBER IT... JUST LIKE YESTERDAY...

...I HAD JUST **OPENED** THE DAM TO DRAIN THE LAKE-- AND SHE STARTED **SCREAMING** AT ME--

--WHY HAD I OPENED IT AND I HAD TO CLOSE IT AGAIN **IMMEDIATELY**--

--SHE **DIED** SCREAMING AT ME.

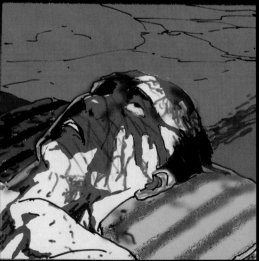

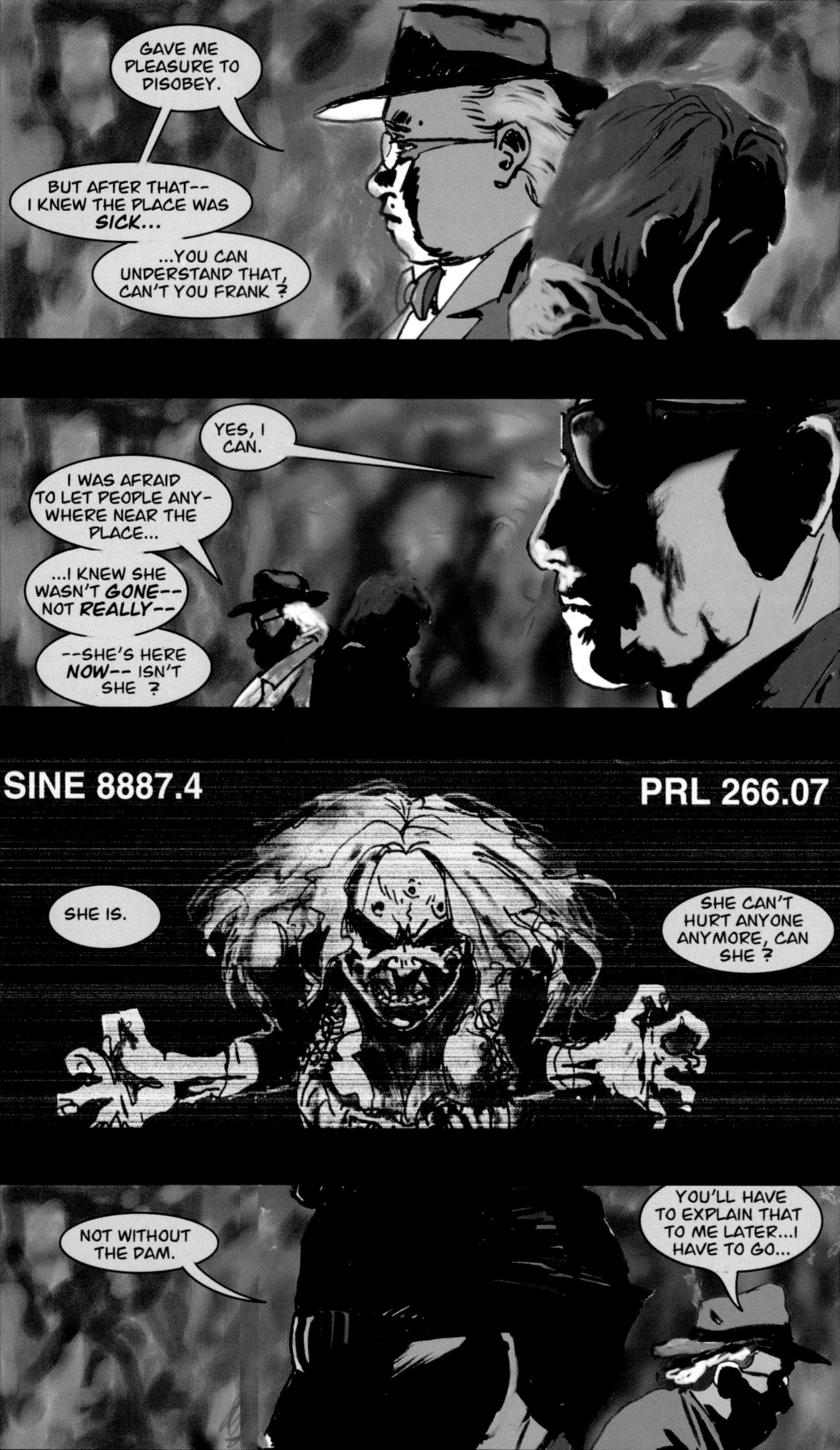
GAVE ME PLEASURE TO DISOBEY.
BUT AFTER THAT-- I KNEW THE PLACE WAS SICK...
...YOU CAN UNDERSTAND THAT, CAN'T YOU FRANK ?
YES, I CAN.
I WAS AFRAID TO LET PEOPLE ANY-WHERE NEAR THE PLACE...
...I KNEW SHE WASN'T GONE-- NOT REALLY--
--SHE'S HERE NOW-- ISN'T SHE ?
SINE 8887.4
PRL 266.07
SHE IS.
SHE CAN'T HURT ANYONE ANYMORE, CAN SHE ?
NOT WITHOUT THE DAM.
YOU'LL HAVE TO EXPLAIN THAT TO ME LATER...I HAVE TO GO...

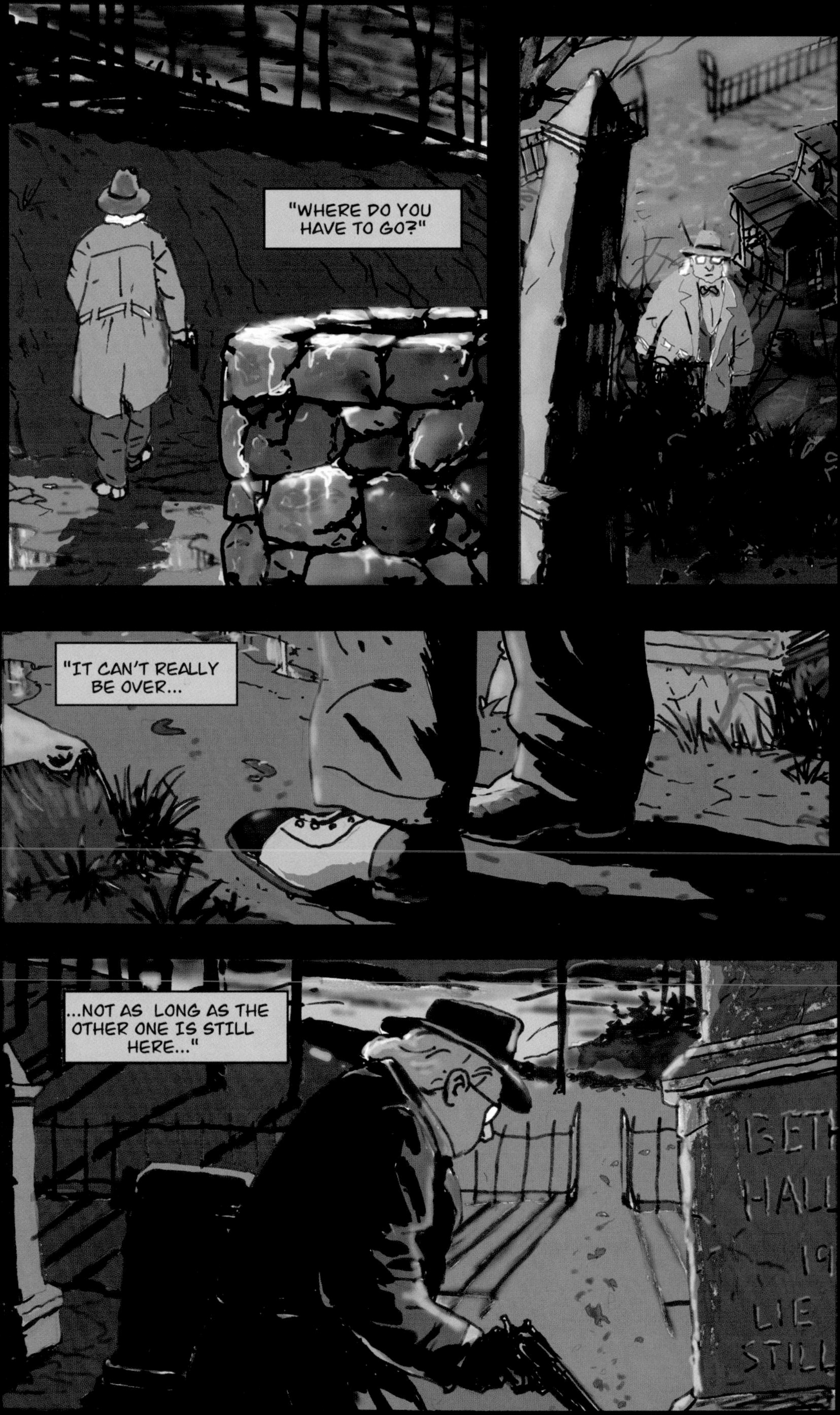
"WHERE DO YOU HAVE TO GO?"
"IT CAN'T REALLY BE OVER...
...NOT AS LONG AS THE OTHER ONE IS STILL HERE..."

"...AND I DON'T KNOW WHAT ELSE TO DO..."

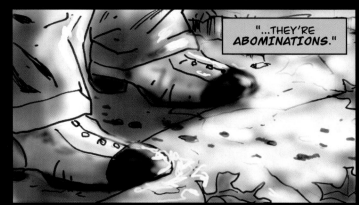

"...THEY'RE ABOMINATIONS."

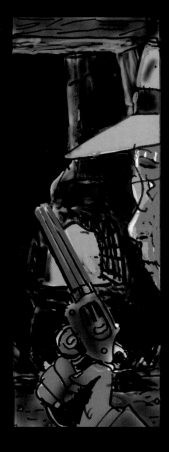

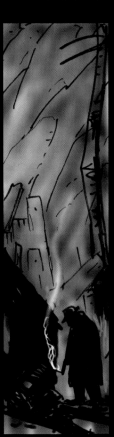

131

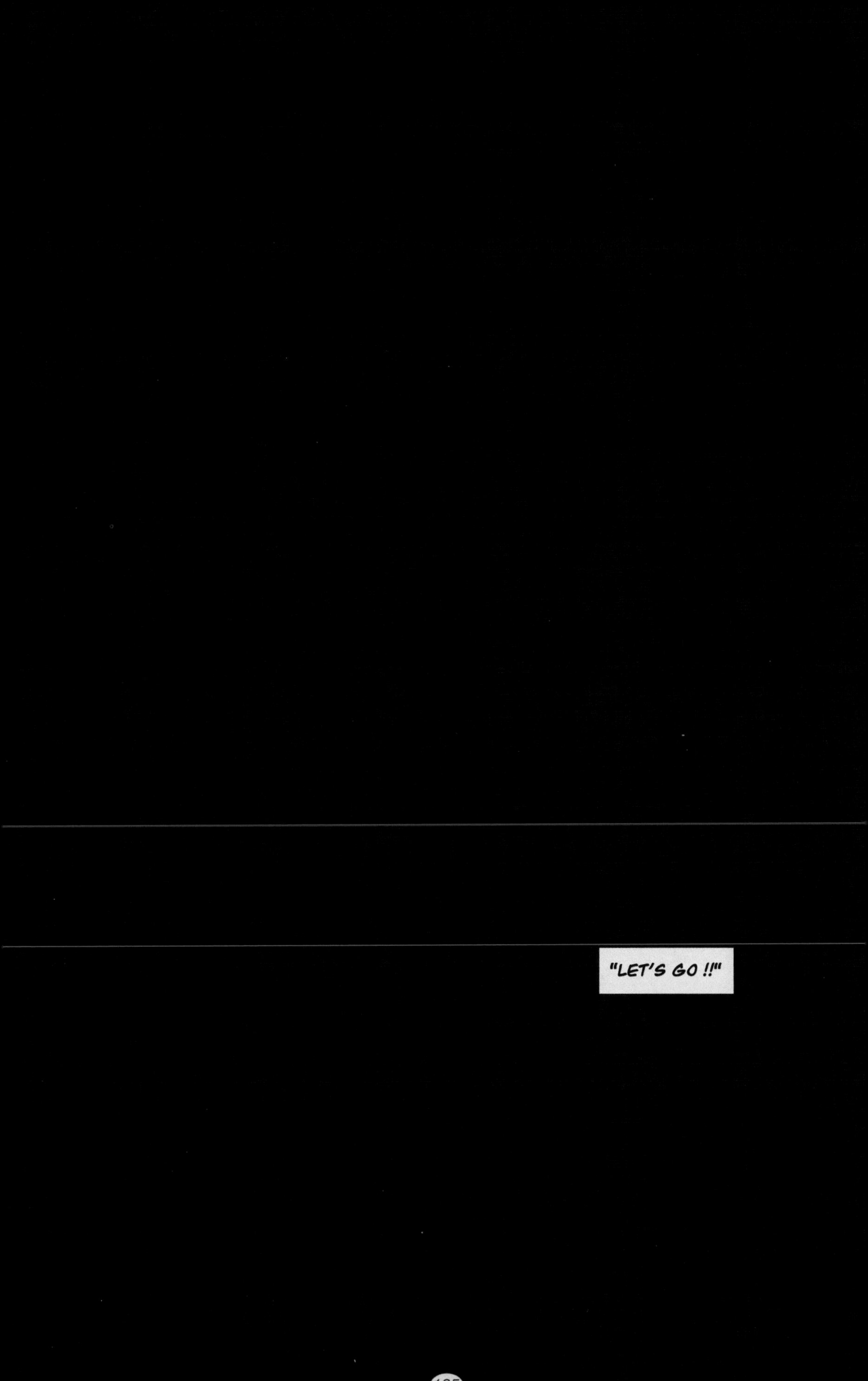
"LET'S GO !!"

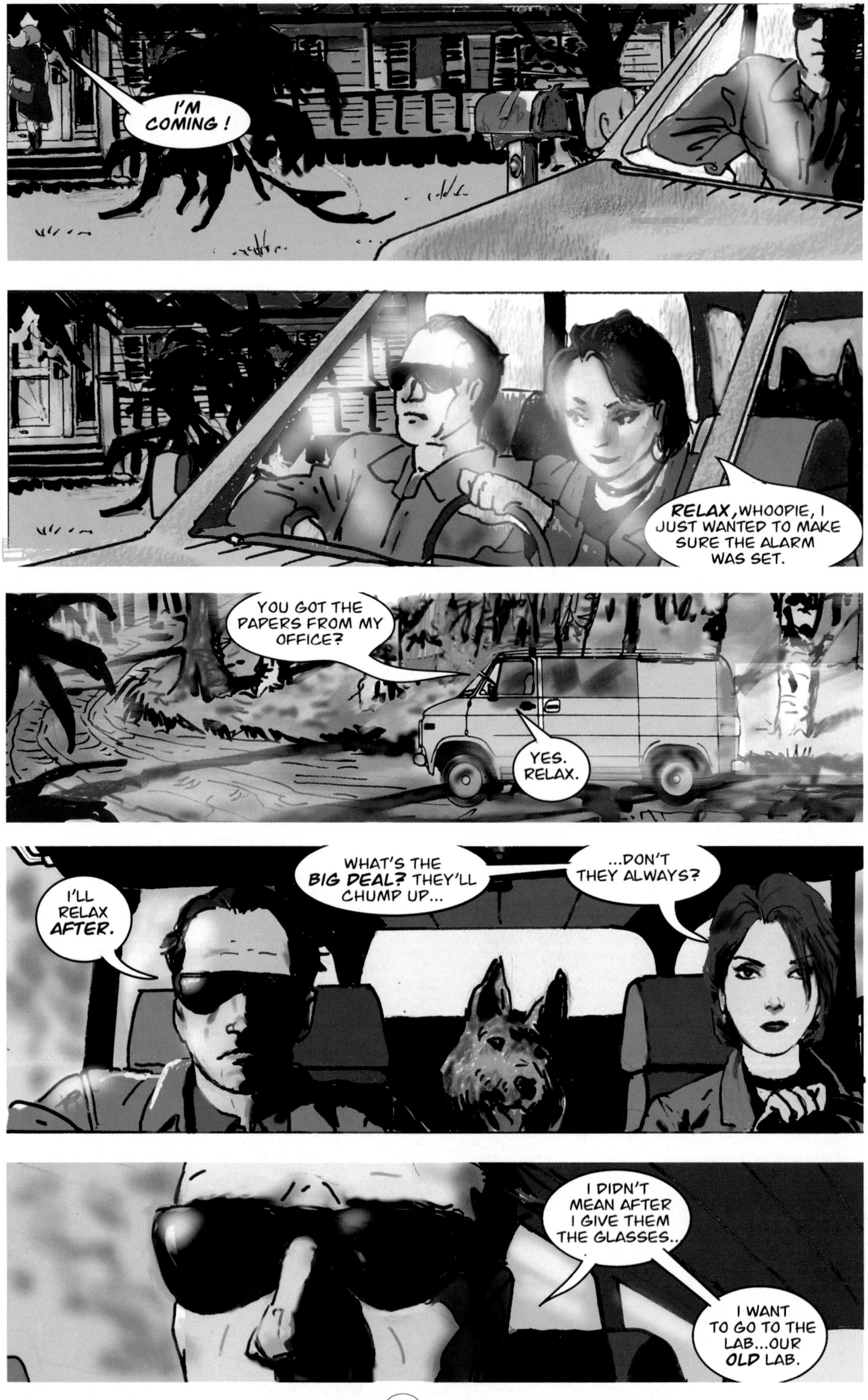
I'M COMING!
RELAX, WHOOPIE, I JUST WANTED TO MAKE SURE THE ALARM WAS SET.
YOU GOT THE PAPERS FROM MY OFFICE?
YES. RELAX.
I'LL RELAX AFTER.
WHAT'S THE BIG DEAL? THEY'LL CHUMP UP...
...DON'T THEY ALWAYS?
I DIDN'T MEAN AFTER I GIVE THEM THE GLASSES..
I WANT TO GO TO THE LAB...OUR OLD LAB.

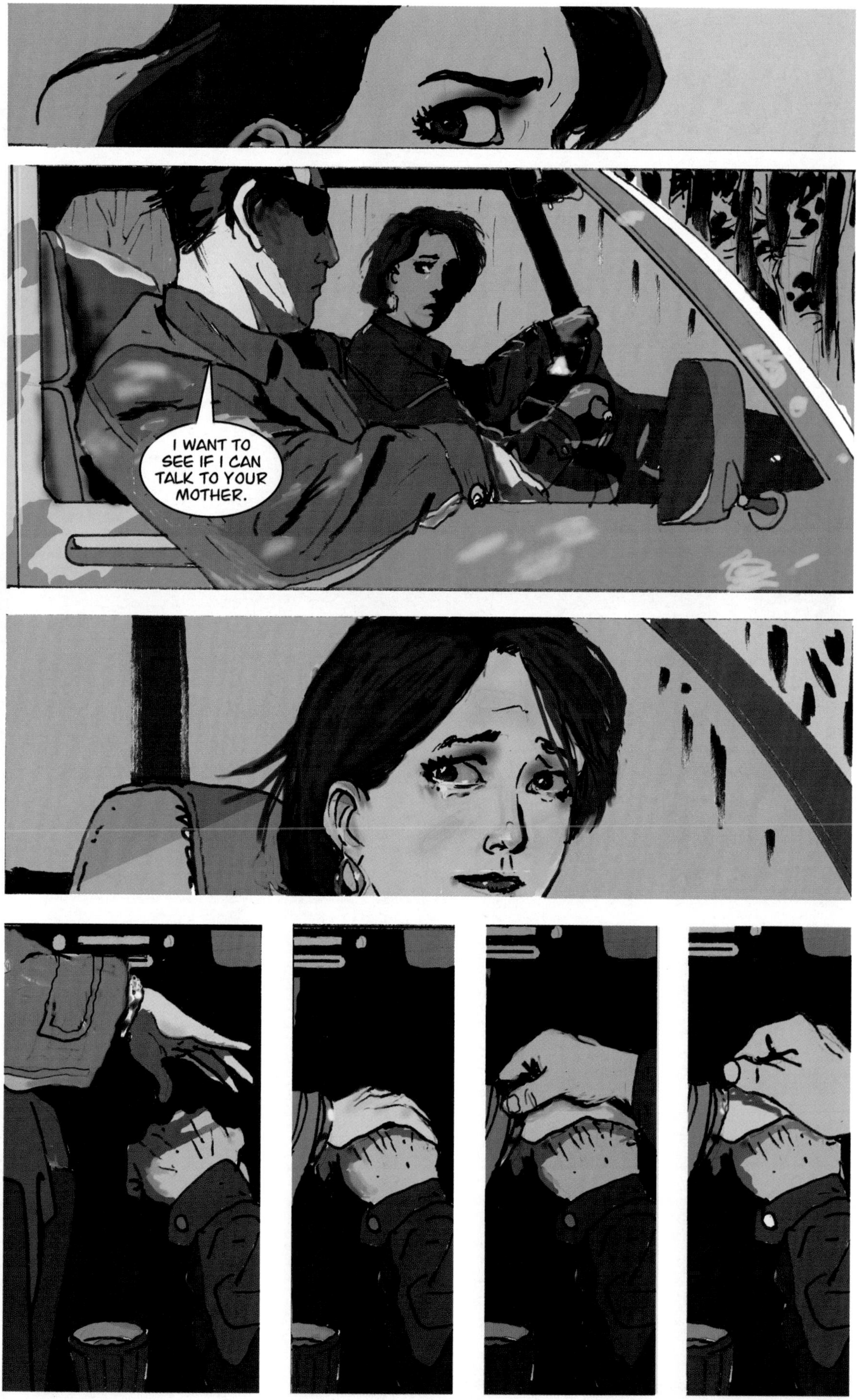
I WANT TO SEE IF I CAN TALK TO YOUR MOTHER.

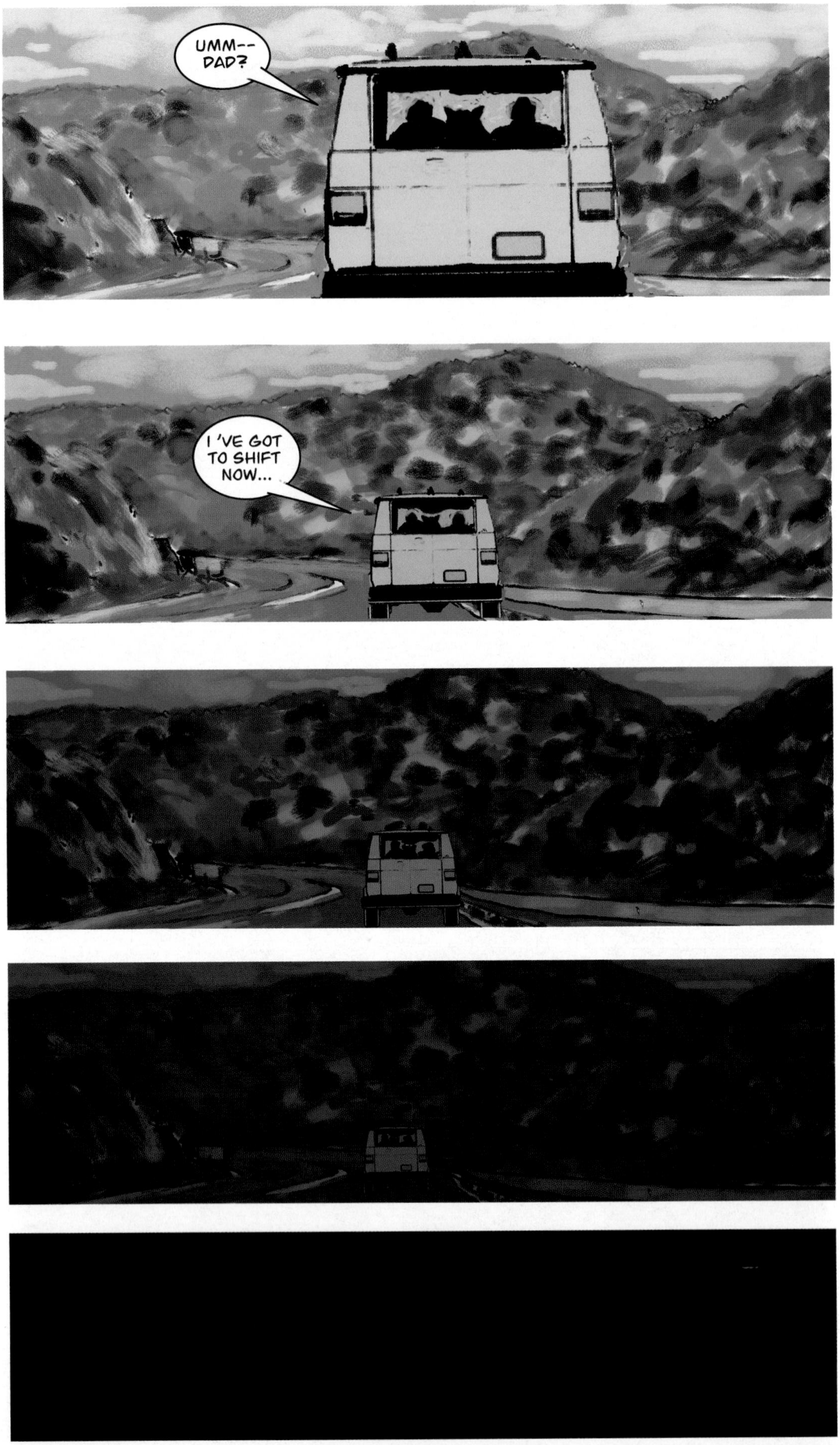
UMM--
DAD?
I 'VE GOT TO SHIFT NOW...

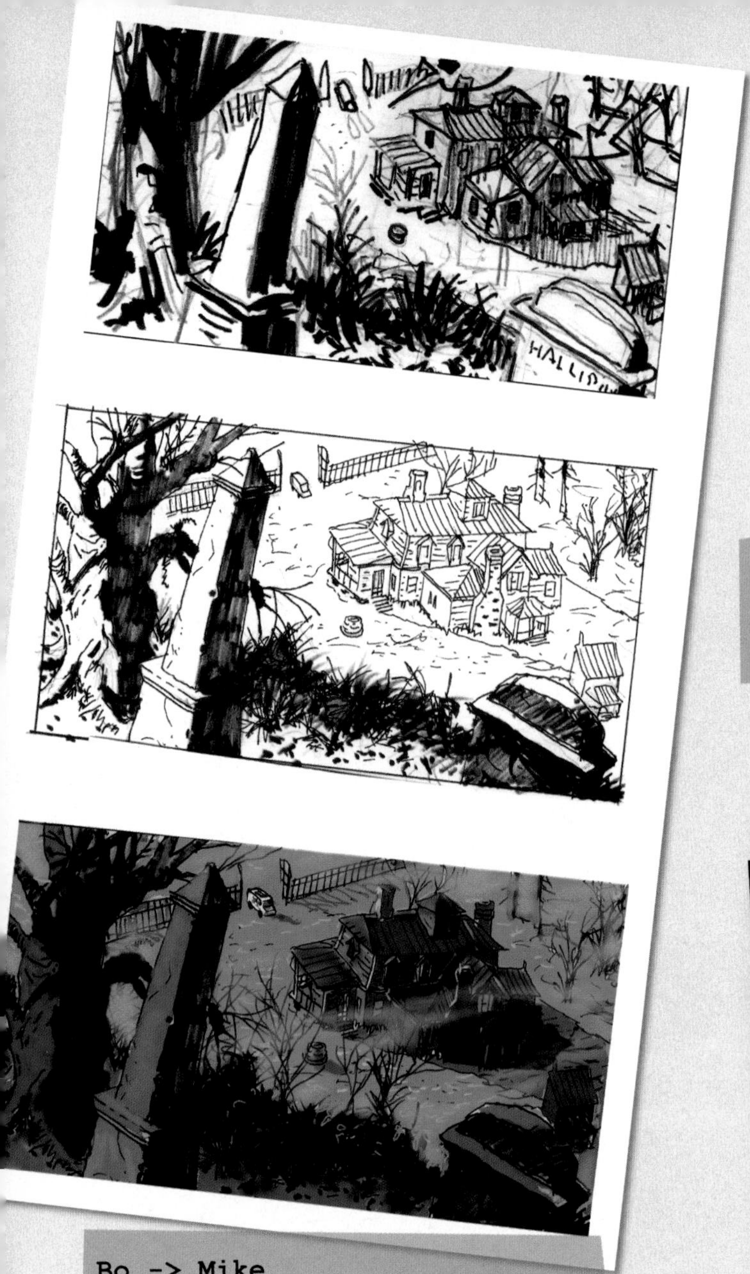

Bo -> Mike

"I thought showing how a panel goes from sketch to color would be good -hence the first attachment."

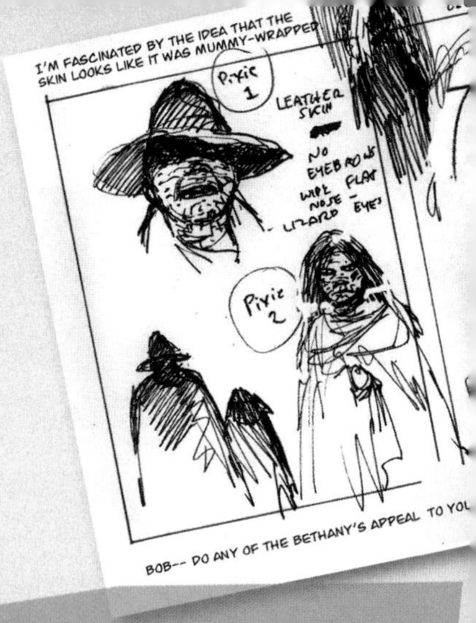

I'M FASCINATED BY THE IDEA THAT THE SKIN LOOKS LIKE IT WAS MUMMY-WRAPPED
Pixie 1
LEATHER SKIN
NO EYEBROWS
WIDE FLAT NOSE
LIZARD EYES
Pixie 2
BOB-- DO ANY OF THE BETHANY'S APPEAL TO YOU

Bo -> Bob

Character sketches

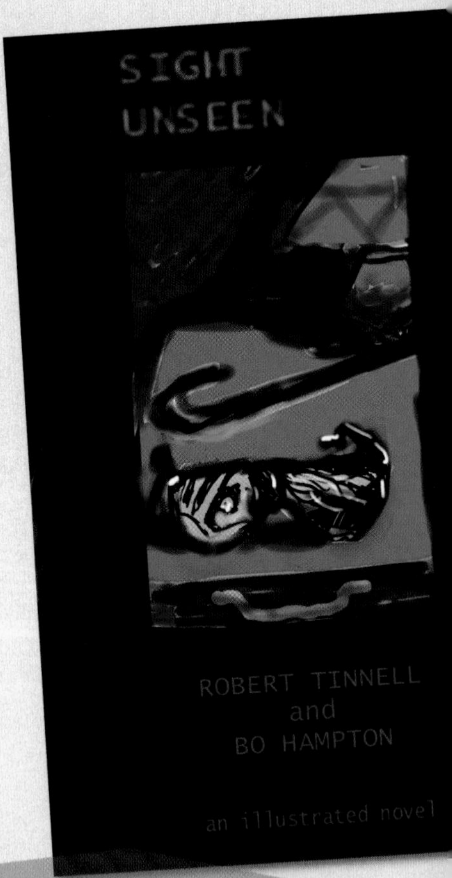

SIGHT UNSEEN
ROBERT TINNELL and BO HAMPTON
an illustrated novel

Bo -> Bob

Early Cover Sketch

sights SEEN

Bob & Bo look at the fear, foundation and creative friendship that forged Sight Unseen

Essay By Jim Bissett
Sketches By Bo Hampton

If Hell has a Sunday newspaper (and we've already got a call out to Hunter Thompson on the Ouija Board to see if it does), you can bet your brimstone that The Birches is the kind of property that would absolutely burn a hole in the real estate supplement.

With the blurb copy penned by Satan, his own damned self.

After all, it's not every day in eternity that a listing like this one comes along.

Location, location, location? Oh, yeah. The house that's the centerpiece to *Sight Unseen* is a hydroelectric conduit to the netherworld, with a sophisticated dam and turbine configuration that can scare up more undead than the ones who showed up at your last high school reunion.

And talk about amenities: You've got your hardwood floors. You've got your wood beam ceilings.

You've got your razor-packing poltergeist with murderous intent and a moldy death-smile that could chill the tan off Wayne Newton … *his* own damned self.

The Birches would do the Dark One proud, indeed.

Satan, we mean. Aw, heck —Wayne, too.

Bob Tinnell and Bo Hampton worked pretty hard to do *you* proud —but you already know that, since you just took *Sight*

Unseen down in one sitting with every light on in *your* house. The authors are understandably grateful, because hey, a book without readers is like the Frankenstein Monster without jumper cables, right?

So they wanted to reward you with a little backstory on just how this tale of real estate, adrenaline-running fear and redemption got past the e-mail, line drawing, plot outline stage.

Like that lightening bolt to Ben Franklin's kite, the project surged with the current of an idea after Bob and Bo struck up a conversation at a comic convention in Philadelphia.

"So we're talking," Bob recalls, and Bo comes up with this pitch: 'A blind scientist who can see ghosts using technology based on his seeing-eye dog's visual processing. I was in. Immediately. Well, not quite 'immediately' —first, I had to get over the fact that an artist of his stature would even want to work with me."

Bo was just as impressed with Bob.

On the flight home after Philly he read *The Black Forest*, Bob's World War I graphic novel with zombies and stitched-together denizens of graveyards who suddenly find themselves as undead draftees in the German army. He was taken by the tale.

"I knew I had to work with the guy," Bo says. "I called him at home the next day and tossed the idea. He came right

```
Bob -> Bo

> -----Original
Message-----
> From: Robert>
Sent: Sunday, May
08, 2005 9:48 AM
> To: bo hampton
> Subject: Re:
Woo hoo!!
>
>
> Okay, let me think
- the next time he
sees her isn't that
after the dam
> is stopped? I
mean, she's bright
initially and then
he can just see
> her? Or should we
just have Derek "re-
calibrate" the specs?
>
> At the end when
he can't see her
- I just checked
that - she'll only
> be the ball of
white when Frank
sees her - not us.
So only in the pov
> shots is she
that bright. BTW I
noticed I didn't
mention that Frank
> puts the glasses
back on - and of
course he must.
>
> I think the whole
ball of white
light thing works
perfectly. It's the
> only way we'll
know the power died.
And since it's only
the pov's we
> can limit them.
>
> Make sense?

> -----Robert Tinnell
```

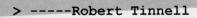

N- NOO -
NN
MISS -
bob---on next pg leaves have blown away---no Da

back and added the town setting, the Confederate battleground angle and the whole thing with the dam. He had that in his head from another story. And we had ourselves a book, you know?"

Damned straight.

And in this one, high-tech ghost busting meets Southern Gothic to do a deft "Monster Mash" on our psyche's dark side of the moon.

Panels pop with crackling dialogue and believable characters, including three of the most inspiring, unlikely heroes you'll ever meet in any medium.

The artwork is so stunning and startling that it almost draws blood. And wrapped through it all, like the Mummy's winter coat, are scary, scary scenes, comic relief and conflicted relationships. Just like real life, actually —right down to the spooky relatives who appear unannounced at the door.

Just plain atmosphere, too, from the cast of the afternoon sun to the full pages in nothing but black to show the perspective of Frank, the blind scientist who can sneak peeks at the mortal-challenged with a specially outfitted pair of glasses wired to the Other Side.

A graphic novel, that's, well, a *novel.*

"Bob has a tremendous ability to create believable, character-driven scenarios," Bo says. "That's what drew me to his work. This collaboration, I have to say, has been the most engrossing I've ever had. We both sacrificed our egos at the altar, and the book, I think, is better off for it. I'm just glad he can't draw."

Well, the beauty of it is that Bob, of course, *can* "draw" with words … the same way Bo *writes* with images.

Slide back to Page 17 for a perfect example. That's the beginning of the chilling sequence where contractor Danny Atkins discovers too, too late that The Birches is a fixer-upper straight from the bowels of the Bad Place. That's when we first meet Bethany, and she's not there to talk about carpet swatches or county building codes.

And forget any ham-handed, "Arrgh! I'm being chased by a ghost!" dialogue. Bob and Bo let the whole thing slither out with nary a word. Just Danny's mute terror.

"I don't have to write panel breakdowns with Bo," Bob says. "I really write in screenplay-style, and he 'directs' the sequence. Bo's also an accomplished storyboard artist and a pretty serious student of cinema, and it really showed with the Danny scene. Very, very effective."

"I set that bit up to intentionally be as cinematic as I could make it," Bo says. "That's why you see the black fields around the panels. I wanted to simulate the darkened theater and 1.85:1 ratio of a widescreen movie."

Dialogue would have destroyed the illusion, he says. And if you felt Bethany's breath on the back of your neck … well … let's just say you weren't alone.

"In case you're wondering," Bo confesses, "I did scare the bejesus out of myself when I had Danny turn the apple over to see the bite marks."

Which is precisely what you need with a good ghost story, even if you're one of the guys creating it.

The same thing happened to Bob. He had himself a little goose flesh, take-a-gander-over-the-shoulder situation, too. It came when he penned the scene where Bethany's reflection appears in Crawford's driver's side

```
Bob -> Bo

> I'd like to - as subtly
as possible - work in
more eye imagery. Maybe
> even stuff you
don't recognize as
eyes at first. Like
maybe something
> at the house - some
sort of image. Maybe that
last beat with Danny in
> the basement we
see one of the feral
eyes?  I don't know...
```

window as he's doing a *Dukes of Hazzard* to get away from The Birches, and his past.

"It did scare me while writing it," he admits. "I know it's kind of a cliched moment —you know, trying to start the car while danger approaches, that sort of thing —but I thought it worked. It's elemental. So I let my mind go there and creep myself out."

Elemental, indeed. Back in the day as impressionable youngsters, Bob and Bo were both tattooed by fear at a formative age. And junkies that they are, they've spent their professional careers trying to recreate that first rush.

As a youngster in small town West Virginia, Bob was spooked by news accounts of a killing in his home county —a crime that ended up being a demented point of pride for the perpetrators. The man's murderers, it turned out, watched from a wooded area as his body was discovered by passers-by. They wanted to see the reaction, and the enormity of that evil is something Bob still can't shake when he thinks back on it.

"The details of it, as a child, were just so horrifying," he says. Add in the victim's

Bob -> Bo

>> Re: Frank, Molly, and the accident. Derek would only have limited
>> details on that, I think - and I don't want him fighting Frank's
>> battles more than he already has. But that could change as they
>> evolve. One of the reasons I'm desperate to sprint ahead of you is I'm
>> certain Derek is going to change. I don't know EXACTLY who he is yet -
>> and most likely won't until the moment of his death and ghostly visit -
>> and I want to have the freedom to get back and massage if necessary.
>> Anyway, I'm rambling. Back to your question - Right now, if you don't
>> mind I'm going to reveal that later in the flashback to the accident -
>> and I HOPE come up with a touching way to underline that Frank was
>> blinded in it (actually I've pretty much already figured it out). Okay
>> with you? I want to see it and I think this scene has enough talking
>> about what happened.

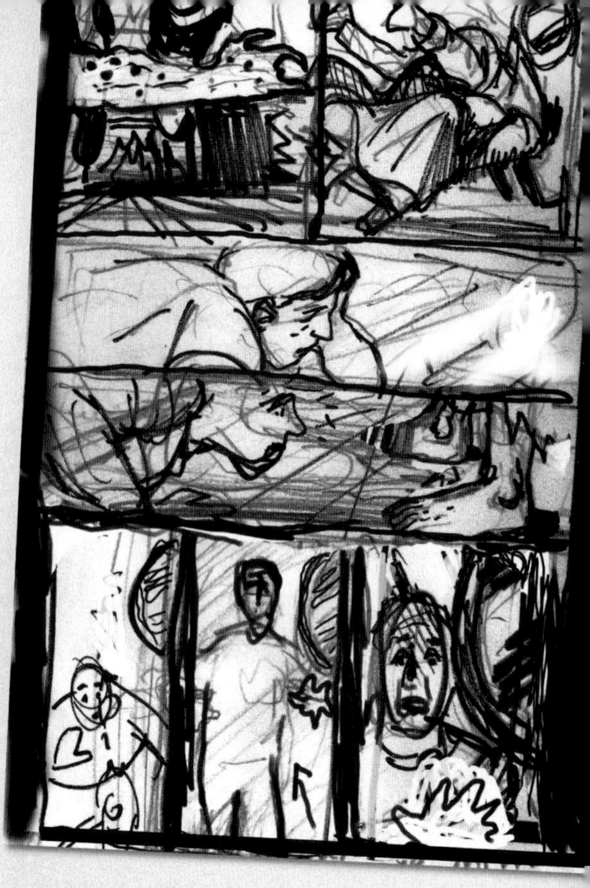

convoluted personal life with enough Southern Gothic to keep Dr. Phil in syndication until the 22nd century and you've got a tale people in the region are still telling.

And that's more than 30 years after it happened.

"There's always the supernatural angle or mystery element to these tales," Bob continues. "I think that's the big reason why writers like Peter Straub and Robert McCammon and of course, Stephen King, made such an impact on me. They have a way of connecting the reader to a time and space … particularly in the way a small town can be so affected by a tragedy or event, that the whole thing is elevated to mythology."

The killer who haunted Bo's boyhood isn't really "real." At least, he hopes not.

He can still generate a shudder when he looks back on that urban legend that took root when he was a lad back home in High Point, N.C. There, according to the tale, a

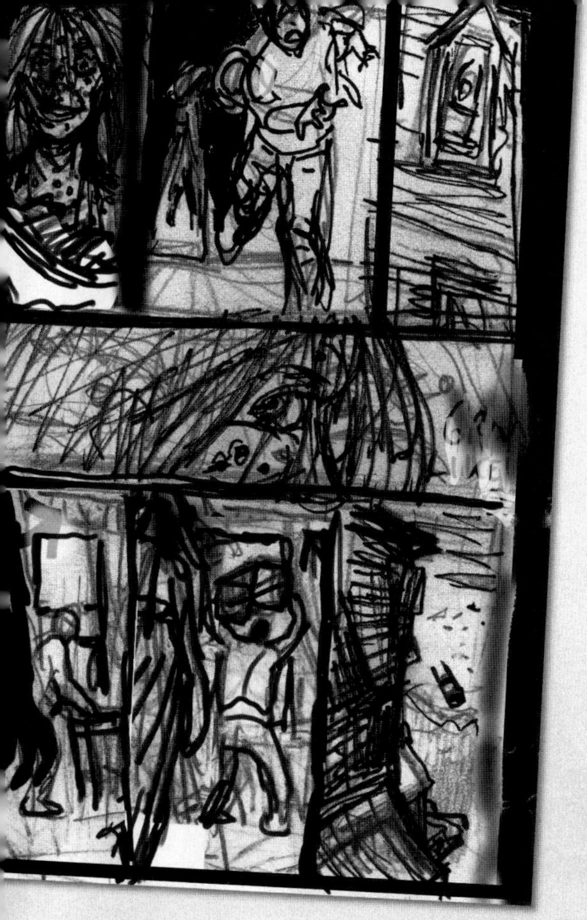

murderer of
children from generations before could still be seen at twilight in the branches of the stately oaks and elms that line the town's inviting thoroughfares.

"Don't look up," the big kids would warn. Because if you did, you just might spy the killer himself, rocking back and forth, almost absently, in the bough. Cradling the decapitated head of one of his victim's in his lap.

"That's an image I've never been able to draw," Bo says. "Just the raw insanity of it scares me to this day."

It was easy to draw out the paranormal science that anchors the book. And its authors aren't shy about admitting they believe in ghosts, no sir.

A lot of the technical particulars practiced by Frank and Derek in *Sight Unseen* are, in fact, based on the principles and findings of real-life paranormal researcher Dr. Dave Oester, whom Bob got to know while directing the fright feature "Believe" in Canada several years ago that starred Ben Gazarra.

While the doctor has his detractors, he answers with evidence (volumes of it) that gives pause to even the most hardened of skeptics to the haunted world. He links ghost sightings to spikes in electromagnetic frequencies and Civil War battlefields, where so many young men died way too soon.

That's why The Birches boasts that dam and turbine set-up to garner the ghosties. That's why Frank and his daughter, Molly, live close to a site where Yankees and Confederates clashed.

When we first meet Frank, in fact, he's engaged in a gentle debate with a one-armed Rebel soldier —who still can't believe he was actually a casualty of war.

"Believe me," the scientist has to say, "you're dead. If you weren't, there's no way in hell I could see you."

Bob and Bo knew they could scare you. Bethany rising from the creek bed behind Frank's back (as Eugene, his faithful seeing-eye dog growls at the menace) would make

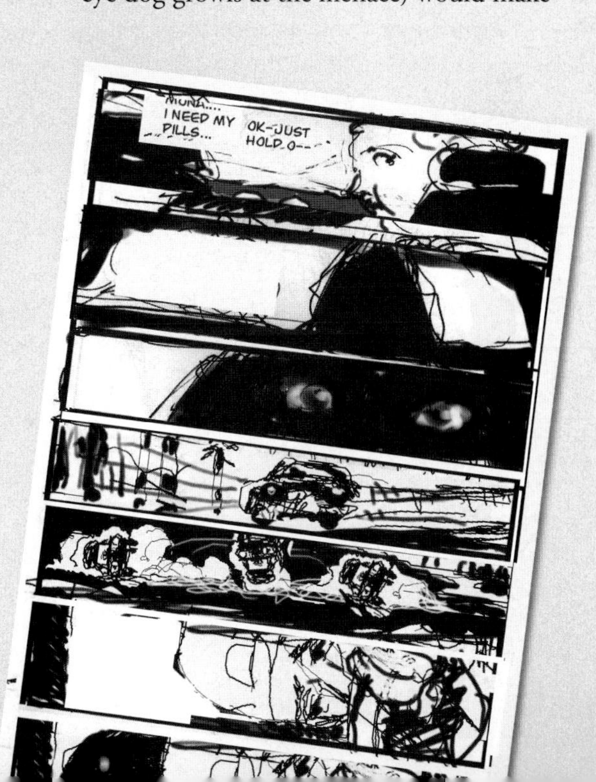
I NEED MY PILLS...
OK--JUST HOLD O--

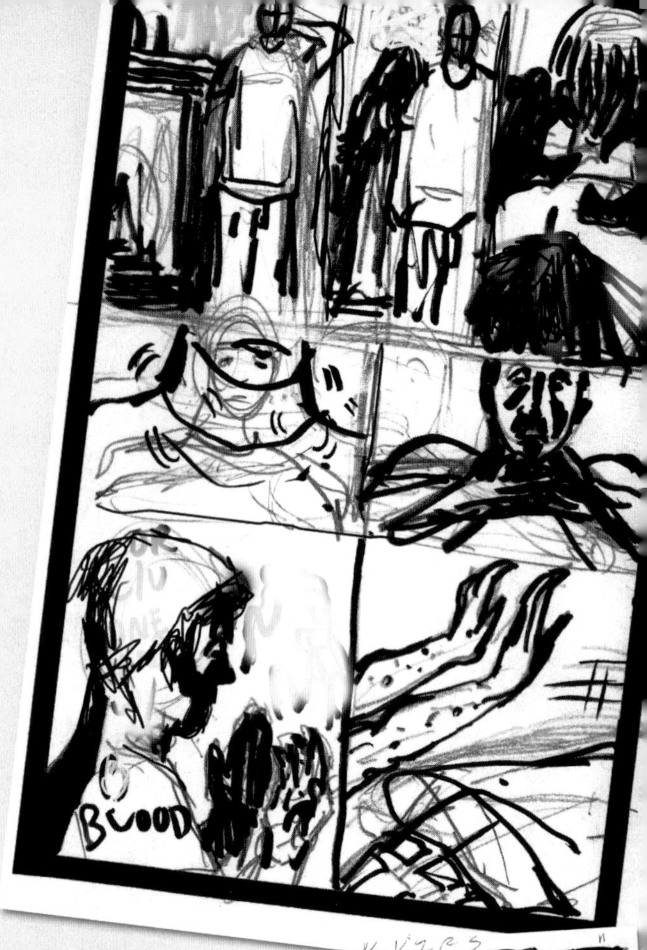
BLOOD

you put a stranglehold on your popcorn if you were watching it on the (not so) widescreen at your local multiplex.

And believing in ghosts is one thing—but the authors also know there's no way in hell you'd be reading this far if you didn't believe in the characters, and the ordinary interactions surrounding their extraordinary circumstances.

That's why they had Frank and his embittered daughter, Molly, sniping at each other for much of the book. That's why Derek flipped off Frank (he was chided by his boss for scurrying for a flashlight, but damn it, *he's* not the one who's blind).

That's why Frank, a learned man, still displayed a little veiled homophobia—or disdain, at least—at Crawford's sexual orientation.

And that's why they gave us Jimmy and Sheryl, who are hoot while they last … which, sadly, isn't long.

The portly, party couple with the bottle of Bacardi and oh-so-hip CD collection adds some much-needed comic relief to the nightmare-inducing tale. Bo gave birth to them—he sketched them out in the early days of *Sight Unseen*, wrote their dialogue and had the idea of opening the book with their sequence.

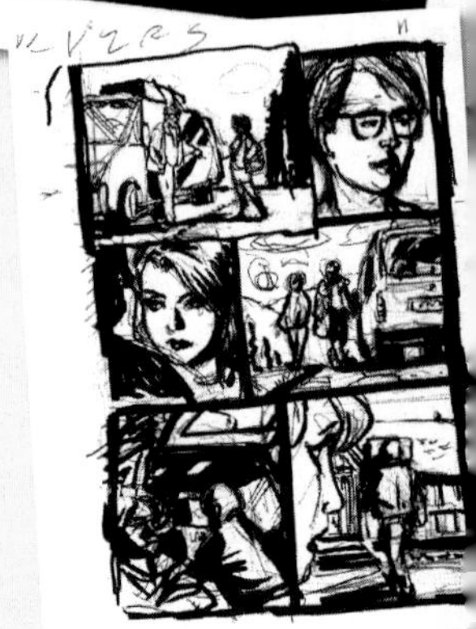

"Bob suggested otherwise," Bo says, "and he was right. They play better in the middle of the book, which was heavy drama up to that point."

Jimmy and Sheryl are like that Everyman couple you knew in back in college—slightly wasted soul mates who never fully got past cinderblock bookcases and Boone's Farm and blowing off finals because there's always another semester and Mom and Dad are paying for it anyway, so who cares?

"Jimmy was modeled after me," he deadpans, "and Sheryl was Bob before he had the stomach stapling and the other procedure. ...oh yeah, the hair-tinting. Bob's actually a brunette. A lot of people don't know that. Nah, Jimmy and Sheryl are no one and

```
Bob -> Bo

  >>> I've had more trouble
  with the script post
  Danny and the razor blade
  >>> than anything
  in quite some time.
  I'm wrestling with
  pinning down
  >>> Molly and Derek and
  Frank and not having
  too much on-the-nose
  >>> exposition and
  blah blah blah.

  Robert Tinnell
```

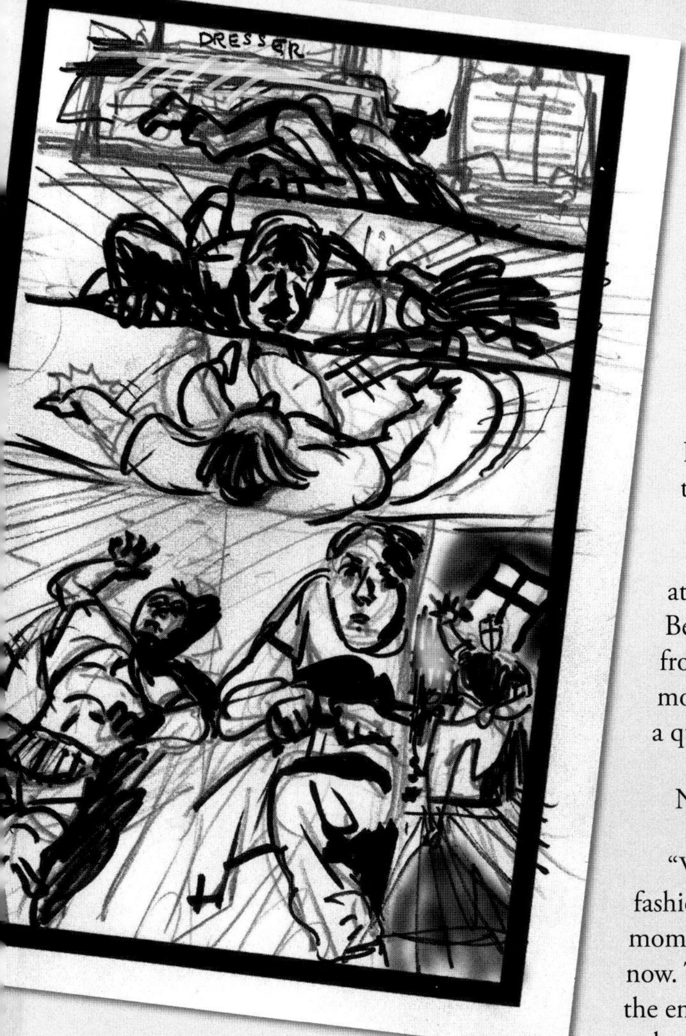
DRESSER

surprised and impressed by that one guy who steeled himself to do what should have been done years ago.

And you had to root for a tender reconciliation between a father and daughter that was unfolding like an origami cutout.

Here's what you won't see: The shock/schlock ending, which, for Bob and Bo, is about as welcome as a tanning bed at a vampire convention.

That means nothing going bump at The Birches in the last panel, or Bethany's rotting hand reaching up from the fender as Molly and her dad motor through those autumn hills on a quest to set other things right, too.

Nope, nope, nope.

"We were trying to work in a novelistic fashion here," Bob says. "As far as the 'Carrie' moment goes, it almost works against you now. To throw in a little extra bump at the end just really felt false. And you had to look at what Crawford went through. The horror and emotional devastation of that would have been trivialized, had we jumped out and said, 'Boo.'"

It also insults the reader, Bo says.

"There's this thing and it's called an 'ending,'" he says, bristling just a bit. "Stories everyone who ever pretended to be young."

We already told you Jimmy and Sheryl aren't going to be around when you close the cover.

But otherwise, we don't necessarily want to rehash the ending, here —just in case you're reading ahead. (And if you are, shame on you. May Leatherface come to your house and carve up your Christmas turkey and the guests who go with it).

Anyway, you had to count on knowing that some nasty, nasty events boiled over at The Birches and that some people you really liked (including Jimmy and Sheryl) became ghosts, themselves. You were no doubt

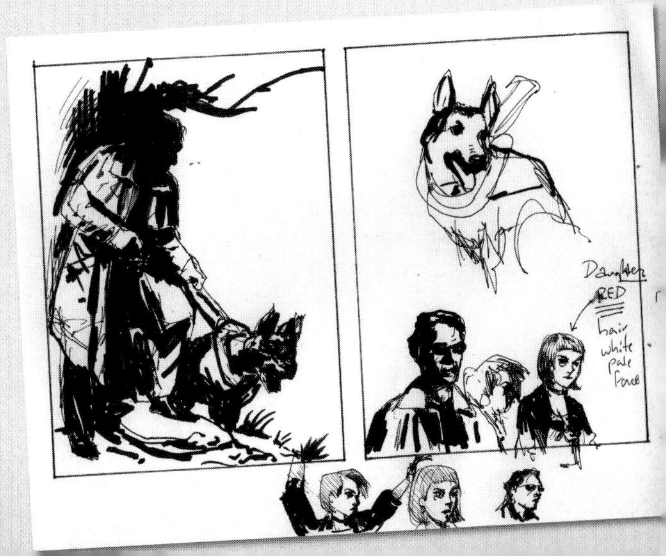
Daughter
RED
hair
white
pale
face

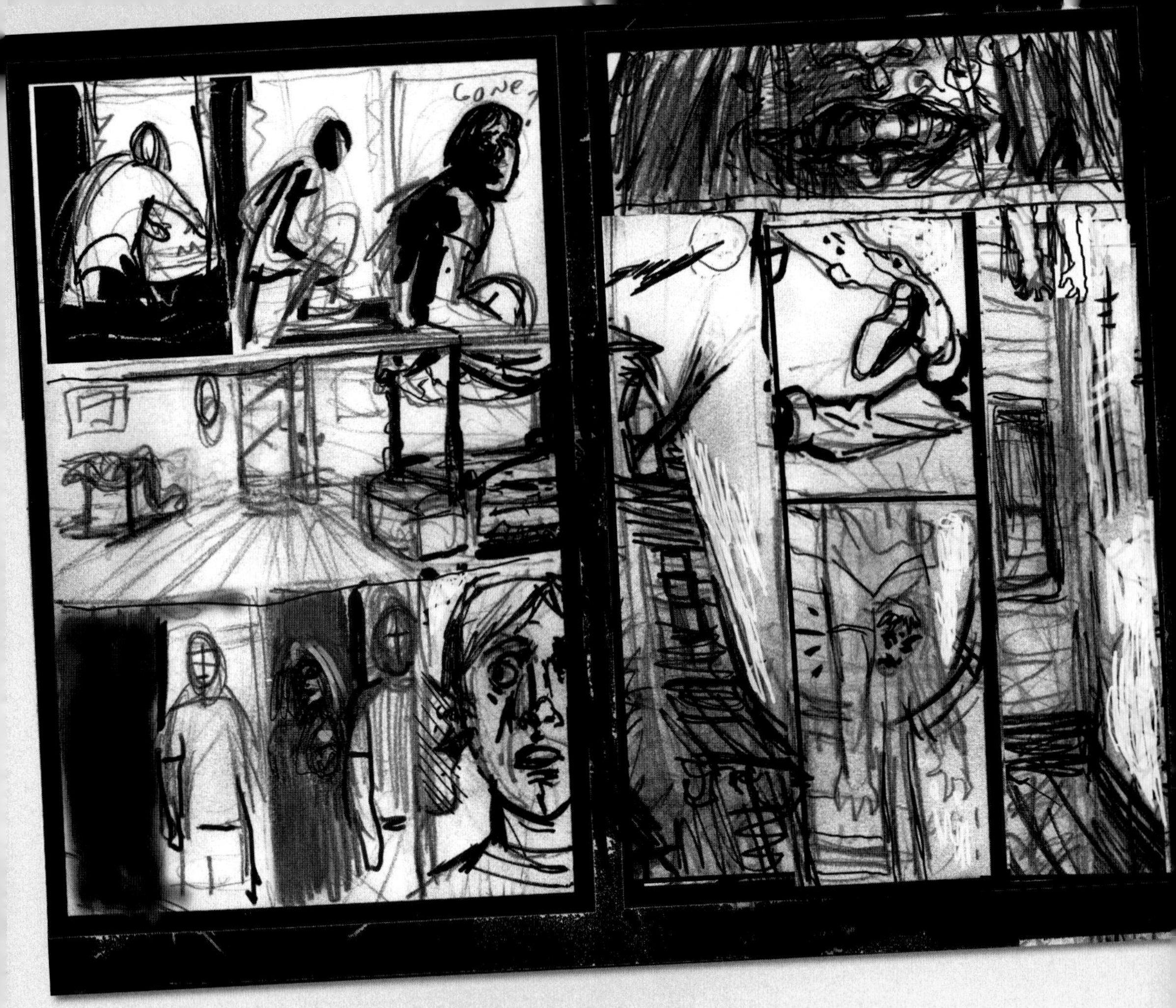
GONE!

have them and when they come around they should be recognized as just that. If the reader has been satisfied up to that point, there's no need for a teaser to make them 'want more.' That's what the story should have done. Frank and Molly had to go through some really bad stuff to get their moment. They earned it, and that's why we just pulled back to let them have it."

While it's hardly a happy ending, the book does end on a relatively upbeat note, what with all that "bad stuff" Bo was talking about. And as Bob says, "Good may not triumph over evil, but I have to hope that it will … or I'm going to end up in my car in the garage with the motor running."

So there it is, and so it goes.

Oh, and the next time you're house-hunting? If there's a dam in the backyard, pass.

If your realtor turns out to be in possession of a razor, pass.

If she walks on walls, make that counter-offer on the condo, instead. After all, there's no law that says you have to buy the first property you see, in this life or the other one.

Robert Tinnell was born and raised in West Virginia. An award-winning director and screenwriter, Tinnell has also authored several acclaimed graphic novels, including FEAST OF THE SEVEN FISHES and THE FACELESS: A TERRY SHARP STORY. He co-authored THE BLACK FOREST, THE WICKED WEST and THE LIVING AND THE DEAD with Todd Livingston. Tinnell resides in West Virginia with his wife, Shannon, and their two children.

Bo Hampton hails from High Point, North Carolina. Since 1983 he has worked for every major Comics and Graphic Novel publisher in the U.S. and a couple in Europe. Works include BATMAN:CASTLE OF THE BAT with Jack Harris, VERDILAK [NBM] with Mark Kneece and THE LEGEND OF SLEEPY HOLLOW [Kitchen Sink]with Washington Irving—thanks, big guy—as well as the current mini-series BOOK OF SHADOWS [Desperado/Image] with Mark Chadbourne.

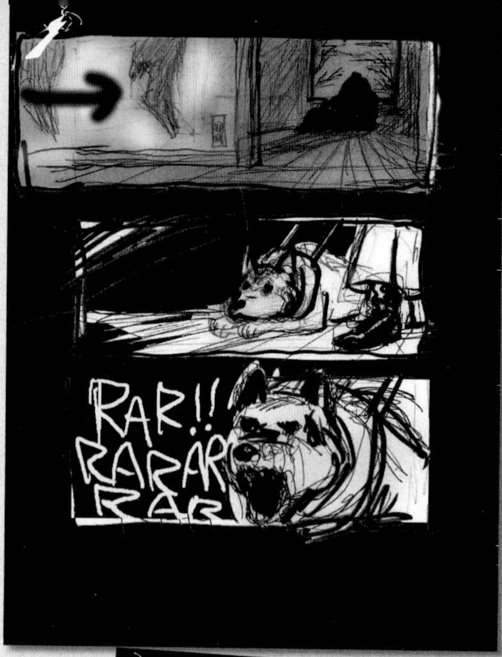
1
RAR!!
RARAR

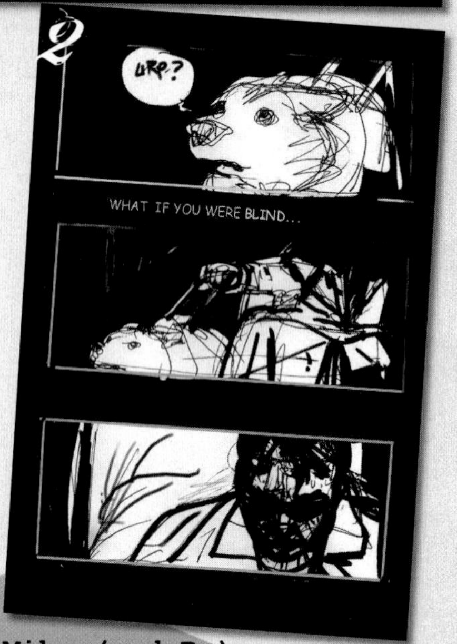
2
URP?
WHAT IF YOU WERE BLIND...

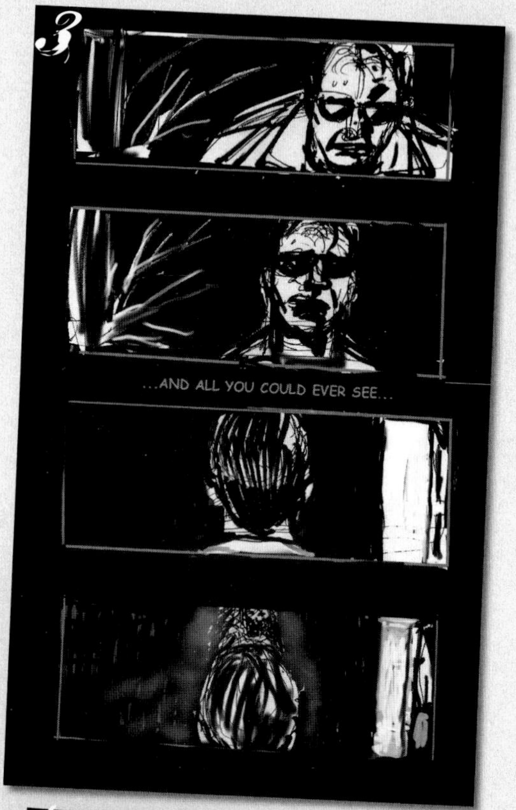
3
...AND ALL YOU COULD EVER SEE...

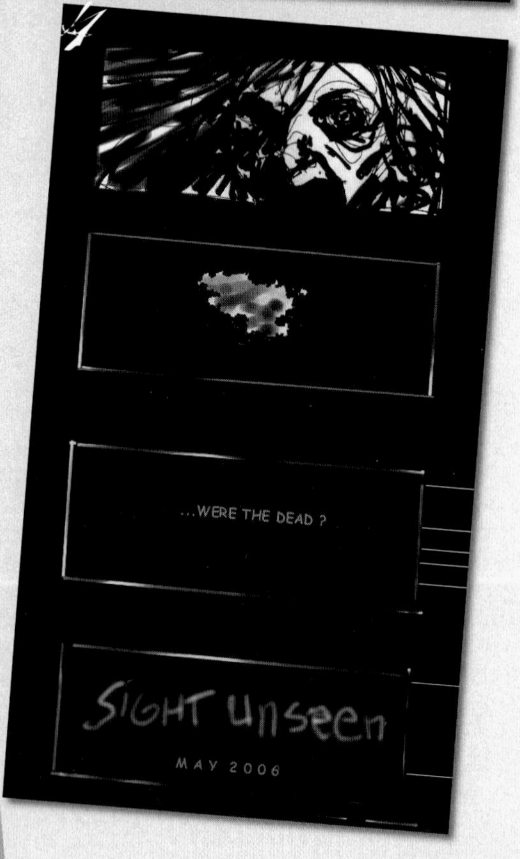
4
...WERE THE DEAD ?
SIGHT UNSEEN
MAY 2006

Bob -> Mike (and Bo)

Here is the "behind the scenes" essay that will go in the back of SU. What I'd like to see is a nice mix of text and graphics - Bo has some marvelous conceptual sketches and layouts that would be really effective. Plus, in the margins I'd like to run snippets of our emails as we worked out the book - in sidebar fashion. Somewhere here I have Bo's proposed page by page breakdown of the book that I will forward...